CORRECTIONAL POLICY AND PRISON ORGANIZATION

correctional policy and prison organization

DAVID DUFFEE

Pennsylvania State University

SAGE Publications

Halsted Press Division
JOHN WILEY & SONS
New York – London – Sydney – Toronto

Copyright © 1975 by Sage Publications, Inc.

Distributed by Halsted Press, a Division of
John Wiley & Sons, Inc., New York

Printed in the United States of America

Library of Congress Cataloging in Publication Data

Duffee, David.
   Correctional policy and prison organization.
   Bibliography: p.
   Includes indexes.
   1. Prisons. 2. Corrections. I. Title.
HV8756.D82   364.6   75-17575
ISBN 0-470-22372-3

FIRST PRINTING

To the men and women, convicted and employed, in the Connecticut Department of Correction

ABOUT THE AUTHOR

The author received his A.B. in English from St. Lawrence University in 1968 and his M.A. (1971) and Ph.D. (1974) in criminal justice from the State University of New York at Albany. He is co-author with Robert Fitch of the forthcoming *An Introduction to Corrections: A Policy and Systems Approach* and the author of numerous articles and government reports. He is currently Associate Professor of Criminal Justice in the Division of Community Development, and a Faculty Associate of the Pennsylvania Field Research Laboratory, the Pennsylvania State University.

CONTENTS

PREFACE

The work reported in this volume is the product of the combined efforts of university research and development staff, correctional administrators and front-line staff, and inmates in the Department of Correction, state of Connecticut. While the outcomes and the procedures for achieving them were a combined effort, it was not always a combination of concerted energies. There were at all points in the three years of research and action conflicts open and submerged, misunderstandings, careless planning or the lack of planning altogether. Lest my readers misunderstand, it must be said that at all times this was a *cooperative* project, in which the first Commissioner of Correction, Ellis C. MacDougall, invited Vincent O'Leary to come into the Department, and provided O'Leary and myself, and his own administrators, a relatively free hand in defining and changing the boundaries of a problem, about the existence of which there was clear consensus. The problem was one of improving the working relationships among central office and field staff who became the members of one bureaucracy only in 1967. Many of these people were new to each other, or, as with the officers in the institutions which were autonomous previous to the formation of the Department, the same officials suddenly found themselves interacting in an entirely changed organizational structure.

A majority of the work reported in this volume was conducted in one institution whose ability to host such activity was itself a product of these new system relationships. The minimum security prison had been, until 1969, a satellite institution administered as part of a single, adult male prison complex. Ironically, the addition of new bureaucratic layers at a central office level resulted for this institution in a new autonomy.

While there are many limitations to this study, one I am critically aware of is that this research has as one goal some generalizations about prison management as organizational systems, but has taken as its main data base a newly autonomous institution in a newly created department. How severe this limitation is, readers will have to judge for themselves. I think that the construct validity of the major theoretical framework is adequately supported both in Chapter 8, and in other research in different settings that has succeeded this project.

One highlight of this study that I care to call attention to is the running report on the derivation of satisfactory outcome to both researchers and administrators although both groups clearly had independent and different motivations in their collaboration. I am pleased that some sense of these joint payoffs, as well as differences, are kindly recorded in the Foreword by Vincent O'Leary and in the Postscript by Richard Steinert. It is not often that such a report as this may be sandwiched between the contributions of both a professor and an administrator.

That their comments are both inherently relevant is perhaps the major point of this book: this is a study of penology for which the foundation is organizational sociology. While this mix may be unfamiliar to many correctional specialists or criminologists who may be struck by the book's title, it is, I hope, such a mix that enlivens both academia and the realities of administration.

I wish to express my gratitude to the officials of the Central Office of the Connecticut Department of Corrections, to the administrators and to the correctional officers and inmates throughout the Department who cooperated in this study. To the staff and inmates of the Enfield Institution I am especially grateful for their hospitality, cooperation, and encouragement. I owe special thanks to the officers of the "research team" of that institution. Although I began work with them after completing the data portion of this study, their creativity and dedication has certainly influenced the final version of this book.

For reasons that I no longer think are clear, all names of institutions, towns, and people in this report are fictitious. At no time during my work has anyone in Connecticut seemed concerned with anonymity. I felt that the role of the people in the Department deserved recognition in this preface, yet I feel strongly that privacy is due those who desire it, within the text.

Last, I consider the Superintendent of Enfield not only a collaborator, but I am very glad to consider him a friend. It will be through efforts of men such as he that corrections, if it can improve, will do so.

I am indebted to all the faculty and students of the School of Criminal Justice of the State University of New York. Even those with whom my contact was only marginal contributed to the climate that makes the school one of the finest places of academic study in the country. To Michael O'Neill I owe special thanks for many informal talks that clarified my thinking and for generous help with the computer that at times I faced as a stumbling block rather than as a tool.

Special appreciation is due Leslie Wilkins, Donald Newman, and Vincent O'Leary who have been tireless in their helpful criticism and encouragement, from discussions of the initial project to their suggestion that the combined report of several projects was worthy of publication.

I also wish to thank Walter Freeman, Director of the Division of Community Development at the Pennsylvania State Universtiy, for his kind understanding and encouragement, which allowed the writing to continue for two years past the actual involvement in Connecticut. To all the secretaries of the division I am also indebted, but particularly to Kay McClellan, Aline Mabon, and Jackie English, who have seen as many drafts as I have.

Lastly, I want to thank my wife, Cyndi, for being human and making the completion of this volume as difficult as it should have been. With the help of Cyndi I think I remained a human being rather than becoming an extension of my work.

David Duffee
State College, Pa.

April 24, 1975

ACKNOWLEDGMENTS

Grateful acknowledgment is made for the selections from the following material: *Correctional Policy Inventory*, by Vincent O'Leary, published by the National Council on Crime and Delinquency, reprinted by permission of the author.

"The Assessment of Social Climates of Correctional Institutions," by Rudolph Moos, *Journal of Research in Crime and Delinquency*, Vol. 5, July, 1968, pp. 74-88, reprinted by permission of the publisher.

Some of the activities, both of research and of an action nature, were supported by three separate grants: (1) "Management Training Program," Connecticut Committee on Criminal Administration, 1969-1970; (2) "Management Training Program," Connecticut Committee on Criminal Administration, 1970-1971; (3) "Using Correctional Officers in Planned Change," National Institute on Law Enforcement and Criminal Justice NI-71-115 P.G.

The fact that this work was supported by these funds does not imply that the findings and conclusions are those of the Connecticut Committee on Criminal Administration or the National Institute on Law Enforcement and Criminal Justice. The opinions expressed herein are solely those of the author.

INTRODUCTION

The prisons of this country are under sharp attack and, while such criticisms are hardly new, their extent and intensity have risen to levels not known in recent decades. Their sources are disparate—ranging from a national commission organized by the Nixon Administration to a working group supported by the Quakers—but conclusions have been generally uniform: Prisons fail to rehabilitate, they are inhumane, and they contribute to the exacerbation of the problem of crime rather than to its abatement. The general force of these criticisms has been to encourage community-based alternatives to supplant present-day prisons.

Arguments such as these pose a dilemma familiar to the reformer: To what degree should efforts be made to improve prisons at all? One runs the risk that any such efforts at amelioration are likely to be no more than cosmetic and will simply prolong the general use of such institutions. Balancing this concern is the fact that, although it has been demonstrated for juvenile systems that an extremely limited use of incarceration is possible, few of even the most outspoken critics of institutions for adults realistically expect that a substantial number of prisons will be closed in the near future. The public's response to the needs for prison reform will not likely overshadow its even greater concern for stricter measures of crime control. In short, the probability is strong that prisons will remain part of the American social profile for many years, and efforts directed toward their improvement remain a part of a realistic agenda for correctional reform.

David Duffee aims to increase our understanding of the means by which at least some of these needed changes can be accomplished. Following in the tradition of Clemmer, Sykes, and others, he analyzes the forces within the prison organization which impinge upon the "keepers" and the "kept" of that alienated world. What distinguishes this book is the emphasis which he places upon uncovering some of the strategic levers which might be employed to modify those organizational arrangements. For while this book is grounded in the tradition of studies of the "prison community," it is also related to a distinct and newly emerging body of knowledge which emphasizes systematic organizational change. That literature develops the premise that the behavior of the members of an organization, while linked to the individual characteristics, is significantly shaped by organizational constraints, and modification of those constraints is required before the behavior of individuals and groups within this organization can be altered.

The identification of a problem and the strategy for dealing with it are important first steps, but there remains the long step of developing practical intervention pathways. This book describes how ideas of organizational theory and change may be forged to develop such pathways. It is an outgrowth of an action research project, funded by the U.S. Law Enforcement Assistance Administration and the RANN program of the National Science Foundation, on which David Duffee and I served as collaborators for almost three years. In the course of that effort, David spent many months in the prisons of the host state where the research was conducted. He developed not only a rich insight into the prisons as organizations, but also a real understanding of the people, guards, and prisoners who live in them. It is an example of the kind of work which can result from careful field research, a concern for theory, and most of all a deep commitment to human beings.

Most importantly, this book is a tribute to the men and women responsible for operating the prison system of the host state. To assure confidentiality to inmates and line staff, anonymity as to the source of data for this book was promised. What should not go unrecorded, however, is the willingness of these correctional managers to support an action research effort which caused them a good deal of inconvenience and, on several occasions, real difficulty. Not nearly enough credit is given to correctional managers such as these, who have the dedication and courage to fight for a decent correctional system and who are willing to open their programs to researchers, and the consequent risk of criticism because of that dedication and courage.

—Vincent O'Leary
School of Criminal Justice
State University of New York
Albany, New York

CHAPTER 1

CORRECTIONAL POLICY, MANAGEMENT, AND PRISON RESEARCH

For many years, prisons have pricked the curiosity of poets, novelists, journalists, philosophers, political scientists, sociologists, and certainly other groups too numerous to mention. A particularly recurrent theme for many of these people has been incarceration as a rape of the human spirit. Whatever manner of act—brutal, selfish, or merely stupid—that has justified society's incarceration of a man has, under the weight of prison time, made the offender feel like a victim. This basically retributive relationship to society in the mind of the male offender has had the frequent effect of justifying for him his future as well as his past criminal acts.

Other writers have concentrated on the corollary of this social process and have emphasized the extreme efforts of the incarcerated man to overcome the negative effects of incarceration. How even the lowest of human beings has been able to scrape together some semblance of integrity and independence in the coercive atmosphere of the prison has at times been a remarkable and heroic story. Ironically, society has found the same qualities of leadership, honesty, and courage in some of the men it has condemned as it has in some of the men it has rewarded and applauded.

Until recently, this kind of irony could be enjoyed because it had been nonpolitical. Cagneys and Bogarts were perhaps acceptable because they were models that few people would really try to adopt and they did not come complete with causes that free citizens would actually champion. But the power groups that influence social action have changed, and the accepted methods of becoming powerful have changed to the extent that Huey Newton and George Jackson, or the dead inmates of the Attica uprising, speak not only for other inmates, but also for large groups of disenchanted citizens.

Perhaps more important, these men also speak to government commissions and shocked legislators, who find that the responsibility for prisoners' actions rests not solely within the male prisoner as part of his personality, but rests also with the governments and their official representatives. For wider and wider segments of society, the interconnectedness and interdependencies of social action are becoming accepted as matters of fact.

As the popularity of this explanation of social function and dysfunction increases, it becomes possible for citizens to demand of their officials more demonstrable and effective change in convicted offenders and in the institutions that have as goals the protection of society. As this demand has increased and has become legitimate, officials in organizations of criminal justice have taken a new look at their roles and at the ways these roles contribute to social order.

This new trend in understanding social responsibility has led to a new importance for social research in prisons as well as other areas. For years, social research in prisons concentrated on the offender group, on the social processes of that group, and on the effects of those processes. The new emphasis on accountability of officials has had its effect on research as well as on public policy. Most recent prison research has frequently concentrated on the prison as an organization, as a social stage filled not with captives and captors, but with the interaction structure that includes both groups.

This study of one prison combines correctional theory and research with applicable material concerning organizations and management. The argument is made that neither area of social science alone is adequate to analyze the behavior of inmates and staff, nor satisfactory in describing the systematic implications of planned correctional action. The interweaving of correctional and organizational theory yields testable hypotheses that, if supported, suggest that attention accorded the manner in which prisons are organized should increase and the attention given the differences between staff and inmates as distinct castes should decrease, if correctional goals are to be more effectively achieved.

Most of the hypotheses of correctional organization were tested during research and organizational development activity conducted within one minimum security prison. As always, when research is limited to one location and one set of observed phenomena, it is an assumption that the hypotheses supported by this research are generalizable to other places and times. And yet this research has the advantage that the hypotheses are drawn from the meta-theory of systems analysis and that all but one of the questionnaires used have also been used elsewhere, independently of each other and of this study. Moreover, since the activity within this one prison was part of a larger departmental program, the opportunity did occur to test some of the hypotheses developed with a wider sample of people and institutions.

In the study of management, there has been a stabilization of the pendulum that swung from the concept of scientific management, functionalizing the components of an organization and compartmentalizing the functions,[1] through the human relations school in which the desires of personnel for support, satisfaction, and interesting work were considered the primary factors in successful administration.[2] Current management theory suggests that the concerns of personnel and the concerns of organization need not be contradictory.[3] Maximal production may be achieved through maximum attention to the social situation of personnel, but in such a way that employee norms support task completion.[4]

Simultaneously, there has been the emergence of correctional studies that emphasize the prison as a community,[5] and inmate entrenchment against staff design as a group phenomenon.[6] As yet, there have been comparatively few studies that actually focus on specifically organizational variables that may affect the behavior of staff and inmates. Recently, there have been several studies demonstrating that different types of institutions produce consistently different inmate populations[7] and that relatively similar populations will be treated with significant dissimilarity by managements with contrasting perceptions.[8] A national survey has been conducted of the behavior of correctional administrators that utilizes a measure of managerial styles. Some assumptions are made about the type of style most compatible with the correctional model most likely in the future.[9] But the connection of managerial style and correctional practice remains an assumption in the national survey, and the formality of the managerial models[10] is not integrated with a formalized system of classifying correctional organization.

With the exception of one work that treats the relationship between managerial action and inmate and staff behavior in an explanatory fashion,[11] there have been no major studies that apply a theory of organization to the correctional enterprise. Under the topic of prison management, correctional analysts usually speak of the management of inmates and rarely of the management of staff as productive of particular types of inmate populations, or recurrent inmate problems.[12] One exception is a study demonstrating that prisoners are moved about the prison for administrative ease, and while officials state that prisoners are moved as their behavior improves, the behavior is actually a product of staff and inmate perceptions about the relative status of different cell blocks.[13] Experts in administrative behavior, when addressing strategies of correctional administration, usually tend to ignore information about deviance, coercive supervision, punishment, subcultures, and the law, which are available in correctional literature.[14] What is lacking is a careful analysis of the organizational assumptions under which different prisons are run, and from which various groups within a prison view each other.

Undertaking this analysis should be greatly aided by two sets of organizational literature. First, Argyris[15] and Selznick,[16] among others, have identified three core activities of all organizations. These are (1) goal-directed or production activity; (2) internal maintenance activity; and (3) adjustment-to-environment activity. Analysis of prison behavior with these concepts in mind would probably reveal that most prison activity has been determined largely by its internal maintenance and environmental needs. In other words, the prison as a collectivity of people has spent most of its time developing an organizational identity. Little attention has been paid to the needs of prisoners except as those needs advanced the status of the prison. The goal of making inmates in some way "better" at release than at entry has usually been implemented by prison officials in such a way that the well-established maintenance patterns and adjustment-to-environment activities were a priori appropriate. The recent developments in the theory of changing inmates, as a goal of the prison, affixes higher status to the first core of activity of organizations, that of "production." But if the personnel and inmates of the prison have for years spent most of their time solidifying their positions, and identifying and stabilizing resources, it is likely that most of this behavior has become routinized and ingrained. As departmental and social forces call for more proficient strategies and techniques for altering offender behavior, it is probable that organizational routine and organizational desire for achievement will be at cross-purposes. While routine seems undefeatable in many bureaucracies, the force of the cultural mandate for change, by society externally and by the staff internally, is likely to create considerable friction in critical areas of prison organization.[17] Symptomatic of that friction are the correctional uses of "bureaucratic gobbledygook,"[18] emphasis on goals that cannot be evaluated,[19] and concern for ideological battles that do not reflect the real consequences for offenders.[20] The principle of homeostasis, by which changes in a system are controlled, can be used to demonstrate how the organizational goal-directed activity can be rechanneled into activities of maintenance and environmental adjustment that are more rewarding for power organizational groups than the originally intended action of changing future offender behavior.[21]

As long as correctional administrators perceive inmates as the raw material of prison production activities (and, hence, increase the division of staff and inmates to the detriment of organizational unification), they are faced with difficult problems of organizational control and coordination. So far, the goals of corrections have remained so intangible, or control of crime has been so defined, that the offenders themselves rather than correctional organizations have been seen as totally responsible for future failures in the behavior of released inmates.

But it may be possible to define correctional goals in such a way that inmates are no longer seen as *in* but not part of the system,[22] (or seen as acted *upon* but not interacting with the organizational network). If correctional goals could be formulated in such a way as to include the desires and initiative of offenders, then the statement of goals could be more directive of organizational activity, and the discrepancy between purpose and practice might diminish.

Of course, there cannot be complete independence among the production, maintenance, and adjustment activities. They are inter-related. The goals of the prison, for example, are greatly affected by the adjustment to environment made by accepting incoming prisoners. But that external determination of input need not delimit within-prison activity so much as it does now. Formulating correctional goals that (1) do not conflict with internal mainte-nance constraints and (2) are not a mere restatement of adjust-ment-to-environment activity may be a highly valuable step in the clarification of the interrelationships of different prison behavior patterns. Stated another way, researchers in criminology have frequently observed that the prison attempts to change the future behavior of offenders, and thus to reduce crime, are typically not rationally planned for their own hypothetical or demonstrated merit, but rather serve as the current and popular justifications for the prison to continue whatever actions maintain the internal social structure or enable the prison to accommodate the demands of a changing external culture and social structure. In contrast, this research program began with the guiding hypothesis that the activities and techniques effective in changing human behavior in desired directions should become the principles upon which cor-rectional organizations were designed and that the maintenance and adjustment subsystems should be designed and planned to support the primary aim of changing future behavior.

Corrections may develop change techniques and standards for crime reduction that exist independent of political or maintenance concerns without concentrating directly on the importance of that independence.[23] If so, the correctional organization may be healthier than critics suspect. But if changes in correctional organi-zations have this trend toward behavior-change proficiency, there is no reason to permit haphazard organizational development when prediction and control of the trend may be possible.[24] The establishment of goals in which correctional personnel can be active and reactive rather than passive may be advanced by a systematic comparison of various correctional philosophies and the organizational variables associated with each of those different perviews.

In doing so, there is another body of organizational literature, rapidly growing of late, that may help to clarify the relationship between goal-directed activity and the organizational adjustment to its environment. Briefly, researchers in the nature of organizational environment have now identified a new type of environment in which social interaction is turbulent and complex.[25] In this setting, simple cause-effect planning by organizational executives no longer makes sense.[26] However, officials in the criminal justice system still frequently operate as though it does.[27] From this perspective, one could surmise that correctional goals are left intangible because concretization would bring immediate evidence of failure,[28] or because the dominant control mechanisms so important to the maintenance of the organization are predicated on simple cause-effect relationships.[29] In either or both cases, comparisons of the traditional correctional management practices with the requirements of open and complex system management should demonstrate that prisons are managed so that the organization is generally incapable of influencing the very variables upon which success in behavior change would depend. Or, to restate the problem, new correctional goals, such as behavior change, must include organizational redesign so that goals are implemented effectively.

SIGNIFICANCE OF THE PRESENT RESEARCH

The studies of both the correctional and the organizational area have now been developed to such a point that it is possible to combine in a single analysis the variety of managerial behavior characteristic of many complex organizations and varieties of correctional behavior recurrent in many correctional institutions. This study employs measures of managerial behavior that can distinguish autocratic from democratic approaches to the management of an organization. At the same time, a means has been established of identifying and measuring the commitment of these managers to particular correctional policies, or specific correctional goals and associated implementation patterns.

Some assumptions may be drawn about the relationship between the way in which a correctional administrator manages employees and the way in which he or she attempts to govern inmates through the employees. It would seem, for example, that a manager who is extremely autocratic with employees might also take a rather punitive orientation toward inmates. By using the instruments reported in this research to measure correctional policy and managerial style, it is possible to test some specific hypotheses about the relationships. Therefore, it becomes unnecessary at this date to leave the judgment about the connection between goals and implementation strategies to a clinical assessment of the particular behavior patterns of particular managers in interaction with particular inmate and staff groups.

In addition to demonstrating that there are some rather natural relationships between particular approaches to staff management and particular goals for inmates, this study is also useful in exploring the opposite. What happens when a manager subscribes to a correctional policy that is contradictory to his or her management of employees? What would happen for example, if a warden espousing a flexible, problem-solving correctional policy for inmates continued to manage his staff in a strictly task-oriented manner, allowing little participation of staff in planning and listening to feedback from neither correctional officers nor treatment personnel? While the correctional programs run at such an institution might "publicly" perform the functions of resocialization, group problem-solving, and behavior-testing, it is likely that these programs would be so directed in the official rhetoric only. Managed in the style of "comply or else," staff might not cooperate adequately with the warden to implement successfully the warden's correctional goals. It is an unsafe (and in terms of this study) an unsupportable assumption that common sense and intuition will lead wardens and other correctional managers to the optimum approach to employees as they try to implement their correctional goals, particularly since correctional goals are now changing rapidly.

Traditionally, prisons have been managed as paramilitary organizations in which inmates were punished for wrongdoings. As the impact of the behavioral sciences upon both the general social ethic and officials of government makes the concept of willful wrongdoing (or sin) less supportable, the idea that inmates should be punished for wrongdoing may change. Currently, there is much concern with the efficiency of our institutions of government and therefore with the future behavior of punished offenders. As old ways of punishing (or as punishing altogether) seems ineffective for the protection of society, new ways of dealing with criminal offenders will be sought. Therefore, new ways of managing and organizing correctional institutions might also be sought.

The formal hypotheses about the relationship of management and the achievement of correctional goals must await a fuller description of the analytical tools employed. However, among the kind of information that an organizational analysis of prisons may yield are the following. The first group of hypotheses will deal with correctional policy or correctional goals alone. Of major interest in this exploration is the possibility that preferences in correctional policy will be increasingly dissimilar as the hierarchical levels are more divergent. For example, administration and captains may be closer in their preferences than administration and officers. It is also possible that, within each organizational level, there may be differences as great as there are between echelons. For example, while inmates and officers may have relatively similar viewpoints, it is possible that officers and inmates working in the dairy have very different correctional preferences than officers and inmates assigned to a special program of high school lectures about crime.

The second group of hypotheses has to do with the relationship between the patterns of managerial behavior and the response to correctional goals. It is quite likely in the great majority of cases that the individual's managerial and correctional choices will largely conform to the compatibilities described by correlation of the two classification schemes. A captain with an autocratic managerial approach is not likely to favor a client-oriented therapy as a correctional goal. The examination of those cases in which preferences of correctional goals are not compatible with managerial behavior should disclose conflicts with staff or inmates that are organizationally disruptive. Furthermore, a particular kind of disruption to expect when preferences of superiors and subordinates conflict is the psychological if not physical withdrawl of the subordinate from prison activity and his or her increasing lack of commitment to the organization.

Certainly one may expect significant differences to appear between inmate and staff perception of organizational goals. But the reliance upon traditional correctional explanations of these differences may be misleading, or at least overly simplistic. In a national survey of correctional managers, for example, differences in managerial style and basic attitudes were found even among the top two positions in correctional departments.[30] Hen the difference between inmates and all other people who are members of a correctional system may simply be one mark of organizations in which there are fundamental rifts among all hierarchical levels.

THE TOOLS OF THE RESEARCH

In the effort to expand upon the presently available research, several different research tools were used. As the study began, in 1969, a series of interviews was initiated to obtain a general impression of the perceptions and problems of the personnel and inmates within the correctional department in which the study took place. As the project started, the top thirty managers in the department were interviewed concerning their thoughts on the goals of the department and their feelings about the major problems and avenues of improvement in the agency. Then a series of group interviews was conducted for correctional officers in the seven largest institutions in the department. As much as possible, the correctional officers were asked the same questions as their superiors were asked in order to see whether they had similar or divergent views of the situation. After these introductory interviews, one institution was selected in which most of the research on the officer and inmate levels would take place. Within this institution, more systematic interviews were conducted. A team of seven managers in the prison was given extended interviews twice. During the three years in which most of the research was conducted, the author also had daily contact with these men on an informal basis. The prison managers were interviewed on such topics as management-staff and staff-inmate relations, the effectiveness of certain goals of the prison, and the relationship between the prison program and the eventual release of inmates to the community.

In addition to these interviews, several questionnaires were also used in the attempt to look at correctional policy, managerial behavior, and the organizational effects of both. One questionnaire in a variety of forms was administered to correctional managers, officers, and inmates in order to gain a multilevel picture of the perceived goals in the institution. This questionnaire was given to all the central office and prison managers and to random samples of officers and inmates in the one selected prison. In addition to this instrument, two different questionnaires were administered to a random sample of all staff and inmates in the entire department. This last questionnaire measured the social climate of the organizations in question. It was evident that staff and inmates with differential perception of correctional goals and managerial behavior also felt that they were living in rather dissimilar social environments.

THE OCCASION AND SITE OF THE RESEARCH

The opportunity for the research described came about when the Department of Correction in a northeastern state invited consultants from the School of Criminal Justice of the State University of New York at Albany to conduct a management training conference for the central office staff. In June of 1969, the first sequence of interviews was conducted in an attempt to get the lay of the land with which to design a management training program relevant to the needs of the department. This conference took place in two stages in October and December 1969. Following the successful completion of this program, the department requested a similar program for middle managers selected from institutions and field services throughout the department. This conference took place in March 1970. In the meantime, some of the correctional managers who had attended the first session became rather excited by the potential of the training materials and the process by which these materials were presented. Because the training consultants saw a long-awaited chance to transform these training devices into more accurate and reliable research instruments, it was mutually beneficial to continue the training program in such a way that inmates would eventually be involved in the organizational development activity. In order to keep the effects of the training activity focused rather than diffused throughout the department, one prison was selected for the continuation of the training and research at the lower levels of the department.

Hilltop,[31] a minimum security farm, was selected for a number of practical and theoretical reasons. The first consideration was size. The site houses between 350 and 450 male inmates with an average population turnover every eight months. The staff numbers approximately 150, with little turnover in personnel. The prison's minimum security status had research advantages in the maneuverability of staff and inmates and the general lack of tension. The superintendent was open to research in his institution and five of his middle managers had attended the training conference for middle managers in March 1970. In the survey of social climates,[32] Hilltop was about average for all the institutions studied. It was the most middle ground in terms of custody, intensity of treatment programs, and size, which the state had to offer.

Hilltop is a recent addition to the correctional institutions in the state. It was built in 1961 when the old maximum security institution was abandoned and a new maximum security complex built at Winters, a mile away. Those inmates classified as low security risks were transferred to Hilltop from the maximum security unit. Now prisoners are almost automatically transferred to Hilltop from Winters as they near parole status.

From 1961 to 1967, Winters and Hilltop were administered by the same warden, who was responsible directly to the governor. In 1967, the Department of Correction was formed, and both institutions, still operating under a single budget and table of organization, were transferred to the Department under the Division of Institutions. In November 1969, they were formally separated, and the Winters Deputy Warden for Treatment and Training became the Superintendent of Hilltop.

Two possible disadvantages because of this history of the institution must be mentioned. Hilltop received its first direct commitments in June 1970, in the midst of this research. This change in commitment procedure created two sets of related problems. For the first time, the institution was dealing with some offenders who were not "prisonized" to some degree at entry. This change may have produced some short-term administrative problems that influenced in some unknown direction the collection of data. Second, officers, who are also generally transfers from Winters, were for the first time dealing with a subordinate group whose members were not all arriving with maximum security experience.

These problems, however, may also have had advantages. None of the questionnaires utilized is very sensitive to these phenotypical changes. Therefore, while organizational conflict may have increased from some "normal" state, it is not likely that the organization moved in directions different from those that could have been predicted from trends measured by the instruments anyway. Moreover, the temporary heightening of conflict may have highlighted relationships crucial to the hypotheses and, therefore, increased the power of discrimination, although the number of people surveyed remained unchanged. Nevertheless, these particular events at Hilltop made it paramount that our research findings at Hilltop be compared to findings at other institutions. These comparisons are reported in Chapter 8.

IMPLICATIONS FOR FURTHER RESEARCH

This combination of management and policy material is rather new in the correctional area. Whether the hypotheses are supported or not, it will open many questions that need greater study, and perhaps many answers that will need greater amplification. If hypotheses about prisons as complex organizations are *not* supported, the most important question is: Why not? What is it about the total institution, about the prison community, that makes it so different from other types of organizations? The general hypotheses that behavior of managers will affect the behavior of people at the lowest echelons of the organization would have a high expectancy of empirical support if tested in other types of organizations. Perhaps the answer, in essence, would be that the prison really is distinguished from other organizations on the issue of treatment versus punishment, and that this organizational schizophrenia is really qualitatively different from inter-echelon conflicts and informal countercultures found in other kinds of organizations. If so, correctional administrators and academicians will have a considerably more difficult time than they do even now in supporting the type of operation we call corrections.

If the hypotheses about organizational behavior are supported, beyond necessary replication, three major challenges immediately appear.

(1) There may be at some time the opportunity to specify as a prison is built that selection of staff and inmates will be determined by correctional and administrative measurements in such a way as to increase the likelihood of achieving objectives chosen as desirable.

(2) There is the entire issue left open here, of changing an ongoing operation by using as measures of desirable variance the questionnaires used here, or reorganizing the available personnel in such a way that a more productive interaction pattern is achieved. Some of the focal points in the issue of correctional change are discussed in Chapter 9.

(3) There should be the possibility of a comparative study, provided that a method of measuring total effect of a greater number of individuals could be achieved, in which end product measures (recidivism or success on parole) could be contrasted for different correctional organizations. Work on this point is being undertaken by the author now.

In addition, there is the largely untouched area, whose investigation is mandated even now, wherein this material should be of considerable relevance. As Professor Wilkins has pointed out on several occasions, when techniques are available in the correctional area for measuring acceptable and unacceptable variations in behavior patterns at various decision points, administrators and academicians will have a better chance of concentrating on the ethical dimension of policy considerations. There is at the present stage of guess-and-guess-again little in the way of policy-making that rises from the morass of belief and, sadly, from the rhetoric of hypocrisy to the properly ethical sphere. We have too little information about the effects of our present activity.[33] Choice becomes rational when the action predicates of our propositions are not so long delayed or widely diffused that the connection is an effort of faith. A researcher, if one were an inmate or an officer, would not like to depend on the faith of superiors.

A SPECIAL NOTE ON IMPLICATIONS FOR
THE CRIMINAL JUSTICE SYSTEM

Perhaps unfortunately, this research has dwelt upon corrections alone and upon one prison specifically. The nature of the research so demands. In the study of industrial management, by way of contrast, progress in research has been such that there is an admirable combination of the specific nature of particular manufacturing processes and the general theory of organizations. But that, for the most part, remains the integration of one body of sociological theory with advanced knowledge of a body of techniques, such as the assembly-line process, the engineering of an airplane engine, the budgeting of piecework. In this study, there is a combination of organizational and criminological theory and research. The bite is quite as large as can be chewed.

However, it is possible to conclude with a note of systemic scope: the criminal justice system as a system must be studied in terms of the organizational behavior that militates against or facilitates cooperation among agencies. That problem will not be ignored in this study largely because the organizational theory we use demands close scrutiny of organizational environments. Any prison does much adjusting to the environment that includes the police and the courts. In this connection, no data will be collected for this study, no formal hypotheses will be drawn. But special attention will be accorded the processes of the system as they impinge on prison organization, and as the findings about prison operation impinge upon the policy and the courts, and on the community in general. This system of study is, of course, circular. If corrections is the end of a criminal justice system, it may also be the beginning, particularly, it would seem, if correction is to take place, rather than just incarceration.

THE CLASSIFICATIONS OF PRISONS BY ORGANIZATIONAL STRUCTURE IN ORGANIZATIONAL AND CORRECTIONAL LITERATURE

There are many possible angles of vision from which to view prison organizations. Each may be helpful for particular studies or social purposes. A politician, for example, may be more interested in how his or her constituency views prisons than in what a prison may look like to correctional officers and inmates. A journalist might be interested in general living conditions, in histories of interesting individuals, or in reports of crisis situations. For many years, sociologists seemed interested in describing the human interaction processes in the prison and drawing hypothetical explanations of how those processes began and were maintained.[1]

For many years, the scientific interest in prisons was rather academic. While Clemmer humanistically deplored what "prisonization" did to a man, he did not present alternatives to the situation he witnessed, nor did his brand of sociology offer much aid in seeking these alternatives.[2] Gradually, however, the social sciences have become interested not only in understanding complex phenomena but also in seeking the kind of understanding that will allow some changes to take place. For example, Clemmer concluded that while prisons were awful, he was not sure how important that awfulness was in the total picture of the world.[3] The world has in 1975 answered him that prisons are indeed important. On the other hand, the social sciences have turned to the examination of some variables, the manipulation of which is not totally dependent on general social approval, or upon a political referendum. We have learned in the study of organization that

[16]

isolation can be protective as well as damaging. If inmates, correctional personnel, and wardens arrive at a consensus about the awfulness of the present situation, there are some ways in which they can change the internal order of that prison without changing the social mandate under which they work. There are also some ways in which they can affect political and social opinion so that the experts can innovate in desired ways.

The sociological study that contributes to the change in organizations generally focuses on the structure of those organizations as it is delineated and elaborated by the people who live and work inside it. The present report is not a study on changing a prison, but it is a study of existing variations in prison structure that are manipulable by those who seek change.

In order to provide a sound basis upon which to analyze these organizational variables, it will be helpful to review previous prison studies that were concerned with organizational structure. To obtain a balanced perspective, four studies by recognized leaders in organizational and prison analysis have been selected. Daniel Katz and Robert Kahn discuss prison in the context of describing the social system as an organization. Amitai Etzioni discusses prisons as a prime example of his coercive type of organization. In a series of articles, Donald Cressey discusses differences in goals and management patterns in custodially and treatment-oriented prisons. Finally, David Street, Robert Vinter, and Charles Perrow conducted a comparative study of six institutions for juvenile offenders in which the classifying variable was the correctional goal chosen for implementation by the institutional executive. Thus, this review can provide us with a brief look at the major ways in which the organizational structure of prisons can be analyzed.

POLITICAL OR MAINTENANCE ORGANIZATIONS

Katz and Kahn[4] frequently mention prisons in their opening chapters as they discuss the theory of open systems in relation to organizations. It is somewhat difficult to abstract from their discussion an integrated look at prison organization, because they use the prison as an example of more general points. Since their analysis of prisons is fragmentary, it is not as successful as their discussion of other organizations later in the work. Nevertheless, their novel approach must not be ignored.

Prisons, along with social welfare organizations and schools, they suggest, differ from factories or mining operations in that their product involves the processing or manipulation of people. "Because human beings are reactive, and will interact with the organization during any molding process, the cooperation must be gained of the persons subjected to the change process."[5]

All prisons differ from object-processing organizations in two major ways. First, staff at the lowest level direct the activity of other people in prisons. Because other people, as compared with inanimate objects, may behave in variable manners, staff at the lowest level must be able to respond in a number of ways. Hence, the lowest staff echelon needs discretionary power and the stability and confidence to use it.[6] Second, the prison will differ from other organizations in the way in which external transactions with other agencies and organizations are managed. Since prisons are not primarily concerned with exporting commodities, the institution is less open to immediate external influences, such as market fluctuations or boycotts.[7]

People-processing organizations may be distinguished from object-processing organizations by the level at which discretion may be officially sanctioned or planned and the type of exchange with the environment. Variations in these two key structural factors may also distinguish prisons from other people-processing organizations. Katz and Kahn suggest that organizational structure will vary with the social purpose of the organization, since purpose will determine amount of discretion and type of environmental exchange. They distinguish prisons from other people-processing organizations on the macro-organizational level, in terms of how prisons usually fit into the larger social system. Most organizations take on one major social function, of which they see five: political, educational, production, research and adaptation, and boundary. Prisons, until lately, they suggest, have served political ends by maintaining order in society. Those persons who could not accept the normal social order are punished and controlled by incarceration. The structure of prisons servicing political goals is dominated by the control theme. The prison in this case is likely to have a steep hierarchy, with executives holding the power both to decide on goals and to implement them. In other words, persons who have decided what the organization should do also possess the operational responsibility.[8] Inmates, of course—but officers and other staff as well—have no say in formulating policy or program. Power of the top echelon is total,[9] and top staff will be considerate of the wishes of those persons or groups who are perceived as a source of that power: governor, legislature, politically powerful business groups, and so on. The prison function is political, and the prison operation largely one of exile, or the keeping of people who have been deemed society's enemies.

With the political prison, Katz and Kahn compare the rehabilitative prison. This type of prison does not serve the political subsystem through the achievement of order, but the educational subsystem through the achievement of rehabilitative goals. The educational prison cannot be total and autocratic because the inmates need to be involved to a much greater extent in the organization.[10] The staff in a political prison could do well without much attention to the needs of inmates, since their job primarily is administering to the needs of the society rather than to the needs of the incarcerated population. But the staff in the educational prison need to obtain from the inmates certain changes in the prescribed direction. This "means some obscuring of the line of cleavage of power and privilege."[11] But Katz and Kahn state that most educational prisons have taken over much of the physical trappings, as well as administrative patterns, from the political prison. Therefore, most prisons find themselves serving the two conflicting functions to varying degrees, with a considerable program of integration.[12]

The analytical treatment of prisons by Katz and Kahn would have had greater utility if they had followed the open system format that they apply with admirable skill to other organizations, by narrowing their sights and focusing on organizational rather than social system goals. But their discussion of prisons occurs in their analysis of the larger social system, and the relative deficiencies for the study of prison structure are apparent. Their distinction between educational and political functions, or between the kinds of prisons that manifest either, are not always clear.

In summary, Katz and Kahn analyze prisons in terms of how those organizations function for the larger social system. Dependent on social function, prison structure differs in two major ways: (1) use of discretion and the level at which it is found, and (2) interchange with other organizations. Katz and Kahn would predict greater discretion and more discretion at lower organizational levels in educational prisons than in political prisons. They would expect more variable interchange in educational prisons, with more emphasis on development of inmate services in educational prisons than in prisons with political functions.

COERCIVE ORGANIZATIONS

In his theoretical work on organizational structure, Etzioni gives prisons rather extensive coverage.[13] Developing a structural comparison of prisons from Katz and Kahn involves the risk of extrapolation because their concern for prisons was largely exemplary and subordinate to their wish to develop a theory of behavior in any organization. Etzioni has his sights set lower. He desires to develop testable propositions about organization, and his format is that of serial comparison. Hence, abstracting his analysis of prison organization is largely a mechanical task.

Etzioni classifies organizations in terms of their compliance type and distribution of power. His constant focus is on the compliance patterns associated with the lowest echelon of the organization, and the effects of that compliance upon the commitment of the echelon to the organization.[14] His three compliance patterns are: (1) coercive, in which control is by force, and the coerced members are alienated; (2) utilitarian, in which control is by monetary reward, and members have calculative commitment; and (3) normative, in which control is by manipulation of status, prestige, or social acceptance, and members are willingly involved.

Prisons are distinguished from other organizations in that the compliance is coercive and lower groups are alienated from superordinate levels. Types of prisons are differentiated according to the amount of force used and amount of alienation found. Etzioni arranges prisons on a continuum according to the amount of force used to gain compliance from inmates. At the more severe of the two poles, Etzioni places concentration camps that are instruments of mass murder. At the mild end, he puts correctional institutions in which force is tempered with some rehabilitative attempts. Between these poles, going from the severe to the mild, Etzioni sets prisons, many mental hospitals, prisoner of war camps, relocation centers, and delinquency rehabilitation centers.[15]

He then suggests a relationship between the compliance structure of the organization and the goals an organization accomplishes. As there are coercive, utilitarian, and normative compliance patterns, there are order, economic, and cultural goals. He postulates that most organizations have one primary goal and one dominant compliance pattern. Compliance patterns and goals tend to be congruent so that in prisons, with coercive compliance, the goals are those of maintaining order.[16]

Some organizations, however, have more than one goal, and where prisons have multiple goals, Etzioni suggests that multiple compliance patterns will also be found. For example, he hypothesizes that in prisons that have a heavy emphasis on prison industrial production, the compliance structure will tend to be utilitarian.[17]

The congruency between compliance and goals is based on effectiveness. Coercive compliance is most effective in attaining order goals, since the inmate economy will not sustain utilitarian patterns, and normative power is blocked by alienation of the inmates. Since order goals are largely evaluated in terms of "total success" (no escapes, no riots), all inmates must be treated as potential risks and all equally coerced to comply with regulations.[18]

Etzioni maintains that the social structure of prisons is also related to compliance. Suggesting that there are two types of leadership skill and opportunity, forming expressive and instrumental elites, he proposes that, as coercion increases, the membership in these elites becomes more distinct. Inmates develop their own expressive leaders ("right guys") who govern in matters of inmate norms and ideology and the distribution of status and prestige. The instrumental elite is necessarily the official staff who have the commodities for subsistence and the force to control physical activity. The inmate group develops its own instrumental elite, however, who have some control over the redistribution of instrumentalities—goods and information. The inmate instrumental elite is controlled, however, by the inmate expressive elite, who do not stop to do business with officials. As the amount of coercion is reduced, so is the split in the elite structure. Hence, instrumental inmate elites are less evident in relocation centers and correctional institutions than in maximum security prisons. In the least coercive institutions, the officials (Etzioni suggests counselors) may have some expressive power, or, at any rate, the expressive inmate leaders are not so alienated from officials.[19]

Etzioni also proposes that the variables of consensus, communication, and socialization vary in the expected fashion. The more coercion, the less consensus between staff and inmates.[20] Distribution of downward instrumental communication narrows with increase in coercion, but upward instrumental communication and expressive communication are relatively unvarying.[21] In almost all cases, expressive socialization (what ought to be done) is left to inmates, while instrumental socialization by inmates by staff (such as vocational training) is possible in rehabilitation centers, where there is less coercion, but is not so possible in more coercive institutions because inmate instrumental elites are more dominant. Etzioni concludes that dissension among ranks will be maintained as long as staff are socialized by staff and inmates are socialized by inmates. Dissension will be reduced when the socialization of expressive norms, particularly, has some vertical scope within the organization. As long as expressive norms are spread horizontally within a rank, the inmate-staff conflict will be visible.[22]

Etzioni perceives the atmosphere within the organization as an important organizational variable.[23] He divides this atmosphere into two independent parts, its pervasiveness and its scope. The scope of the organization refers to the number of activities that organizational members do together. Pervasiveness refers to the number of norms set by the organization for its members, or the number of activities of members that the organization seeks to influence.[24] Scope and coercion are directly related; the more totalitarian the prison, the more activities inmates are forced to do together or the greater the scope. Coercion and pervasiveness are inversely related; the less the coercion, the more the organization affects inmate norms and the more official behavior patterns are internalized by inmates, or the greater the pervasiveness.[25] Etzioni has the important insight that highly coercive organizations have little control over inmate norms, and also little control over community belief about the proper treatment of inmates. There is little to buffer inmates from community resentment in coercive prisons—these institutions are pervaded rather than pervasive.[26]

In his last two chapters, Etzioni switches from a static to a dynamic perspective in his analysis. He attempts to show the interaction of his interrelated variables over time. Normative organizations, he points out, frequently exhibit intermittent structures. They disband periodically except for a skeleton maintenance crew, and then they reform for periods of heavy activity. Charity drives and churches have this characteristic in common. Prisons, however, never take on an intermittent structure because order goals demand continuous surveillance. The objective is to prevent certain things from occurring, and this cannot be done periodically.[27]

In his last chapter, however, Etzioni modifies the unrelenting nature of prison compliance. He points out that, within this century, there has been a marked increase in normative compliance and a similar decrease in coercion. Since this change is sweeping and unrelated to any particular type of organization, Etzioni attributes the change to outside influence, or to the external environment of all organizations. He suggests that the boundary processes of all organizations are concerned with the external factors producing the common trend. The organizational variables immediately related to the boundaries or the organization are scope, pervasiveness, and recruitment.[28] While Etzioni's recognition of the prison as a system in constant interchange with its environment is brief, he makes the important point that the atmosphere within is related to the atmosphere without.

In summary, Etzioni's analysis of prisons begins one step lower than the analysis of prisons by Katz and Kahn. He is concerned with comparing organizations to other organizations, rather than with integrating all organizations of a particular type into the social system. He states that prisons differ from other organizations based upon the kind of compliance structure utilized with the lowest echelon of the organization (inmates). Because all prisons have coercive compliance structure, he states that they are most likely to have order goals. This analysis is fairly satisfactory on the macro-organizational level, but it begs many questions about differentiating between prisons or dealing with variability within one prison. It would not appear to be a useful analytical tool in distinguishing between prisons, because it does not allow for a sensitive differentiation among the many operational prison goals that must be understood in order to make much sense of different management patterns and a growing variety of correctional programs.

A PRISON FEEDBACK SYSTEM

Donald Cressey's analysis of prisons does not attempt to do so much as the studies of Katz and Kahn and Etzioni, and perhaps partly for that reason, his set of articles[29] on two West Coast prisons seems to accomplish considerably more than the first two studies. Cressey is not using prisons as examples of types of organizations, but rather tries to use a theory of organizations to explain behavior that he has observed in prisons. The theory on which Cressey relies is the theory of bureaucracy developed by Blau, Gouldner, and Merton.[30]

In general, the bureaucratic model usually represents the use of bureaucratic authority by superiors and the unintended consequences that occur within the organization that reinforce the superior's original action.[31] For example, Merton studied employment agencies in which the superiors' desire for control of the organization resulted in their demand for increased reliability of procedures. The added emphasis on rules had the intended consequence of providing easy evaluation of employees and defensibility of individual action in terms of the promulgated rules. However, the expanded attention to rules also increased rigidity of employee behavior and client complaints about the agency. Additional client complaints intensified the felt need for defensibility of individual action, which in turn increased the emphasis on reliability of procedures. Hence, the dysfunctional aspects of the original action fed back into the system in such a way that the problem-generating behavior continued.[32]

Cressy suggests that prison structure differs from this general model of bureaucracy, because, rather than consistent methods of employee evaluation applied to the detriment of the organization, the goals of correctional agencies are contradictory and result in conflicting control mechanisms. All prisons, he states, have both treatment and custodial components. In any particular prison, one goal may predominate, but never can the treatment-oriented prison operate without regard for the crisis such as an escape or violent rule infraction, and never can the custody-oriented prison ignore demands for humanitarian treatment of offenders.

Evaluation of officers proceeds in either type of prison under multiple criteria. The custodial guard must enforce all rules, but at the same time he must treat prisoners with respect and watch carefully that too severe domination does not stir up revolt. The treatment officer must relax stringent conditions so that prison atmosphere is compatible with counseling requirements, but he must at the same time remind prisoners that they are being punished and regulated for criminal acts.

Under these conditions, officer deviations and considerable organizational inefficiency are related to contradictory directives. In the custodial prison, the officer can only receive demerits, and in the treatment prison, the officer is never punished.[33] Officers in the treatment setting can use their discretion to exact their own informal punishment upon inmates through ridicule or by withholding their affection. Hence, they are able to use the treatment setting for their own purposes, but there are no ways of evaluating which uses of discretion aid rehabilitation and which uses retard it.[34] At the custodially oriented prison, officers are strictly forbidden from using such discretion. They are permitted to do something to an inmate only after an observed infraction of the rules. However, the officer must also prevent disorder by interacting with offenders before an infraction takes place. This kind of interaction can only take place if officers defy regulations, according to Cressey.[35]

Cressey is at his best in analyzing the relationships between values of power and participation and the nature of exchange with the environment. For example, he suggests that the unstated prison goal of protecting inmates takes various forms depending on these values. In the custody prison that he studied, managers viewed themselves as public servants who were open to political influence (compare with the Katz and Kahn political prison). Hence, inmates were constantly on display to outside groups who were curious about prisons. In the treatment prisons, managers viewed themselves as professionals who sought different outside support. Prison tours were a rarity, but academic research programs were common.[36]

Perhaps it is Cressey's desire to make a unique case for prisons that hinders him from drawing the strongest conclusions available in his own analysis. These conclusions are ones that might be suggested by the more global but less stringent analysis by Katz and Kahn. Primarily, these conclusions would involve the study of the prison as an open system, in which the internal activity of a prison organization is directly related to interaction with the environment, and the inability of most prison managers (in either custody or treatment prisons) to recognize the behavior most effective in an open system. In other words, most of the conflict that Cressey attributes to contradictory goals of prisons might be more effectively analyzed in terms of correctional managerial practices that detract from the natural operation of open systems. In the custodial prison, close surveillance seems to have too costly a price in both officer and inmate commitment to the achievement of order, which is usually a political goal demanded by outsiders. In the treatment prison, new treatment professionals have been added to the organization at too high a price in terms of treatment-custody conflict. In either of these cases, the significant point is not the impossibility of achieving the goals, but the inaccurate implementation of goals by presently available control and evaluation techniques.

ORGANIZATION FOR THE ACHIEVEMENT OF GOALS

Street, Vinter, and Perrow's major comparative study of six institutions for juvenile delinquents also begins with the common assumption that certain organizational structures are correlated with certain organizational goals.[37] Street, Vinter, and Perrow begin their organizational analysis by examining the nature of organizational goals, and they proceed to discover the structural implications of these specific aims. They complete their analytic cycle by establishing the way in which daily operational patterns reinforce or alter the goal-formulation activity, further changing the organizational structure.

Street, Vinter, and Perrow achieve considerable success in their organizational analysis because of the care with which they select the type of goals upon which to build their analysis. They discuss four major conceptions or organizational goals:

(1) Goals as official mandates (such as legislative preambles to statutes establishing correctional organizations).

(2) Goals as outputs to external agents or larger social structures (such as keeping order in society by removing disruptive people).

(3) Goals as personal and group commitments (such as religious sect's desire to save wayward youth, or a desire of prison guards to demean and punish inmates).

(4) Goals as the essential constraints built into the organization (such as the structural configurations established by executive managerial strategies).[38]

All four conceptions have been used at various times for different analytic purposes. Katz and Kahn and Etzioni use the second concept (goals as functions of the organization in the larger social system).[39] But while organizations may be viewed as they function for the social system, this is a descriptive view that does not consider the organization as it operates to do real work (transform an input into an output), and, hence, does not provide an adequate base from which to study the structure through which the work is accomplished.[40] Viewing the organizational goals as social functions may allow broad classification schemes of different types of organizations, but we agree with Street, Vinter, and Perrow in assumption that "the analysis of differences in organizational goals, as a means of distinguishing organizations, is *most* useful among organizations that are very similar in purpose."[41]

Street, Vinter, and Perrow adopt the fourth goal perspective— "goals as the essential contraints built into the organization."[42] This framework relates structure and goals by definition, because organizations are structured for production rather than for the coincidental consequences that they may serve for society. In other words, organizations are truly future-oriented, and should be studied as such.

Street, Vinter, and Perrow suggest that goals, as the structural constraints of an organization, are formulated, within limits, by the executives (policy-makers) of an organization. In addition to legal limits, political influence, and so on, one important limit to this formulation is that the executive, in making primary decisions, has alternatives constrained by his or her own value system. This value system has been learned through past professional experience, in past employment, collegiate reference, and professional perspectives about how best to change people.

Regardless of the specific prison structure that develops, all prisons have in common with welfare agencies, schools, and churches is that their organization is arranged to change people. This is the primary task. But this task may be accomplished in many ways, with many different results. Thus, the executives must decide what kind of change they value, how they should articulate that change goal to the public and the staff, and how they should arrange and manage staff for the achievement of the desired change.[43]

The authors develop three institutional models into which they classify the six institutions under study, according to organizational goals.[44] They state that these models are roughly spaced on a "custody-treatment" continuum, but they are careful to explain that the continuum should signify an alteration in the way inmates are perceived, in the method of change chosen, and in the complexity of organizational structure. The three models are:

(1) *Obedience/conformity.* Habits, respect for authority, and also training in conformity are emphasized. The technique is *conditioning.* Obedience/conformity maintains undifferentiated views of its inmates, emphasizes immediate accommodation to external controls, and utilizes high levels of staff domination with many negative sanctions.

(2) *Reeducation/development.* Inmates are to be changed through training. Changes in attitudes and values, acquisition of skills, the development of personal resources, and new social behaviors are sought.

(3) *Treatment.* The treatment institution focuses on the psychological *reconstitution* of the individual. It seeks more thorough-going personality change than the other types. To this end, it emphasizes gratifica-

tions and varied activities, with punishments relatively few and seldom severe.[45]

Using these models as a framework by which to distinguish consequences, the authors structure their research around four basic assumptions:

(1) that the substantive goals will have many consequences for organizational behavior;

(2) that the executive strategies make these goals operational and hence will have important implications for structure and conflict;

(3) that different change strategies will evoke different responses in inmates with further implications for structure, in terms of staff relations with inmates; and

(4) that different organizational patterns will have different consequences upon the inmate group itself, with additional feedback to staff structure and goal formulation.[46]

In general, these hypotheses were supported by the year of research in the six institutions. As the goals progressed from custody to treatment, they found (1) that inmates were perceived more as sick than as unwilling to cooperate or change; (2) that inmates were perceived and treated more on an individual basis; (3) that staff were younger, better educated, and professionally trained; (4) that executive reference and activity changed from political to professional groups; (5) that relations with other organizations were more varied; (6) that staff had more varied tasks, more interdependent tasks, and were more often in conflict; (7) that staff changed from action upon inmates to engagement of inmates; (8) that inmate leaders were less often antagonistic to staff aims and less coercive in dealing with other inmates; and (9) that, in general, inmates were less alienated and more committed to staff values, norms, and official programs.[47]

While different methods have been devised to measure variations in managerial philosophy, Street, Vinter, and Perrow use a clinical assessment of the key executives in the institutions rather than more rigorous, replicable methods. Therefore, the strength of the comparative study of delinquency institutions lies in the utilization of an open system theory that remains incomplete, and an insightful treatment of managerial behavior that remains anecdotal. The study, however, should be considered seminal in the field, because the completeness and openness of the design allow for emendation where other studies beg for contradiction.

PRISON GOALS AND PRISON STRUCTURE

There are some obvious common threads running through these four different studies of prison structure. The simplest way of stating the major point is that prisons will differ according to variations in goals. Evidently, prisons can be structured to serve a variety of different purposes, or they can be described as performing several different functions. It is also quite clear that the description of prison structure and its relationship to goals will vary with the purposes of analysis.

For their purposes, Katz and Kahn's discussion of political and educational functions of prisons was very much to the point. We also saw that, on this level, the prison is a vague generality and that contradictions develop between the definition of a prison as a people-processing organization and the structural characteristics of a politically functional prison. We saw similar problems arise in Etzioni's comparison of the gross differences in organizations. What further complicates Etzioni's treatment is that the goals he uses in his analysis are again goals-as-social-functions. From time to time, he speaks of organizations as planned units at least partially reactive to their achievement of goals, or to their effectiveness. The behavior of personnel in working for effectiveness is not easily explained in terms of social functionality. Cressey focuses on organizational effectiveness (while infrequently mentioning the concept) by studying the planned managerial attempts to achieve both treatment and custodial goals. He demonstrates that these two purposes frequently contradict each other, or that correctional officers frequently violate the evaluation criteria of one goal in order to achieve a good rating by the evaluation criteria for the other goal. Last, Street, Vinter, and Perrow go further than any of the other analysts in clarifying the executive strategies used to operationalize policy. In doing so, they study the executive as an organizational gatekeeper to outside influence and as a major determinant of internal organizational activity.

Since the purpose of the present analysis is to select and study those variables manipulation of which promises the potential of planned change, a first step is to identify those organizational goals that have a direct bearing on organizational structure. Hence, we should choose a method of studying prison organization that allows us to begin with the kind of goals that Cressey and Street, Vinter, and Perrow found important. These goals should be stated in such a way that they connote executive choices in interaction with an outside environment and executive strategies in organizing personnel and inmates. This study of organization should also capitalize on the functioning of the prison as an open system in which the internal, goal-directed or production activity is related to the outside world. Last, this study should allow us to look at the ways in which correctional managers recognize and accommodate the interdependence of all the people within the organization, including the people who are processed through the prison.

CHAPTER 3

THE PRISON AS AN OPEN SYSTEM

The review of the prison analyses by Katz and Kahn, Etzioni, Cressey, and Street et al. has demonstrated that, even though formulated under widely varying concerns and traditions, those authors' distinctive treatments of prison organization probably have more commonalities than contradictions. The basic difference stems from the type of goals around which each study is structured. Goals as functions in the larger social structure seem less effective than goals as policy or structural constraints, when the purpose of the study is differentiation among prisons. All four analyses agree that prisons should be studied as organizations that change people, but only Cressey and Street utilize that fact to any advantage. Except for Etzioni, all these studies find environmental-organizational exchange of utmost importance, but only Cressey and Street, who combine that exchange with goals-as-policy, make much headway in classifying the environmental exchange. Only the latter two studies give much attention to different styles of managerial behavior and consequent staff and inmate reactions. The ability to use this material seems to hinge significantly on (1) viewing the prison as a system of activity in which internal action is related to action in the environment, and (2) choosing to study the type of goals which are theoretically related to systemic behavior.

A more complete theory of prison organization that capitalizes on both the strengths and the deficiencies of former studies would now seem possible. In general, this theory should permit analysis of the prison as an open system and facilitate the systematic observation of managers as they react to that situation. While there can be no set rules on the most effective way to perceive organizational variables, the more successful studies of Cressey and Street et al. suggest that managerial behavior may be treated as an independent variable. Considerable attention must also be given to the way in which organizational behavior at lower levels feeds back into the system and changes managerial action. The relationship between managerial and officer behavior in a prison, for example, may actually be one of mutual causation. However, in such a relationship, it may be helpful to consider as the independent variable the managerial behavior, because that is the variable most frequently available for manipulation by the investigators. In day-to-day prison operations, it may well be that officer or inmate behavior influences the behavior of managers as much as managers' behavior influences subordinates' activity.

Where the causal arrows go both directions simultaneously, traditional causal analysis is of no use. However, it is becoming increasingly important now in the criminal justice field for social scientists and managers to be able to change the present structure of the system. As a change strategy, it is wiser to begin at the top of an organization than at the bottom, if only to gain *first* the commitment to change from the persons who have last say in organizational behavior. The requirements of planned change are different from the requirements of a more traditional social analysis that did not have as its motivation changes in the system being studied.

THE PRISON AND TYPES OF SYSTEMS

There are several system frameworks within which to fit the behavior of correctional managers and its consequences. A closed system is a self-contained organization, the parameters of which are unchanging. An open system is an organization whose boundaries are changing during its operation, and thus during the study of its operation. A learning system is a type of open system capable of changing its own internal structure of such alterations are needed for continued production or goal achievement.

Whether to study the prison as a closed or an open system is not a clear-cut decision. If a prison is to be studied as a closed system, then all the external variables affecting prison operation must be constant during the study. If the prison is to be studied as open, then some of the parameters of the system are allowed to vary during the study.[1] Thus, the decision of open or closed depends upon what kind of prison operations we are interested in, whether it is known which parameters have effects on these operations, and whether there is some way of controlling these parameters.

In all these regards, the knowledge and skill of social science researchers is rather incomplete. The prison has not often been studied as a system where external variables were thought to be important. As a result, we have rather incomplete knowledge of the parameters of internal variation in the prison system. For many years, the prison was studied as a closed system—to the extent that the major studies *assumed* that the parameters were constant. The two primary examples of this approach are the analyses of prison social systems by Clemmer[2] and Sykes.[3] Clemmer rarely mentions the outside world at all, let alone variations in particular parts of it, or of any attempts to control them. Sykes' study of the Trenton prison rested on the assumption that the general social ethic did not permit gross brutality by guards. This demand for simple humanitarianism on the part of prison officials was a constraint on the prison system and had the effect that custodial officers did not have the full range of techniques of control that they would have needed to make the totalitarian scheme of government effective. Hence, it was a parameter of the prison system that brought techniques and strategies of control into conflict and pressured the guards to accommodate certain rule infractions by inmates. It is this relationship between the prison world and the outside world that Sykes labels the "limits of the totalitarian regime."

Another external variable that presumably is important to both studies is the characteristics of offenders upon entrance to prison. Clemmer and Sykes both spend considerable time describing the ritual of initiation that occurs when an inmate first enters the prison. Clemmer concludes that the process of "prisonization" affected inmates in various ways, depending on such characteristics as family ties and time to serve. While Sykes spends more time describing the pains of imprisonment than he does noting the variations in their felt intensity, presumably he, too, would agree that such pains are relative to the background and references of the inmates. It was not until some years after Sykes' study that the suggestion was made that too little attention was given these variations. Autobiographical works of people subject to the pains of imprisonment suggest that lower-class people who go to prison most frequently have anticipated prison as part of their life cycle.[4] A more recent study of the prison and the parole process suggested that the uniqueness of the process of incarceration was overemphasized by Sykes and Clemmer. The counter-suggestion was made that prisonization is just an institutional form of deprivation felt by lower-class, uneducated, and black offenders most of their lives. If the prison is not a totally isolated life event, then it becomes very important to know what kinds of variables in the larger social system affect the prison organization.[5]

Finally, another external constraint that has been receiving increasing attention is the rate at which the community reabsorbs offenders into the social system. It is only in conjunction with an examination of reentry difficulties that the prison can be understood as a system with input, throughput, and output. The methodologies in studies of recidivism rates have varied considerably, but it probably is true that failure rates vary from one type of prison to another and from one type of inmate to another. The most complete study of recidivism yet done produced the rather unexpected failure rate of approximately thirty percent in the federal prison system. Many experts had expected that the rate was actually much higher.[6]

One commonly cited article suggests that the failure rate itself is not so important to internal prison structure as is the available information about reentry. This study suggests that the inmates' culture is generated when the inmates' desire to conform to staff norms is undercut by information that the results of rehabilitation are unrewarding. Inmates in prison receive most of their information about parole from recidivists and parole revokees. Therefore, no matter what the rate of success on parole, inmate behavior in prison is affected by biased information.[7] Like the other studies, the works by Glaser and Cloward treat these variables of recidivism and information as rather stable quantities. There is no report of the effect of variations in informational feedback or variations in the recidivism rate.

One of the few analyses of the prison system as an open system is the rather thorough examination of the Oahu Prison riot of

1960.[8] Although this is basically a historical rather than a sociological account, the riot is clearly related to changes in the political environment of the prison that had disruptive consequences within the prison social structure. In a more recent study of peaceful changes in prison social structure, the tightening of prison security regulations is attributed to changes in a department of corrections headquarters and to gubernatorial campaign promises, rather than to changes initiated within the prison itself.[9]

The major differences in these two studies from the previous examinations of prison social systems is the interest in *change* in that system. In the prison studies that are concerned with understanding the internal social processes of the prison, the prison is usually viewed as a closed system (i.e., one in which the environmental parameters of the prison are assumed to be unchanging). In the studies interested in variations in the social processes of the prison, the prison is usually viewed as an open system (i.e., one in which the environmental parameters of the prison are changing, or are changing more rapidly than was the case in the other studies).

The dimension of change is rather new to the social science of organizations. There have been many haphazard studies of organizations in change and many hypotheses about why they change. *Planned* attempts to change organizations, however, are rather new, and many have been unsuccessful. Frequently the "changers" have sought to vary organizational behavior by altering variables that were not organizational in scope. For example, it has been reported that positive changes in individual managers at training conferences have even produced negative changes in the organization.[10]

Reviewing the checkered history of planned change in organizations, Katz and Kahn conclude that the most significant changes in organization are caused by alterations in external events.[11] This conclusion leads us to an even less well known area of organizational study, particularly when the organizations in question are prisons. If the most significant changes in organizations come about by alterations in system parameters, to what extent is it possible for organizations to change these parameters deliberately? For example, if Etzioni is correct that the amount of coercion in organizations has decreased because of changes in external society, could it be possible that prison managers who favored less coercion in their prisons could effect certain alterations in the external society?[12] If a prison system can behave in such a way that it continuously changes itself in order to do its job more effectively, that open system would be a learning one. It would be a system that had the ability to adapt to predicted changes in its parameters, or one that could even change its parameters.

THE LEARNING SYSTEM

Whether or not the average prison is now an open system with a capacity to learn is debatable. Without question, there are learning systems within a prison. New inmates learn to adjust to their circumstances in ways calculated to reduce strain.[13] Officers learn to adjust to conflicts in executive directives so that one message cancels out another.[14] A manager learns to invite different groups to the prison dependent on the goals he has chosen for the prison. Managers seeking political support may conduct tours for a curious public while managers seeking behavioral change in inmates may abhor tours and encourage visits from social scientists.[15] It is less certain that the prison system as a whole changes in response to information about the imperfect reception of prison output in the community. The answer to this question in part depends upon the purpose of the analyst.

In a broad historical perspective, the prison institutional structure has changed from penitentiary to work house to more varied present modes that in the extreme may approach either a hospital or a job-training and referral service. Different ways of treating the offender have demanded different styles of management and different responses in both staff and inmate populations. The structure was changed, and the system has adapted as the punishment of criminal offenders has reflected changes in social ideas about society and about punishment.

To the historical analyst, then, the prison system has learned. For example, Alcatraz is no longer operated because the benefits of that type of prison no longer are worth its operational cost. Or, as another instance, the U.S. and Pennsylvania prison systems have been experimenting with the provision of community sponsors for each inmate, so that the prisoner will return to some ties in the community that have grown up during his or her prison stay. However, the historical perspective may seem trivial to the male inmate who cannot receive the services he deems he needs within his own three-year prison stay, or to the police chief who finds that his officers spend an important part of their time working on crimes committed by criminal recidivists. For the purposes of either that inmate or that police chief, the learning technique of the prison system is inadequate at best. For the social scientist, there are also certain kinds of learning that a correctional system might do that are inadequate or uninteresting. The inadequacies considered may or may not be different from those relevant to the inmate and the police chief. When is the kind of learning that open systems may do of enough significance to make the system worthy of being called a learning system?

For the purposes of this study, the prison as a learning system would be a prison in which the goals are sufficiently clear, the deviation from goals sufficiently measurable, and strategies to be employed at the occasion of deviation from goals sufficiently certain, that fundamental changes in prison structure, particularly in power and decision relationships, could occur within a matter of months. Just how many months is unspecified, but a method of analysis that considers adaptability in years is insufficient for the problems of modern society. Indeed, in a country where a "cultural generation" is now shorter than a biological generation, the need for increased rapidity or organizational response becomes crucial. For a country where the dominant ideas about right and wrong can be expected to turn about within a man's lifetime, the sensitivity of prison organization may become particularly important to the maintenance of social control and stability. More mundane, perhaps, but certainly related to the nation's increasing cultural complexity, is the demand on the prison system to respond rather rapidly to fluctuations in criminal statutes, police practices, court procedure, federal, state, and local politics, the job market, and any other variables that may affect the input or the output of the prison system.

One good example of a contemporary prison system with an inability to respond is Attica prison, which erupted in riot in September 1971. In the "manifesto" sent to Correctional Commissioner Oswald before the riot were demands for better food, medical facilities, and a training program for guards.[16] While it is true that at the time of the riot Oswald was initiating programs that would presumably have answered some of the demands, Attica had been without any significant changes for many years. Another major difficulty frequently cited as a spark to the revolt was the absence of black officers in the Attica guard force and predominance of ghetto blacks in the inmate population. In other words, in a variety of ways, the prison had not responded to major shifts in the demographic characteristics of the incarcerated population or to the increased legal and social awareness of the inmates. When the prison management did respond to changes in the prison population, and the changes in the society from which the inmates came, it did so clumsily and on the verge of the riot that finally erupted.

Correctional administrators have typically responded slowly to both internal and external evidence that change in prison structure and prison operation are necessary. In most cases, the prison as it stands is changed bit by bit, begrudgingly and slowly. As one experienced correctional administrator recently put it:

> Correctional innovations usually set things right—they reform rather than form. Commonly generated by crisis, they seldom go beyond readjustments in the existing system. In our recent work (a planning committee), we used the term "adaptive" for this kind of innovation. The adaptive innovation is a reaction to a situation rather than a response to a need, and it is almost always adapted to the system rather than the other way around.[17]

In other words, the usual changes in prisons are unplanned. They are examples of the prison as open systems, reacting to an environmental alteration, but they are not changes related prior to the crisis to some overall design that incorporated a procedure for change.[18] Many prisons are difficult to change not only because of the physical facilities that must be used, and meager budgets that must be met, but also because of the kind of organizational designs which are often used. Prison plans frequently adopt a bureaucratic and paramilitary organizational form without deciding which organizational design is most clearly related to the goals of the particular prison. If it is the goal of a prison that inmates learn new behavior patterns, a military operation is not satisfactory, because that model does not allow for role experimentation.[19]

VARIATIONS IN ENVIRONMENTAL CHANGE

It would seem unlikely that many prisons could now be considered learning systems. But if it is true that the most significant changes in organizations have external antecedents, it is quite possible that prisons will become learning systems. There seems at the present time to be a trend toward accountability in government and public administration. Politicians are making campaign promises that public bureaucracies will serve the public more effectively, and legislatures and funding sources are demanding more measurable proof of output than they used to demand. The trend, in part, may stem from frustration with action programs in the 1960s that failed in spite of good intentions and a great deal of money. The impetus may also come from the increased visibility of organizational actions that may highlight contradictions between organizational rationale and practice. In any event, there is an observable move from unregulated problem-solving forays to more carefully monitored activities capable of evaluation.[20]

Another way of explaining this kind of trend is that organizations are growing less autonomous, more interdependent, and more complex. It used to be true that a prison did its job if there were few escapees and no riots, and if the methods used to gain these objectives were not so inhumane as to become visible and reflect negatively on society itself. Now it is expected that a prison can and will make society safer not by holding onto inmates, but by releasing people who feel differently about themselves and society and demonstrate that difference by behaving differently. The prison has become accountable for the people who pass through it.[21] This new accountability means that offenders, prisons, and the society that surrounds both, are now much less distinct things. People are less willing to identify an act of a parolee solely as a manifestation of internal psychological processes. That act is now also seen as a manifestation of the way in which the offender has been prepared for parole by prison officials and the way in which the parole officials react to both the parolee and the prison. Last, society also views itself as responsible for parolees who "go straight," for parolees who do not, and for prisons and parole systems.

As the interdependencies of different organizations and actors in the criminal justice process become more apparent, the prison *will* change. But the change at some point is likely to be different in kind from changes that the prison has undergone in the past. As the prison organization reacts to the sanctions for its failures to meet the new accountability, it will strive to learn the kinds of internal operations that have effects on the behavior of people it releases. The dearth of information in this area is immense. Current statistical categories that are used to predict behavior of offenders on parole usually utilize pre-prison characteristics of parolees, because the behavior in prison is much less predictive of behavior on parole. Moreover, these statistical predictions are usually more accurate than the clinical assessments of parole board or prison officials who are knowledgeable about inmates' prison behavior and any changes that may have taken place there.[22] Although we may now consider that situation deplorable, it is not surprising, when consideration is given to the short amount of time that correctional officials have attempted to affect behavior of the offender upon release. Both their attempts and their sophistication will increase if the trend toward accountability and interdependence of organizations continues.

It will become important to separate this trend toward complexity and interdependency from moral judgments about the value of such a trend. Within a system framework, organizational environments are also organizations of a larger order. Like organizations, they tend to evolve. The study of organizational planning and interorganizational behavior has led to the identification of roughly four types of organizational environments that vary in complexity and activity and in the kind of organizational responses required, if the organization is to survive.

The latest, or emergent, environment has been called "turbulent," to refer to its primary characteristic that environmental changes occur spontaneously or by chance.[23] There is, of course, no denying that things happened by chance one hundred or two hundred years ago, also. The important difference between the environments of organizations today and environments that organizations had to contend with in, for instance, colonial America, is the consequences to the organization for not accommodating the planning for the uncertainty of chance variation. Since organizations are more interdependent and complex today, small chance variations in one part of an environment can be followed by relatively large variations in other parts of the environment. While in the past, successful organizational managers could plan a sequential pattern from A to B to C and feel successful if each step proved satisfactory, managers in a turbulent environment discover that many obvious but short-run successes become long-run failures.[24] In the long run, organizations that can adapt to turbulent conditions will tend to survive.

Trying to analyze and in some ways predict evolutionary progressions is a different sort of activity than defending or detracting from a particular prison or correctional system. It is one thing to say that if prisons continue to exist for very long, then one will notice in them more and more learning system characteristics. It is quite another thing to single out an institution in which to build a learning system, or to decide what kind of adaptable system should be encouraged. If a learning system can change its internal structure in order to achieve a certain goal more effectively, it is quite possible that a correctional system that learned would never utilize a prison facility. Perhaps it would employ only ex-offenders. Or perhaps in response to a different set of goals, the correctional systems of the future will close up even tighter, and in some manifestation of Orwell's fears, project propaganda about crime and punishment that is geared to keep the normal population at bay. In other words, the trend of correctional institutions is not set. Institutions will not get better because organizations normally tend to improve. Very simply, they will become more complex and interdependent because organizations tend to evolve. If the changes that take place are good, it is because the organization serves a purpose for the people doing the judging.

THE CORRECTIONAL MANAGER AS A CONTROLLER OF CHANGE

More than any other role in the correctional enterprise, the one role that will be essential to the construction of an adaptable correctional system is the role of correctional management. This role is crucial because of the function it performs in the organization. The manager is the gatekeeper controlling the quantity and quality of interactions between the organization and the environment. Essentially, it is on the ability of correctional management to adapt and improve that the evolutionary fate of correctional organizations depends.

Why the correctional manager is so important may not be immediately clear. There is not at present much information about the background of skills or behavior of people who are correctional managers. One major finding of the most complete survey is that correctional managers are not professional managers, but persons who have come up through ranks of correctional departments. Their behavior in the management task is rather varied and correlates more with their previous correctional jobs than with a specific concept of management per se. In other words, they may know much about corrections, but the source of their organizing behavior has usually been tradition or intuition.[25] Many of these, who have been successful correctional officials, whatever their characteristics as managers, were in favor of changing the present correctional system.[26] However, it is unlikely that correctional managers would be the most accurate source in an attempt to understand their function. In order to analyze correctional management qua management, it is necessary to raise to a conceptual level the behavioral patterns and attitudinal consistencies that have usually remained unspoken and unstudied.[27]

Since the role of managing primarily involves the task of directing or controlling, one way to conceptualize the correctional manager is as the "regulator," "governor," or "control" in a system. How the control differs in closed, open, and learning systems is not so great that a very simple system model will not suffice for this exploration. In this model, there are five important points. There is (1) a situation with boundaries to which there is (2) an input and from which there is (3) an output. There is a measure of the output by (4) the control that through (5) feedback adjusts the input to the situation in accordance with some standards that are to be met or some goal that is to be achieved. In a very simple correctional example, there is (1) an inmate to whom there comes (2) information about the prison, its staff, and inmates and from whom there evolves (3) behavior. The behavior is measured by (4) the officer who through (5) rewards and punishments regulates the messages from the inmate's environment in accordance with some standards for inmate behavior or some goal that the inmate is to achieve.

It is in this way, Cressey argues, that the correctional officer is the lowest-level manager in the correctional organization, because he performs the "regulator" or "control" function over the inmate. To a higher-level manager who is responsible for more complex control, the inmate and the officer together may be taken as the "situation." The input then is no longer the messages to the inmate or to the officer, but the information that structures the interaction of the dyad, and the output is the behavioral result of the dyad. The feedback of the manager into this situation is not necessarily information to either party, but a new way of handling the two of them together so that some standard is met or some goal achieved. If we kept building on this model, we could conceivably build an entire prison without changing our principle of construction.[28] A major distinguishing characteristic among prisons, if we were to flesh out the model, would be the nature of the feedback used in achievement of some particular goals or standards. In short, the difference is in the nature of the correctional manager.

The two most important aspects of correctional managers' role in the system model would be (1) the goals or standards to which they are comparing the output of the correctional organization below them and (2) their particular methods of regulating the inputs in order to reduce the disparity between output and goal. The first part will be called a manager's *correctional policy* and the second aspect will be called the *managerial style*. It will take some research to elaborate the varieties of correctional policy and managerial style. But in order to place those managerial characteristics in proper perspective, it will be necessary to have a more complete description of the "situation" or "organization" that is under control.

AGGREGATING AND INTEGRATING SITUATIONS

The difference between the system model explanation of the manager's role and more commonsense explanations from practicing managers is the content of the situation that the manager is, and should be, controlling. Frequently, a manager thinks of his or her job as making sure that everybody else is doing his own job correctly. To do so, the manager usually separates the organization into several different units such as "production" and "sales" or "custody" and "education" and places a subordinate manager in charge of each division. The underlying theory behind this kind of organization is that "if people will simply do their own work and follow their own specified rules, then the organization will function properly." How these pieces fit together, even if they are all working well, is often left unstated and unplanned. The problem is compounded because frequently all parts are not working properly, and so the problem of coordination is complicated by intradivisional malfunctions which in turn can cause malfunctions in other parts. A *good* manager operating with this organizational strategy usually finds that his or her job is one of putting out fires between divisions, and thus becomes the compromiser or adjudicator. Frequently, one can find oneself doing much of the work of subordinates because what had originally been an interdivisional problem has fouled up separate processes within divisions, but the technicians responsible for the separate processes find the solutions beyond their control.[29]

A common correctional example of this kind of management is the organization in which custodial and counseling staffs are managed, and are supposed to work, separately. The supervisors of these two groups are both responsible to the top manager, but they have no structured responsibilities to each other. There is no "legal" way for them to settle their problems. As a result, there may turn out to be many security problems that experts cannot solve because the needed information lies with the counseling staff, and vice versa, there may be many counseling problems in which the effective approach to the inmate lies with the custodians. The higher-level manager to whom the custodial and counseling supervisors report often finds his days filled with short-term problem-solving activities that arise from independently managing these separate parts. Frequently, the manager does not locate the source of these problems either. If a counselor does not "reach" an inmate, the manager is more likely to blame the counseling technique than the inmate-officer-counselor situation, and is likely to recommend a new counseling approach rather than to reorganize the institution. Likewise, if officers on a certain shift cannot stop rule infractions by inmates, the manager is more likely to review the shift personnel and their adherence to post orders than to review the organizational design in which the rule enforcement is to take place.

In many ways, this kind of correctional management is analogous to the social action of sending a police officer and a social worker to clean up gang violence in a city neighborhood. The techniques available to the officer and the social worker do not manipulate the variables on which the gang behavior is dependent. As a result, many correctional counselors and social workers, many correctional officers and police officers, develop by necessity new techniques of their trade that are, in effect, secondary manifestations of the same organizational problems that they were sent to control. The problem is not controlled, but a host of new security and treatment practices are advanced as "new and different" and then, after a while, are quietly dropped.

Managers of a system, in contrast, are much less concerned with the parts and much more concerned with the way that the parts fit together. They are interested in integration rather than aggregation. For them, the relevant situation is the interaction networks that join components rather than the processes that may go on within each.[30] Because of this interest, traditional or intuitive managers may complain about a system manager that he or she "does not know the business." They mean that he is not so knowledgeable about the particular practices or techniques of individual divisions. Indeed, the system manager probably depends very heavily on subordinates to know their own disciplines well. It would not, for example, be his primary job to criticize custodial or counseling practices. Instead, he would see his job as managing the situation between custodians and counselors—to make sure that one group is not building a house with wooden pegs because the other group holds the nails.

THE PERSPECTIVE OF THE MANAGER

It is crucial in this discussion to distinguish between *system management* and *managers of systems*. Because all organizations, effective or ineffective, large or small, good or bad, can be analyzed as systems, then all organizational management may be studied as system management. The manager who tries to organize and supervise divisions separately and the manager who tries to integrate divisions are *both* managers of systems. In either case, the selection of goals by which they measure situation outputs and their methods of feedback to the situation can be analyzed as a control process of varying effectiveness. Hence, every correctional policy and every managerial style can be analyzed under a theory of *system* management.

On the other hand, not all managers of systems may understand their jobs as system management. If they do not understand the independent variables in the system to be the interconnectedness of the organizational parts, then their attempts at control will reflect their perspective. Managers who basically see their jobs as integration of a system can be expected to have correctional policies and managerial styles that reflect this perception. Managers who basically see their jobs as holding together an aggregate can be expected to have correctional policies and managerial styles that reflect this perception.

THREE MAJOR SUBSYSTEMS OF ORGANIZATIONS

To understand more fully the expected consequences of aggregative versus integrative control, it may be helpful to elaborate somewhat on the basic input-output-control-feedback model. There are many ways to do this. The elaboration chosen here demonstrates rather quickly, succinctly, and in nontechnical terms the difference between systematic (integrative) and nonsystematic (aggregative) management of systems. It is basically a simplification of the organizational model propounded by Katz and Kahn.[31] Because of this source, the model is particularly useful in the discussion of people-changing organizations and of the relationship between the organization and that important part of its environment that consists of political and other governmental structures.

The basic model of an open system, specifically of human organization, can be elaborated by looking at the three major kinds of activity that managers attempt to control. The various roles and offices structured by these activities form the major subsystems of the organization. These three sets of activity are "systems" because they each have their separate inputs and outputs. They are "subsystems" because they are mutually supportive. Independent of each other, they would fail to function. Integrated to some extent, they function sufficiently to perpetuate the organization. How well the organization as a whole does is dependent on the degree of integration and elaboration of these subsystems—or on the kind of managerial control present in the organization.

THE PRODUCTION SUBSYSTEM

The primary subsystem, or the one from which the others evolve, is the production subsystem. It is made up of the set of activities and the set of personnel directly concerned with the input-output transformation that identifies the organization. In the case of the prison organization, this subsystem is concerned with acting upon offenders.[32] The usual personnel involved in this subsystem, as a prison is customarily structured, are correctional officers, counselors, teachers, and work supervisors. These are the persons who have direct, face-to-face contact with the greatest number of inmates for most of the day. They are also considered the "front-line" workers, or the persons traditionally lowest in the power and decision-making hierarchy of the organization.

A less-traditional view of prisons would place inmates, along with these "front-line staff," on the production line. Why this is so requires a closer look at the production goal of "changing inmates." Whether inmates are the material of production or are participants in a change process depends upon the staff's perception of institutional goals and inmate needs. Frequently, inmates are referred to as "clients" or even "patients" in a therapeutic process in which the criminogenic factors are seen to reside within the person. This orientation by staff is usually referred to as the "medical model" of correctional work. The prison is likened to a hospital, and all necessary alterations in the inmate's condition can take place within that unit. After some form of diagnosis, the male inmate is passed from one person to another as a series of operations is performed upon his character. At the end of the line, he has supposedly been reconstituted. In this model, the offender is treated as a passive host for problems that occur within him. He may not be the material of production, but he is the vehicle of that material.

A second common way of treating an offender is as a "bad" person. This is typically a highly moralistic approach in which the offender must be broken until he "learns a proper attitude." The principal difference between this orientation and the treatment of the offender as sick is that a bad person is presumed to do as he wills. Hence, it is definitely the person himself rather than a condition that he harbors which must be changed.

In a third view of production, the staff and inmates are mutually concerned with changing behavior patterns. Patterns of behavior by which the offender sought reward and status are to be changed, and so are the patterns of other people with whom the offender interacted. In this model, the "product" is neither within the offender nor is it the offender himself. Instead, this model focuses on the interactions between the inmates and the other members of the prison and community organizations. In this view, inmates and staff work together on material that exists between them.

How "productive" any of these different production lines might be depends, of course, on a variety of factors. The first problem is whether any of the models can be made to work, and then there is a second problem, of how well the models have been assembled in particular instances. But this problem of construction is different, as Katz and Kahn point out, in human organizations, than it is, for example, in the construction of a model airplane or the construction of an organism.[33] Human organizations do not have anatomies that may be studied separately from their functioning. A dead frog can be compared to a model frog in a text book. A "dead" organization dissolves. When management, production, and the other operations of the organization cease, it is usually hard to discern from the remains exactly what the organization did.[34] In other words, a clear understanding of achievable goals is very important both to the articulation of a model and to the quality of the implementation. Unless there are clear and precise statements of what organizations should achieve, an organization will tend to produce other things (and, in a sense, become a different kind of organization). In most cases, the organization will tend to produce in the direction encouraged by whatever criteria are used for evaluation. If the indices chosen for evaluation are not reflective of the original production goals, then the organizational activity will tend to cluster around the measurements rather than around the goals.[35]

In comparing the three alternative production processes, only the third seems to offer much hope for clarity of goal statements and accuracy of evaluation. While the "material" of production is not concrete, it is observable and measurable. What inmates and officials should achieve together can be clearly stated. How they will achieve it may vary from task to task, but the principle of organization would seem to be the type of task stated rather than some a priori principle of "good" organization. In contrast, treating the sick or the bad offender as the unit of production makes a statement of what should happen very difficult. If curing sickness is a goal, we presently lack methods of measuring its presence or absence except in some form of inmate behavior, which may be interpreted as a manifestation of a variety of disorders. If destroying a badness is a goal, it is hard to relocate the willfulness separately from the consequences of the willfulness. Thus, if the previously pronounced "bad" person begins to act like a "good" person, two problems arise. Either he is fooling the staff, or the staff had "made" him do something, which is contradictory to the model.

There seem to be two basic kinds of production lines: one in which staff look at inmates and do something to them and one in which staff and inmates look at each other and do some things together. Of these, the latter seems more carefully constructed while the former seems the more commonly implemented. The latter correlates well with integrating management and the former with aggregating management.

THE MAINTENANCE SUBSYSTEM

The maintenance subsystem is subsidiary to and supportive of the activity of production. Involved in the subsystem are the

activities that make organizational processes stable and predictable. Particularly common and important methods of obtaining
stability and regularity are selecting and training of personnel,
socialization of new members into the organizational routine and
value system, and allocating the rewards for organizational membership. This subsystem is obviously subordinate to production
because unless the production activity had already developed and
organizational goals were already fairly well established, the goal-
achieving activities would not be structured enough for rules of
maintenance to develop.

The statement that this or that organization "is only interested
in maintaining the status quo" is one of the most commonly
voiced complaints about bureaucracies. The bureaucratic control
mechanisms force the organizational members away from the
planned goals. A prison bureaucracy has many similar difficulties,
as Cressey's analysis of "treatment" and "custody" institutions
has demonstrated.

A more complete explanation of this complaint about bureaucracy involves a detailed examination of the relationship between
production and maintenance subsystems. In an organization that is
highly productive, the personnel directly responsible for changing
inmates are being effective in achieving change. In this situation,
their activity is supported by organizational processes through
which the production workers are sufficiently trained and socialized that they work together as a unit in effecting change. Moreover, the rewards for behaving in a productive manner are
allocated by methods and in proportions so that there are few
complaints about one kind of staff "getting more than its share."

In an organization that is not so highly productive, the personnel responsible for handling inmates are not achieving change.
Assuming that their change techniques are equal to those in the
productive organization, one explanation of lack of productivity is
that the proper supportive activity is not rendered. Employees
may complain that other groups in the organization have all the
power or get more than their share of recognition and reward. The
method by which organizational members may resolve these and
similar conflicts may be faulty. There may be poor methods of
replacing personnel because initial selection is inaccurate or train-

ing of those selected is inadequate. Last, the informal socialization processes within the organization may be working to increase rather than reduce dissension among organizational divisions.

One important factor in determining just how supportive the maintenance subsystem is, is the extent to which the maintenance subsystem is predetermined or alterable as the production tasks vary. In either kind of prison that Cressey mentioned, staff had fixed positions and fixed operational patterns that they were to adhere to regardless of fluctuations in the inmate population or alterations in the behavior of any particular inmate. Officers were informally punished by their peers and perhaps formally censured by a union if they "worked classification." In other words, officers were not expected to do things that disrupted the social stratification of the prison any more than an inmate would be permitted to disrupt that stratification pattern. The prison, whether "custodially" or "treatment"-oriented, was generally run as if the productive work of changed occurred *after* order had been established. This kind of organizational strategy accommodates normal patterns of learning (or change) about as much as the notorious elementary school teacher who is concerned with discipline to such a degree that there is no time to teach. An alternate pattern would deemphasize the predetermined structures in the organization and let groups of staff and inmates organize around the tasks or patterns of behavior that were to be learned.[36] The groups would govern and reward members in accordance with productivity rather than constrict productivity to conform to standardized rating and reward systems.

THE BOUNDARY SUBSYSTEM

The third subsystem of the organization involves the activity by which the organization relates to its environment. On a very elementary level, this kind of activity takes place whenever any representative of the organization has contact with somebody from the outside world. It is in this vein, for example, that prison post orders may admonish all officers to be clean and neat in appearance, and in particular cases warn officers whose inmate work crews are under public scrutiny to make sure that the inmates "appear to put in an honest day's labor."[37] These kinds of boundary contacts are much less important, because they are less significant to the structure of the organization than are the policy-making bodies who have primary responsibility for integrating the organization with other criminal justice agencies and the surrounding community. Typically, these policy decisions are made at the top of the organization by the person or persons with final authority over operations. The warden or the superintendent, whether he considers himself custodially oriented or inmate-oriented, usually has little direct contact with the activity of production and not much more with the activity of maintenance. While a warden may be proud of his custodial or counseling background, in the top position in the organization, he finds that career is behind him. As the policy originator and the person with most authority in the prison, the warden's primary task involves meetings with departmental commissioners, political leaders, and community representatives. It is his decisions in regard to these different community elements that open the prison to certain kinds of influences and close it to others.

For example, the Pennsylvania Correctional System has long been known as a "political system," because the top positions were awarded to important political supporters of the governor rather than professional correctional careerists. As a result, certain Pennsylvania prisons have had full-time crews of officers and inmates who were solely responsible for organizing and conducting tours. One of the last requests for a tour came from a nursery school class. Shortly thereafter, the new commissioner placed a ban on all tours. The new commissioner, who has had years of experience in different criminal justice positions, has emphasized research and treatment and has repudiated the custom under which any state citizen had the privilege to tour any state institution. In other words, the political and educational prisons hypothesized by Katz and Kahn seem to exist, but their existence is dependent, as Cressey demonstrated, on the policy decisions of officials.

Perhaps at its highest level, this boundary activity of executives does not involve the flow of tangible resources and influences through the prison, but does involve the creation and presentation of an organizational ideology. Alternative ideologies in criminal justice have received some attention lately, but the usual emphasis has been on how the ideology or presuppositions of the system affect participants or academic analysts who are very close to the system.[38] While it is obviously important to study the valuative foundations upon which the officials base the logic of their operations, studying ideology as it is broadcast outward toward a general public is also very important. A common complaint for example, is that criminal justice operations are "invisible" or of low visibility and high discretion. This criticism means that people outside the system only infrequently know what is going on within it.

One explanation of public ignorance is public apathy. While this may be true, it would seem more likely that the public is uninterested in seeking out information to the extent that it seems to be unnecessary. If the prison has not been active in providing to the public accurate information about what goes on within it, it has generally been very active and is becoming increasingly so, in providing explanations of the purpose it serves. Even the statement "out of sight, out of mind" is misleading, because the high stone walls and impenetrability of an Auburn or Eastern State Penitentiary are very vivid statements that what lies beyond *should* be shrouded in mystery.

Prison ideologies have probably kept pace with the times more than internal operations have. As public satisfaction with the message of the wall has decreased, other explanations of prison work have arisen. The prison is now presented as a place of therapy or treatment rather than as a land of the exile. While the older ideology prevented inspection and inquiry by suggesting that prisoners were alien, the new ideology prevents inspection and inquiry by claiming that therapeutic processes will be interrupted. Hence, in either the custodial or the treatment institution, the public's understanding of and information about the prison is rather tightly controlled by information and physical demonstrations sent outward by the prison to the public.

These kinds of ideological messages have usually inaccurately described the prison by understating the inhumanity or overstating the therapy. In either case, the inaccuracies in the public messages are accompanied by low productivity and constrictive maintenance mechanisms. It seems as if, cognizant of low change potential and over-concern with order, the organization "hides" its internal affairs behind a careful manipulation of information.

It may be too early in the evolution of correctional organizations to single out from the new voices that are being heard, the kind of ideology that accompanies an organization which does produce changes and has flexible maintenance structures. It is possible, however, to hear the harbingers of such an ideology from ex-offender groups, legislative reformers, certain innovative administrators, correctional officers who "work classification," in spite of the ribbing they may take, and from particular community groups who are expanding the notions of who is included in "community."

In general, this ideology would seem to involve a filtering-in process rather than a filtering-out process. It would be more dialogue than monologue. Furthermore, it will have less to say about inmates as "bad" or "sick" and therefore will not be a message about how a certain group of people should be perceived. It is more likely that the ideology of the productive organization will in some ways be general instructions about how different groups of people should proceed in working together. The ideology of a "new corrections" would address the value of work and of rewarding people for the uniqueness they represent in terms of the resources that they bring to a particular work situation. In other words, the ideology that joins a change-oriented prison to a community environment is likely to be a reiteration of its production standards. As the unit of work in the prison is behavior shared by offenders and staff, boundary activity will be experiences shared by the prison and the community.

MANAGEMENT OF ORGANIZATIONAL SUBSYSTEMS

Obviously, individual managers in any particular prison are responsible to varying degrees for production, maintenance, and boundary activity. Usually the lower managers are concerned with production and the higher managers with boundary because it is easier to delegate internal roles than roles that link organizations. It is usually easier because production in most organizations involves the activity about which there is the most knowledge and experience. Organizations have technicians to handle what is known and managers to handle what is not known. This principle also holds in prisons—while our ability to change people may not be great, it is far more advanced than our knowledge of how organizations as a whole may be related.

Cruelly or humanely done, changes in individual inmate behavior are more readily accomplished than changes in group behavior, and group behavior is more readily changed if the group is homogeneous than if groups are part inmate and part staff in composition. Moreover, any of these changes is more likely to be achieved once than is an organization likely to be formed that can make these changes repeatedly. Finally, to build such an organization is more probable than to build a system in which that organization is not adversely affected nor adversely affects the other organizations in the entire arrangement.

Since it presently seems to be a goal to make the prison such a change organization in such a change system, the successful manager is one whose major energies are most frequently directed at developing such a system. The managers who are in the best position to work on this task are those who are best able to have the organization below them run itself. The ability to achieve this position is the skill of management. It has, in reiteration, the major aspects of *policy-making,* or the creation of the standards against which organizational output is measured, and *managerial style,* or the manner in which the comparison between standards and output is used to restructure the organization. It would seem that when policy and style tend to integrate the organization, the manager will have a greater amount of time to spend with organizational-environmental relationships than where policy and style tend to aggregate the organization.

In summary, then, the argument in this chapter began with the assumptions that an organizational analysis useful in determining planned changes in correctional organizations should concentrate on (1) examination of organizational goals as the internal constraints built into the organization, or organizational policy, and (2) on the system linkage and process that relates internal organizational activity to the activity of the surrounding environment. Certain crucial distinctions have been made between the *managers of systems* and *system management.* Our most general conception of the organizational system included the primary concepts of input to a situation, output from the situation, a control or governor, and feedback from the control to the situation, which is directed at changing the internal situation to result in more desired output. It was suggested that there are many ways to build upon this bare frame. Chosen here is a fairly common elaboration, in which the overall situation is analyzed in terms of production, maintenance, and boundary activities. These activities may be aggregated or integrated by management, depending on managerial understanding of the nature of the situation and the outputs desired from it. The next chapter expands on one crucial aspect of the managerial role: that of making correctional policy.

CHAPTER 4

POLICY CONTENT AS AN ORGANIZATIONAL VARIABLE

The description of the correctional organization as an open system demonstrates the need for managerial coordination of the several system components and suggests general trends in organizational activity proceeding from different relationships among the components. Most correctional organizations, it has been argued, do not have goal specifications exact enough to allow the optimal ordering of supportive systems. Hence, the activity of production (that of changing people) with undetermined effectiveness, becomes a rationalization for the maintenance activity of distributing rewards and sanctions to organizational members. The release of individual offenders has been subordinated to the transmission of vague and sweeping informational outputs about inmates in general. In most instances, then, the correctional organization has been more concerned with the general legislative mandates of retribution and deterrence, or, perhaps in more general terms, of reassuring interested segments of the public that the moral standards of the community are being upheld.[1]

That the correctional organization usually subordinates offenders' needs to an attempt to serve the community should not be mistaken to mean that the public actually *desires* this system goal, or that this goal is achieved at a sufficient level to gain public approval. Indeed, there is some evidence that outside groups are clamoring for reform of some sort (perhaps in contradictory directions). Concomitantly, most correctional budgets are increasing, or at least have not been as seriously cut as other parts of government budgets, and federal support for state and local corrections is on the upswing. Generally, then, the public seems dissatisfied with the present correctional output.

THE DEFINITION OF MANAGEMENT POLICY

One of the most important antecedents to the understanding of legislative and public relationships with the correctional organization is the behavior of the correctional manager in interpreting and implementing legislative goals. Many organizational analyses in the past, and many administrators presently, have assumed that correctional goals are given, and that it is the job of the administrator to carry them out.[2] The legislative policy, or the public policy, in which these goals are imbedded, is not the administrative policy under which organizational activity actually occurs.[3] These general statements of agency purpose and legislative intent are drawn to justify the creation or funding of agencies. The law accompanying such expressions of intent is also vague and serves to charter the organization, to authorize the appointment of a head administrator, and to authorize the administrator's implementation of the correctional goals. The legislated mandate does not say *how* these goals are to be implemented—it is the first task of the administrator to operationalize these goals, or to formulate a correctional policy. It is only as the institutional policy is implemented that the public and the legislative desires for rehabilitation, punishment, deterrence, or whatever mean anything on an operational basis.[4]

Hence, it is to the examination of actual, operating policy that correctional study must turn in the analysis of correctional behavior. The degrees of freedom any specific administrator has in the formulation of policy is an empirical question. Administrators will variously be limited by their past experience, by their skill in convincing the legislature that the formulated policy is indeed the proper interpretation of public desire, by their own personal characteristics of age, sex, race, and professional affiliations. The invariant constraint, from the open system perspective, is that the formulated policy must in some way arrange, elaborate, and coordinate the major system components.

The administrator may go about the process of policy formation on a number of levels. Some may not even be aware that organizing for the achievement of goals is the restatement of the goals. Some may be aware that policy will reshape the original charter goals, but portions of their policy may be contradictory.

Regardless of how policy is made, it is a major determinant of organizational behavior because it is against policy that organizational behavior is measured, evaluated, and changed. Administrative or organizational policy is defined here as decisions of organizational managers at levels that have implications for organization structure.[5] Or, to use the words of Street, Vinter, and Perrow, policy is the "goal as the essential constraints built into the organization."[6] Policy in this sense is distinguished from policy as the official legislative mandate, and also from organizational goals as the functions the organization has in the social system, and from the service an organization may perform for an outside clientele. Policy as the essential organizational constraints is more closely related to official goals than an executive might publicly state for an organization. The stated executive goal, however, is a more limited concept, best associated with boundary activity. Executive goals may be subsumed under policy as organizational constraints, because it is within the organizational operating context that executives perceive and state organizational goals. Or, if the executive statement of goals precedes the formulation of policy, that statement then stands in the same relationship to policy as do officials' mandates. In either case, whether policy is an accurate working definition of an executive's publicly stated goals, or whether executive goals are an accurate statement of operating policy, are empirical questions. It may, of course, be implicit in operating policy that executive goal statements will not accurately reflect organizational achievement because the policy is based on a belief that the public wants to be protected from inmates and does not want to be bothered by what is actually happening within the prison. Public goal statements may be geared to assuage social guilt rather than to inform the public of actual conditions.

THE FUNCTIONS OF EXTRINSIC POLICY

In utilizing policy as the independent variable in correctional study, the analysis must begin by classifying correctional policy into its possible variations. We may then trace the organizational consequences of one kind of policy or another. Naturally, each prison may have its own unique policy. But one should not be so concerned with the myriad differences as one is with the recurrence of certain underlying dimensions common to all correctional work and with similarities and differences among prisons associated with those dimensions.

The importance of the policy classification, to reiterate motivations behind the open system framework, is twofold. First, in terms of understanding the system, it would seem likely that system parts function differently, depending on the system in which the function is performed.[7] Hence, as policy generates organizational entities with different characteristics, the people in the system will behave differently, and the system will yield different outputs. Second, an ordered classification of policy alternatives is a first step in changing present organizational states. If policy is an inappropriate interpretation of legislative mandate and social desire, or if policy contains conflicting elements, the organization may not be operating as people want it to, or think it is.

> The greater the clarity of goals associated with an activity, the greater the propensity to engage in it. It is easier to attach rewards and penalties, internal as well as external, to completion of tasks with clear goals than to others.[8]

Hence, an organization will be more easily controlled and changed when policy is clear and consistent. Moreover, only when a policy is explicated in a rational manner does the chance arise for persons inside or outside the system to disagree with each other in a productive manner.

> If shared goals are operational, the problem of differential perceptions of the optimal course of action has a logical solution. If the goals are not operational, there is no logical and testable answer to such differences of judgment.[9]

In fact, the suggestion has been made that without an articulated and measurable operating policy, the system may change without noticeable evidence of the fact.[10] This situation of low visibility policy decisions and diffuse policy consequences has disadvantages for both the personnel in the system and the public relating to it.[11] Where either inside or outside groups seek to behave toward a system in misapprehension of its operating policy, they are both shut off from its actual output (either to be avoided or used) and frustrated by believing the system can accomplish the tasks that they might mistakenly bring to it. "Whenever a system of criminal justice takes on an *insular* character, a question is raised as to the degree of justice such a system can generate."[12]

A first step to rectifying the insular character of justice agencies would be to gain a clear understanding of what these agencies are actually doing, or what work they have been constructed to do. In order to understand the administrator's approach to the goals of his institution, a helpful question is which parties or interests the administrator is likely to consider relevant to the construction of policy. If the administrator desires professional assistance from outside research groups or schools, his organization is likely to be arranged to accommodate some common research demands. If the administrator is desirous of a larger budget and the legislature is cracking down on "the coddling of criminals," he is likely to organize the prison in another way. So, the adminstrator is concerned, on the one hand, with some outside groups, the community, and, on the other hand, with the people who will be in the organization—the staff and inmates.[13]

THE PRIMARY CONCERNS IN CORRECTIONAL POLICY

Several recent studies using widely different methodologies in different correctional agencies have all concluded that concern about the community and concern about the individual offender are the two most important variables that, in conjunction, are the frame of reference within which policy is formulated. A recent parole study outlines the parole supervisor's concerns as (1) avoiding public and police criticism, and (2) producing low returns to the prisons.[14] In a recent probation study, it is noted:

> In probation and parole service there exists a contradiction between the agency-centered approach (the concern is the consequence of the clients' behavior), and the client-centered approach (the concern is actualizing the maximum self-potential of the individual).[15]

A recent juvenile study concludes that decision about disposition of boys is made (1) in terms of the juveniles' needs and (2) in terms of protecting the community from the boys.[16] To cite from the prison studies already reviewed, Cressey reaches the

conclusion that the two major focal points of prison administration are concern for the individual inmate and concern for
society in varying degrees.[17] On a slightly different tack,
another prison study emphasizes the dichotomy between feelings
and attitudes of organizational participants and the public behavior required for both.[18]

The dual individual-community concern complex found in these
more or less empirical studies of the system may also be deduced
directly from the open system organizational theory. In that
framework, inputs and outputs must be related (in particular
ways) by a throughput or, in other words, environmental exchange
and internal operations.

A rough and ready framework for policy formulation may then
be drawn by using the two intersecting dimensions: concern about
the community and concern about the individual offender (see
Table 4.1). By dichotomizing the two dimensions, four possible
policy concern complexes emerge:

Consistently high: Simultaneous concern for individual and community.

Mixed: High concern for individual, low concern for community.

Mixed: High concern for community, low concern for individual.

Consistently low: Simultaneous inattention to individual and community.

The two dimensions may also be considered as polar ways of
treating the system process, from a point of view in which the
individual, organizational, and community goals are integrated, to
a point of view in which the goals of individuals and the community are basically ignored and the goals of the organization are
treated in isolation (see Table 4.2).

In Table 4.2, the policy makers' frames of reference are represented. In the top righthand cell, policy is formulated as if the
organizational goals are most effectively met when the individual
and the community goals are approached concomitantly. In the
bottom lefthand cell, policy is formulated as if the organizational
goals can be achieved in isolation from the needs of offenders and
the needs of the surrounding community. Between these two

Table 4.1:   Frame of Reference in Policy Formulation

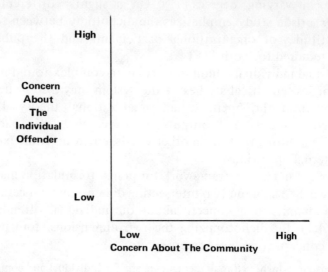

Table 4.2:   The Variations of Emphasis in Policy Construction

		Low	High
Concern for the Individual	High	Mixed, Emphasis on Individual	Organization Treated as a Matrix of Individual and Community Concerns
	Low	Organization Treated as Independent of its Members and the Community	Mixed, Emphasis on Community

Concern for the Community

extremes are two types of "mixed policy." In the top lefthand cell is the policy that emphasizes the individual offender, but without a simultaneous concern for the needs of the community vis-a-vis the offender, or for the needs of the offender as they are modified by the individual's interaction with the community. In the bottom righthand cell is a mixed policy that emphasizes the needs of the community, but without a simultaneous interest in the individual offender, or the way in which the community needs might be met in terms of the offender.

To say that one policy emphasizes one concern at the expense of the other does not mean that the deemphasized concerns are totally ignored. Policies in which the organization is treated as independent must still allow for certain interactions with the community—namely, those directed at blocking influence from external sources. The policy which treats the organization as open to both community and individual influences must still allow for control and governance of interaction—namely, into those channels conducive to productive activity. Between these two poles, there are the two mixed alternatives: (1) policy that treats the community as a given, or a machine, while accommodating the probabilistic nature of individual action; and (2) the policy that treats the individual as a given, or unchangeable, while acknowledging the problematic nature of community behavior.

THE CONSEQUENCES OF DIFFERENT CORRECTIONAL POLICY

Under the assumption that organizations and individuals *do* possess open system characteristics, the two mixed policy frameworks and the policy of isolation suffer from the following contradictions or misapprehensions:

(1) Policy of isolation: that organization and environment are related in an unvarying fashion; that organizational arrangements are not altered by the goal-directed activity of persons who are arranged within the organization or by the changing demands of the community.

(2) Mixed policy with the emphasis on individual offender: that persons once in the organization are not affected by changes in the external environment; that organization encloses its participants totally and can treat their needs regardless of different external demands that are

made upon the organization as it treats, or upon the released individual.

(3) Mixed policy with the emphasis on the community: that the organization can effectively serve the community and be sensitive to community concerns about corrections without being sensitive to the needs and goals of offenders, who eventually will be returned to the community.

These contradictions and mistakes about system relationships will in these three cases have the following uncontrolled results that administrators do not anticipate:

(1) Policy of isolation: the organization will have difficulty adjusting to environmental change, it will not be able to handle new inputs (i.e., in terms of new kinds of offenders) and outputs will be undirected (i.e., offenders will return to the community unchanged and will interact the same way they did before). The internal organization will have to adjust to unacknowledged social systems within itself. Officials will have to accommodate informal inmate and staff norms without having official channels and planned alternatives by which to do so.

(2) Mixed policy with the emphasis on individual offender: the organization will have inadequate base for understanding characteristics of input, changes effected in throughput will be inadequate to community influences upon output, organization will grow cynical, blame organizational failure on community insensitivity.

(3) Mixed policy with the emphasis on the community: the organization will have difficulty changing individuals as the community desires, or of motivating inmates to deal with reactions of community. Although the organization will claim to serve the community, it will maintain low visibility of internal operations. It will ultimately call organizational failure a failure of individual inmates.

In any of these cases, considerable energy will be spent upon maintaining the misconceptions, and less energy will be available for actual change processes.

In contrast with these three frames of reference, the policy of goal congruence would seem to be most effective, if the goal of corrections does involve reduction of future cases of illegal activity by offenders. Policy that treats organization as open to both community and individual variation presents the greatest chance of high effectiveness because it implies that the primary organizational task is achieving congruency between organizational and environmental processes and between organizational and subsystem processes. However, this trend toward high effectiveness, like the contrasting trends toward ineffectiveness, is a proposition that stipulates a considerable duration of organizational life. Sensitive to present realities, the policy of congruence must allow for the longer history and earlier evolution of the other three policy modalities. It is impossible that prison organization can start new and fresh. In almost all cases, this means that a more open policy must accommodate both personnel whose behavior is symptomatic of previous policy contradictions and communities which are habituated to stylized and limited interaction with prison organizations.

Hence, the history of correctional organization places considerable pressure on organizations operating with an open policy to accept the tendency toward closure in one form or another. Persons and organizations are more acquainted with mixed and closed policies and will therefore respond to open policy as if it were overly demanding or surprisingly naive. Social systems built on the adjustments necessary to maintain contradictory policy can be so unequipped for open interaction that primary reactions to the open policy will tend toward rebellion rather than toward acceptance. The open organizational system that has been treated as fragmented *becomes* less permeable and less integrated, and it will react to open policy as an oppression rather than a return to a more natural state. While behavior in the open system will be affected by a secondary reaction to previous closure, behavior in the mixed and closed systems will be affected by secondary reactions to previous openness.[19]

MOTIVATION AND CONTROL STRATEGIES IN DIFFERENT POLICIES

The specific policies of correctional organizations may be elaborated in terms of the control and motivation strategies administrators will use to structure the organization in order to implement the alternative policy concerns for community and offender. That is, the method by which organizational roles are mapped out and integrated is dependent on the system models used. As there seem to be four model complexes, organizational studies have identified four motivational patterns for the production of required behavior. These are:

(a) Legal compliance, the use of machine theory, that rules are sufficient.

(b) The use of rewards or instrumental satisfactions, a modified machine theory of stimulus-response.

(c) The use of internalized patterns of self-determination and self-expression.

(d) The use of internalized values and development of self-concept.[20]

These motivational patterns may be related to the policy frameworks in a consistent fashion. Legal compliance alone is likely to be considered sufficient for control of organizational behavior when the goal of that control is merely the minimum acceptable amount of work. What is really important in this situation is not the actual behavior itself, but the demonstration through the rules that the organization and the people in it are adhering to orders, or, if they are not, that management has publicized the rules. Each level in the organization treats the one below it as a cog in a machine that ought to work properly because the rules of the position have been outlined. Likewise, the organization itself is treated as a cog in the social system, as if it cannot change or be changed since the rules have already been laid down.

The use of rewards or instrumental satisfactions (and the use of punishment or the denial of instrumental satisfaction) is frequently the motivational strategy in the organization where it is believed that the community requires punitive treatment of offenders or when the goals of individuals in the organization are viewed as suspect and their participation in the organization seems to require coercive techniques of control. Individuals are controlled by making their cooperation with organizational goals a more pleasant prospect than lack of cooperation. Whether the organization is a prison or an oil firm, this kind of organizational strategy is frequently accompanied by a strong paternalistic and moralistic tone: the organization can treat its members as it does because it serves a good purpose for society.

Patterns of self-determination and self-expression become a motivational strategy when the perceived importance of the community to organizational operations is decreased. Individuals are encouraged to express their desires and to develop plans of action within the organization that will allow them to experiment with different feelings that they have about themselves and about the organization. The constraint is that the encouragement of individual freedom is delimited by the confines of the organization. The organization is treated as *the* reality into which the individual must fit. It is assumed that feelings that adjust one to the organizational reality enable one to fit into other realities.

In the last motivation strategy, that of internalized values and development of self-concept, the organizational constraints on self-expression and development are lifted. In this strategy, the organizational goals are seen to be congruent with the achievement of individual goals, rather than identical, conflicting, or greater than personal goals. What the individual will do for the organization varies with altering available tasks and individual skills and interest.

For a summary of these four patterns of motivation and their relationship to policy frames of reference, see Table 4.3. In brief, the four policy modes now appear like this:

Low concern for the individual, low concern for the community: The organization is designed on paper to work on paper; rules are written and naturally should be followed, both by organizational participants and by outsiders. The organization is essentially at a loss when someone does not comply, and force is the usual response. The organization is also at a loss to explain why rules should be followed. There is no positive, transferrable value

Table 4.3: Policy Frameworks and Motivational Patterns

		Mixed, Emphasis on Individual	Goal-Congruent
	High	The use of Internalized Patterns of Self-Determination	The use of Internalized Values and Self-Concept
Concern for Individual			
		Organization Isolated	Mixed, Emphasis on Community
	Low	Legal Compliance	The use of Rewards or Instrumental Satisfactions

                    Low   **.High**
                    Concern for Community

in so doing, because the behavior of offenders upon release is an irrelevant criterion in formulating rules.

High concern for community, low concern for individuals: The organization is established to serve the community, but its design does not include a component by which this service may be desirable to participants. Dependency is on outside community values which may be different for different members or completely irrelevant to organizational participation. Roles are played in accordance with arbitrary rewards and punishments, in contradiction to the way roles are usually structured in the society supposedly serviced.

High concern for individual, low concern for community: The organization is designed to benefit members by presenting a stage upon which they may be something other than they were before entry. Experimentation with different feelings and different social relationships offers some reward in the organization, but does not take into account the environmental factors that did not accommodate this freedom on the outside. Hence, the rewards for newfound roles and feelings are not coupled directly to actually available roles previous to or following organizational membership.

High concern for community, high concern for the individual: The organization is designed to change participants; behavior is structured toward patterns that can accommodate value systems of differing sorts. Organizational roles are geared toward the development of self-concept so that the individual may find status upon release that is not dependent upon any *one* way of behaving. Simultaneously, the organization is active in changing community structures that generated deviant responses and to opening new opportunities in the community.

While these policy modes are based in part on years of observation and discussion with executives of various organizations, they are largely developed from the open system theory in terms of how the major system components interact with each other. The policy with high emphasis on both the individual and the community emphasize various production tasks, and the support subsystems are organized around different task needs. The management spends most of its energy organizing this production-support matrix, and engaging external resources that blend with production goals. The two mixed policies and the policy of isolation emphasize heavily the maintenance and boundary activity, and the managerial subsystem spends most of its time balancing power by dividing the change-production process into discrete parts that can be parcelled out to different segments of staff.

CHANGE STRATEGIES IN CORRECTIONAL POLICY

On this level, the policy modes refer to the prison organization in its entirety, and the motivational schemes that administrators use in managing inmates may have certain parallels in the management of staff. In the policy of organizational isolation, both staff and inmates are directed to keep interaction to a minimum. In the policy that emphasizes the individual, both staff and inmates are directed to express themselves and to develop interpersonal relationships. In the policy that emphasizes the community, both staff and inmates are regulated by rewards and punishments in accord with what the community considers a good officer or inmate. In the policy of goal congruence, both staff and inmates are directed to behave in accordance with how they see the world, and these perceptions are tested by inmates and staff in terms of the perceptions of others, and the behavioral consequences.

In other words, this fourfold policy classification, in that it may hold implications for both staff and inmates, may be equally applicable to other organizations, which are also open systems.[21] Verification of the general policy complex and the elaboration of policy in the specific activity of changing people is available in Herbert Kelman's extensive study of change strategies.[22]

This study lists three important variables that together determine the type of behavior change:

(1) the basis for the importance of the induction of change;

(2) the source of the change agent's power; and

(3) the manner of achieving prepotency of the induced response.

Combining these variables produces three change modes:

Compliance: in which the changee is deemed to have done something wrong that must be stopped. The change agent's power lies in the ability to manipulate rewards and punishments. Prepotency of the induced change is gained by continual surveillance. Since the new behavior is in and of itself of no value to changees, they are not likely to continue in it unless they are watched.

Identification: in which the changee is perceived as immature or sick, as unable to form proper human relationships. The change agent wields power in terms of denying or developing a relationship which the changee desires. Changes identify with the agent and change their behavior in order to continue the relationship. The induced behavior will likely last as long as the relationship is salient.

Internalization: in which the change agent believes the past behavior of the changee has been learned as a way of resolving problems that the changee has met in the past. The change agent's power resides in the ability to show the changee other alternatives, or new opportunities that will more effectively resolve those problems. The new behavior is likely to be stable and long-lasting because it has value independent of the change agent. The new pattern is internalized.

These change strategies may be substituted for the general motivational strategies represented in Table 4.3 with the following results.[23] Kelman's change via compliance is a specification of motivation through the use of rewards and instrumental satisfactions. The correctional officer or correctional counselor in a prison with a policy emphasizing the community will frequently attempt to control the changee through compliance. Kelman's change via identification is a specific example of organizational motivation through the use of internalized patterns of self-determination. The inmates will be allowed considerable freedom to express themselves and develop their feelings, within the confines of the organization. Kelman's change via internalization is a specification of motivation through use of internalized values and self-concept. In this case, the inmates' view of themselves is recognized and respected, and alternate means of achieving goals are presented and tested as substitutes for previous criminal methods. The fourth general strategy of motivation, that of legal compliance, has no analogy in Kelman's change typology because correctional organizations that depend on legal compliance or bureaucratic authority do not intend to change inmates (see Table 4.4).

FOUR CORRECTIONAL MODELS

For the sake of expedience, these four correctional policies have been assigned the labels of Reintegration, Rehabilitation, Reform,

Table 4.4: Models of Correctional Policy

	Low	High
High **Concern** **for the** **Individual**	Rehabilitation Identification Strategy	Reintegration Internalization Strategy
Low	Restraint Holding Strategy	Reform Compliance Strategy

Low   High
Concern for the Community

and Restraint.[24] These labels are a shorthand reminder of the frame of reference and change strategy associated with each.

Restraint is the policy with low concern about the community and low concern for organizational participants. There is no change strategy involved. Correction in this mode is a holding action or warehousing of inmates. In terms of traditional legislative and judicial goals for invoking the criminal sanction, this policy probably corresponds closely to the goal of retribution, in which the offender is sent off to prison as a punishment for wrongdoing.

Reform is the policy with low concern for the participants and high concern for the community. The change strategy is one of compliance; people are molded into different behavior reactions according to a well-established set of rules with rewards and punishments freely administered. In terms of traditional legislative and judicial goals, this policy probably corresponds most closely to the goals of specific and general deterrence. The correctional action is supposed to have future effects, such as deterring the offender from future crimes and deterring others from following a criminal example. Safety of society (probably in the short run) is paramount.

Rehabilitation is the policy with high concern for participants and low concern for the community. The change strategy is one of identification; people change through a manipulation of intrapersonal and interpersonal relationships. This mode may be divided into (1) a milieu strategy wherein the individual personality is the dependent variable and the social interaction is assumed to change contingent upon successful internal manipulations. In terms of traditional legislative and judicial goals, this policy corresponds most closely to the goal of treatment of rehabilitation, as these goals have been borrowed loosely from psychiatry and social work. The society is seen as good or functional, and the deviance is seen as a characteristic of individuals.

Reintegration is that policy with high concern for participants and high concern for the community. The change strategy is internalization; people change as they discover and test alternate behavior patterns congruent with their values and beliefs. This policy does not correspond to traditional legislative and judicial goals because it treats criminal deviance as an interactive process that requires changes in both the individual and the system of justice, and also in the external community. As such, it does correspond however, to very recent legislative trends toward social reconstruction and to recent judicial trends, particularly in sentencing practices, where incarceration is viewed as a last resort, usual correctional operations are viewed as failing, and the beneficent purposes of state intervention are viewed as suspect.[25]

POLICY AS AN ORGANIZATIONAL STANDARD

The fourfold policy table will be used as an operational definition of correctional goals against which the correctional manager, operating as the "control" in the correctional system, will measure the output from the organization. Depending upon an assessment of organization behavior, in terms of policy, the manager will then feed back to the organization instructions about changes in behavior. The effectiveness of the feedback will depend upon the clarity of the manager's policy and his or her ability to identify organizational indices of that policy. Whether the manager has a clear or a muddled idea concerning operational goals, it is assumed that a policy profile can be constructed that will consist of the managerial emphasis on community and individual concerns. It should also be possible to measure the perceptions of other people in the organization about the implementation of policy as a check on managerial effectiveness.

CHAPTER 5

MEASURING CORRECTIONAL POLICY

There are many ways to measure correctional policy just as there are many ways to measure other types of organizational goals. It might, for example, be possible to train a small number of judges in what to look for in the correctional system that would distinguish one type of operational policy from another. Or it might be possible to develop a list of observable manifestations of the different policies and to have research assistants count the frequency of the occurrence of these manifestations. It might be possible to conduct a content analysis on written reports, goal statements, and rulebooks. Or it might be possible to develop a questionnaire that would allow correctional personnel to self-report the policy that they attempt to implement.

It is the questionnaire approach that has been taken in this research for several reasons. The development of the concepts that underlie the correctional policy questionnaire took place in many years of correctional training and organizational development. Several forms of the correctional policy questionnaire predated consideration of its use as a research instrument. In part, it was the response of correctional administrators to the questionnaire in the training setting that prompted interest in the potential of the questionnaire as a more rigorous taxonomic device.[1]

As the delineation of the four different correctional systems became clear, the theoretical inquiries as to the reasons for the classifications opened the discussion of prisons as organizations. Finally, it was then the theoretical material on organizations that directed the use of the finalized questionnaire as a research instrument.

THE CORRECTIONAL POLICY INVENTORY

Correctional administrators were asked their policy in twelve different areas of correctional concern. These twelve areas were selected after many training sessions established those areas as of importance to correctional administrators. A subsequent item analysis demonstrated the weakness of the items in two of these areas, and the final questionnaire was cut to ten areas of inquiry. The aim of these questions was (1) to encompass as much as possible the correctional adminstrator's entire range of interest, from probation to release from parole supervision, and (2) to tap the administrator's policy interest in areas in which there was considerable room to maneuver. Administrators' choices concerning escapes, riots, or the use of the death penalty may not vary as much as their decisions about less extreme measures. The lack of alternatives to extreme situations may mask the considerable differences in less extreme and more frequently occurring correctional matters.[2] Since it is quite possible in an organizational system for small actions in one situation to generate large actions in a subsequent situation,[3] understanding differential responses to these everyday affairs may preclude the need to struggle over the responses to extreme and rare events.

The final questionnaire consisted of ten general problems and situations about which it was assumed four alternative responses existed. These areas of inquiry were:

(1) Belief about the chief obstacle for correctional systems to overcome in assisting offenders to avoid further crime.

(2) Belief about the best way to change another person.

(3) Belief about the philosophy of general orientation a correctional institution should have.

(4) Belief about the operating principles of pre-release programs.

(5) Belief about the best way for the parole board to operate.

(6) Belief about the legal rights parolees should have.

(7) Belief about the skills a probation staff should have.

(8) Belief about the way correctional officers should handle inmate challenges to the rules.

(9) Belief about the way citizen volunteers should be used.

(10) Belief about the way parolees should be used to change the behavior of other offenders.

The questionnaire, called the Correctional Policy Inventory, was formulated around these ten areas. The questionnaire consisted of ten statements about common correctional issues followed by four responses to each issue. For each issue statement, administrators were asked to rate all four alternatives along a continuum from a score of ten (most characteristic of a respondent) to a score of one (least characteristic of a respondent). The maximum score for any one policy was 100 (10 x 10) and the minimum score was 10 (10 x 1). For example, the first question area, involving reduction of criminal behavior, read as follows (the policy presumably represented by each choice has been supplied parenthetically):

The chief obstacle for correctional systems to overcome in assisting most offenders to avoid further criminal behavior is:

(1) The existence of poor attitudes and values on their part which must be replaced by more positive ones. (Reform)

(2) The availability of practical alternatives which the community is willing to provide and the offender's perception of those alternatives. (Reintegration)

(3) The maintenance of the correctional system's program from which the offender can benefit if he desires. (Restraint)

(4) The presence of emotional problems within offenders which usually can be traced back to early defective relationships with parents. (Rehabilitation)

The alternatives were to be spread over ten spaces of a continuum:

```
:____:____:____:____:____:____:____:____:____:____:
  10    9    8    7    6    5    4    3    2    1
```

(completely characteristic)   (completely uncharacteristic)

The primary advantage of this questionnaire design is that it is sensitive to administrators' secondary choices, does not force their responses in one direction or another, or, in other words, allows them the kind of discretion that they presumably have in policy formation. It would be possible, for example, that a particular respondent has developed no clear delineation of policy. This lack of clarification should be reflected in relatively equivalent policy totals on the questionnaire. It is also possible that an administrator answers consistently high for one policy, but has second and third choices that are not very discrete. This confusion in a manager's policy profile might have important consequences in an institutional setting.[4] For example, an administrator may demonstrate a clear first choice for Reform (total score = 90), but has secondary alternatives that are not clearly distinguished (Rehabilitation = 50, Reintegration = 48, Restraint = 47). On the one hand, the profile of scores may represent a rather consistent correctional strategy in which staff and inmates are organized around clearly defined areas of activity, power is in the hands of staff, and deviations from the rules are punished in accordance with a list of allowable sanctions. On the other hand, this profile suggests that if at any time the Reform strategy is blocked or frustrated, there is no consistent alternative. If the compliance strategy does not work, the secondary strategy may oscillate from an emphasis on internal personality variables to an emphasis on greater practicality and openness between staff and inmates, to a temporary default of change-oriented policy and the acceptance of minimally acceptable legal behavior.

Because policy decisions may change over time, not only the first choice, but also the entire profile is important in the analysis of correctional behavior. However, the technique for the analysis of the entire policy configuration has not been developed. While there are statistical methods available for handling configurations of characteristics simultaneously, at this date not even the primary policy decisions of a correctional organization have been handled systematically. If policy preferences were to be analyzed as characteristics of individual employees, it might be possible to use particular policy configurations as the criteria in the formation of actuarial tables.[5] Past experience with prediction methods, however, demonstrates that sophisticated techniques have rather limited value because the analysis of the operating system in which these decisions take place is still rudimentary.[6] Policy formation and implementation is a group, if not a subsystem, or total system characteristic. At some future date, it may be possible to analyze correctional policy data for individual respondents to clarify the particular combination of individual profiles that together form an operating policy. This investigation, however, will have to await further study of organizational influence patterns and power structure, among other variables, that might be important in weighting those characteristics of individual personality, role, and office position that affect the impact of individual policy preference upon the organizational scheme.

In the interim, correctional policy data should meet these qualifications:

(a) The questionnaire should be sufficiently reliable to allow the manipulation of policy data for groups.

(b) The questionnaire should have "face validity" or prove useful to administrators in ordering their thoughts on correctional management, and in their judgment provide an accurate summary of correctional policy alternatives.

(c) The policy configurations measured by the instrument should have construct validity, or prove useful in analyzing the structure of the correctional organization.

Of particular importance to the policy construct used here would be the relationship to managerial style, or the way in which managers give feedback to subordinates.[7]

THE RELIABILITY OF THE CORRECTIONAL POLICY INVENTORY

Correctional policy is a complex notion, a construct built of concepts concerning organizational goals and those concerning offenders and community as recipients of system services. Each of the ten issues included in the questionnaire could have been the target of a detailed examination by itself. For example, other investigators have given considerable time to issue 2 ("beliefs about the best way to change another person");[8] there is a lengthy study of the use of citizen volunteers (issue 9);[9] and several studies on the use of parolees as change agents (issue 10).[10] In fact, each of these issues is an area of some controversy in correctional administration. The existence of controversy allows measurement of differences. But it also means that alternative responses in these areas have received lengthy treatment on their own rather than as manifestations of an underlying correctional policy.

Although the principal test of the validity of a construct may be the way in which it relates to other variables, it is sound practice to demonstrate how different measures of the construct yield similar results and to test how the construct can be differentiated from other similar constructs prior to investigating the relationship to other variables of interest.[11] The first of these prerequisites was approached both through an analysis of the internal consistency of the questionnaire and through validation in a series of interviews. The second prerequisite was handled in a demonstration of the independence of the four correctional policies as measured by the Inventory.

The data in Table 5.1 demonstrate that the Correctional Policy Inventory provides a fair degree of internal consistency. The Correctional Policy Inventory was administered to 225 managers and practitioners in several different correctional organizations. Table 5.1 shows the product-moment correlations between each of the ten items and the policy total to which each of the alternatives was assigned. In each case, the item is significantly correlated with its total. Individual items that represent key operational responses to policy formulation correlated more strongly than items that were less essential to the delineated program. For example, the use of the probation officer as an advocate for his charges, who actively intervenes in their behalf, is a primary behavior pattern in Reintegration policy and correlated with the Reintegration total at .62. Likewise, the use of ex-offenders as new careerists, who assist other offenders in changing, is crucial to the Reintegration policy of treating system, community, and individual goals congruently. This item correlated with the Reintegration total at .63. Items with the strongest correlation to the Rehabilitation total also contained key phrases and concepts. For instance, the parole board that "should be modeled closely on that of a clinical review team in a hospital" correlated with the Rehabilitation total at .53. Similarly, the institution as a "kind of hospital" correlated with the same total at .57. The strongest Reform items involved the institution "in which inmates are required to acquire acceptable behavior habits" (.58), and the change style that stressed the "rewards and penalties which will be imposed depending . . . on compliance" (.50). Restraint items proving particularly strong were the institutional model that "operated in an orderly fashion and without disruption processes offenders" (.59), and the pre-release program that encouraged inmates to "cooperate and observe institutional regulations" (.63).

Table 5.1: Product-Moment Correlations of Individual Policy Items with
Total Scores for Each Policy from the Questionnaires of 225
Probation and Correctional Institution Officials in the
Northeastern United States

Individual Items	Correctional Policies			
	Reintegration Total	Rehabilitation Total	Reform Total	Restraint Total
Custodial Officer	.54*	.40*	.45*	.37*
Crime Theory	.53*	.41*	.40*	.44*
Pre-release Program	.47*	.47*	.40*	.63*
Legal Rights	.45*	.39*	.42*	.43*
Probation Officer	.62*	.37*	.31*	.57*
Ex-offender Uses	.63*	.36*	.45*	.34*
Change Style	.40*	.40*	.50*	.53*
Parole Board	.39*	.53*	.36*	.48*
Volunteer Uses	.43*	.33*	.43*	.27*
Institutional Type	.57*	.57*	.58*	.59*

*when r = .23, p. = .01

The reliability coefficient for the correlation of split-halves on
these 225 questionnaires is .80. The halves are hardly identical,
but .80 would seem to be reliable enough for the manipulation of
grouped data. It would be insufficient to depend on any particular
score as the foundation for the analysis of an individual's behavior.[12] The examination of internal consistency, of course,
does not provide an estimate of reliability over time.[13] It has
not been feasible so far to provide such an estimate because the
employment of the questionnaire as a training device has meant
that the respondents receive a full explanation of the questionnaire after they fill it out. A second administration very close to

this training session could not avoid the effects of the training session on the preferences of managers, and a second administration more removed from the training session might suffer from the challenge that the managers' preferences in policy really have changed in the intervening time, particularly if the training has been effective.

Table 5.2 demonstrates that the four policies as a whole are fairly distinct and independent constructs. At the .01 level, there are two correlations of significance, a positive one between Reform and Restraint and a negative one between Reintegration and Restraint. In other words, it is likely that administrators responding highly to Reform items will also respond fairly high on Restraint items. Also, it is likely that administrators responding high on Reintegration items will respond rather low on Restraint items. It is possible that further revision of the Policy Inventory may reduce these policy relationships, but the Inventory in its present form seems usable for two important reasons. First, in no case do the data suggest that the policy alternatives are identical. The four alternative combinations of concern for the individual and concern for the community *do occur*. Second, the three policies with distinctive change strategies (Reintegration, Rehabilitation, and Reform) are independent. It is possible that the relationship between Reform and Restraint may signify that the manipulative change strategy employed in the Reform policy is the strategy most easily isolated from the goal of such behavior manipulations. Isolated from the goal of making good citizens or molding proper attitudes, the continual emphasis on reward and

Table 5.2: Product-Moment Correlations Between Correctional Policy Totals for 225 Probation and Correctional Institution Officials

	Policy			
	Reintegration	Rehabilitation	Reform	Restraint
Reintegration	–	– .13	– .21	– .39*
Rehabilitation		–	.05	.03
Reform			–	.37*
Restraint				–

*when r = .23, p. = .01

punishment may easily become a ritual in which the means are more important than the ends, and the result becomes merely one of keeping institutional order.

Where the administration of sanctions itself becomes more important than the goal of changing behavior by doing so, the policy is in effect one of Restraint, wherein the goal is not changing behavior but maintaining the organization. In similar terms, the negative relationship between Reintegration and Restraint may signify that a policy based on congruence of internal and external goals is least likely to become ritualistic or isolated from the achievement of its goals. The Reintegration policy requires continual examination of behavioral consequences, and the goal statements are likely to be too tangible and practical to be ignored when policy decisions are made.

ADMINISTRATION OF THE QUESTIONNAIRE AND "FACE" VALIDITY

While "face" validity is not in the usual sense possible with the Correctional Policy Inventory, because it is an attempt to measure a complex set of ideas, certain reactions to the questionnaire by the administrators who filled it out lend credence to the instrument and to the dimensions it measures. Once sufficient reliability of the questionnaire had been achieved, correctional agencies were sought in which correctional policy and organizational structure could be studied. Entrance to an eastern Department of Correction was gained in a management training program initiated by the Department Director of Staff Development. At its inception, the training program was conceived as a series of departmentwide conferences in which selected officials would convene with professional training consultants to discuss new information relating to correctional policy and new ways of managing and organizing for the achievement of goals. After several preliminary discussions, the consultants suggested that the evaluation of the training sessions might be facilitated if the training could also concentrate on the personnel of one institution. In that way, training information would not be diffused among individuals throughout the department. This plan was tentatively agreed upon, although a particular institution for the study of lower-echelon employees was not chosen. Two managerial conferences were scheduled for department-wide attendance—one for Central Office personnel, wardens, and assistant wardens; and one for middle managers such as captains, lieutenants, and varied treatment staff (counselors, teachers, and work supervisors).

During the first training session for Central Office staff and top institutional officials, the trainers presented information on the correctional policy classification. Intensive use was made of laboratory learning. The managers were divided into teams and given mock assignments of communication and decision-making. The purpose of negative feedback—how to accept and to generate it—was emphasized. The conference began with considerable nervousness and dissension. The Commissioner, for example, spent a good part of his time the first day calling the office, consulting with messengers from the various institutions, or pulling aside other conference participants to discuss departmental business. He gave up this activity in the morning session of the second day during a game that involved team task accomplishment within given time limits. Once caught up in this exercise, he transferred his energies to the conference content. At the same time, officials from geographically dispersed institutions began to be comfortable together, and an atmosphere of considerable rapport developed between participants and trainers.

The managers had been asked to fill out the Correctional Policy Inventory previous to the conference. Their response forms were scored and the data presented to the participants at the conference. The data were retained by the trainers to be combined with the policy data obtained in similar manner from the middle management conference, and the data from additional administrations by the writer at a yet unselected demonstration institution.

There were both advantages and disadvantages to collecting data in this manner. The primary advantage to the consultants was that it gave them the opportunity to obtain immediate feedback on the validity of the correctional policy material. In this regard, this particular training conference and others like it around the country were successful. Correctional managers were readily able to "see" the four policies as viable alternatives, all of which existed in their department. They also agreed that the ten-item alternatives did, indeed, form a consistent pattern. They did not say that their own policies were as consistent as the models, but they were able to agree intellectually that their individual profiles were relatively accurate, even if they did not like them. Simultaneously, the training consultants, who by this time had extended contact with some of the officials, saw no glaring misrepresentation in the profiles produced. For example, the Reintegration scores were higher among officials in the Central Office than they were among institutional and parole personnel, and it is Central Office personnel who had the greatest responsibility and the greatest opportunity to see the value of goal congruence. Staff, or advisory experts, were also more liberal (open to individual or policy response) than line officials (persons with direct responsibility for custody).[14]

Hence, one advantage of the research-training combination is that, during the training exercise, the research material demonstrated its face validity through the reactions of the administrators. The concepts and their measurement were acceptable to prison managers in that they dealt with familiar problems and perceptions and were exciting in that they helped to order those problems and perceptions in a new way. In other words, the research, which may have been conducted anyway, became more valuable because it demonstrated the probability of being helpful.[15]

PROS AND CONS OF THE TRAINING SETTING FOR RESEARCH

In addition to the immediate positive reaction of the managers, another advantage to this style of research is that administrative personnel become comfortable with the research method early in the program. They learn by examining their own responses in relation to the theory behind the instrument that such investigation has practical benefits for them, and that the researchers have not subordinated them as human beings to their research status as subjects. The research becomes interactive and collaborative; hence, the administrators develop a commitment to the goals of the research project. The value of this commitment was demonstrated in concrete fashion during this study. As part of the year-long training-research enterprise, the consultants desired to

administer several questionnaires measuring organizational variables[16] to random samples of inmates and staff in all institutions in the state. This intent was announced and discussed on the
third day of the management conference and produced considerable defensive reaction, particularly from the wardens. It was
explained that the results of these two instruments would provide
baseline data for the second half of the management conference
which was scheduled a month later. The administrators could use
the feedback from their own institutions in planning training goals
and long-range policy for the department. Largely because of the
success of the in-conference research instruments, the administrators agreed to cooperate with this departmentwide research
plan.[17]

Unfortunately, one warden was unavoidably absent from this
conference. When research assistants were dispatched to supervise
the administration of this survey, only the researcher sent to this
institution met with difficulties. As he entered the jail, he was told
that he was not expected. No one seemed to know of the project.
While the survey was finally conducted there, only thirty percent
of the staff completed the two questionnaires properly. Return
rate at the other institutions was eighty-five percent, so the jail
presenting the difficulties was cut from the survey sample. Except
for the absence of the Centerville warden from the training conference, there was no available explanation for this lack of
cooperation.

Riots had disturbed the summer at both the Newtown and
Shipburg jails, but these jails produced a high return rate. Lack of
cooperation was expected from the maximum security prison,
simply because of the size of the sample population, but the
warden there, who had been one of the most active conference
participants, was strong in defending the need for the survey data.
Therefore, it would seem that, where researchers can be of practical help to administrators, administrators in turn can be of aid to
researchers.

On a more general level, perhaps the most important advantage
of this research format is a conceptual one. The trainers presented
to the correctional managers at the conference information on the
consequences of behaving in a closed and in an open fashion to
other people in the organization. It was also shown that if man-

agers really desired, as they said they did, correctional policies of the Reintegration or Rehabilitation type, then they had a responsibility to behave personally in a manner congruent with that general policy.[18] With the goal of the training program being the creation of congruent behavior patterns at various levels of action, the researchers also had an obligation to conduct the research in a collaborative manner. While research in a training setting has many difficulties, it did provide a rapport with managers that might otherwise have been lacking.[19]

The disadvantages of the dual purpose operation involve, primarily, maintaining acceptable research standards within the fast pace and enthusiasm of the training climate. If researchers who are not simultaneously trainers are often held off by managers who have a negative stereotype of research that is boring, irrelevant, too fancy, or too radical; researchers who are simultaneously trainers often generate a positive halo, in which everything they say and do is acceptable to trainees. The researcher must be careful lest his or her charisma, even if it lasts only as long as the conference, distorts the perceptions of reality. There may be the tendency in this dual role to lower standards for research information to the standards of training information, where it is not so much the quality of the data that counts but the use that can be made of the general concepts and the increase in participation that can be generated by the use of questionnaires and other instruments that draw people into the training activity. It is principally in light of these common conference conditions that the research instruments are sent out ahead of the meeting. Conference participants are at that time anxious about the upcoming event and fill out questionnaires conscientiously, so that they will not run the risk of embarrassment at the conference because they have not done their "homework." A disadvantage of this pre-conference administration is that the managers may fill out the questionnaire defensively in hopes of making a good showing. Even if they fill it out honestly, there is the problem that the researcher has no control over the time spent on the questionnaire by each individual or over the environment in which the instrument is answered. While the advantage of mass administration of questionnaires is the ability to control the test situation, the rapport and good feeling at the conference may not be easily controlled.

Participants filling out questionnaires during the conference may compare answers with their fellow participants. Trainers may caution that the instruments must be answered individually, but this kind of damper may contradict the participants' present feelings about "being open" and able to compare attitudes, feelings, and responses without being defensive about it. Therefore, those training instruments that were also used for research were administered prior to the conference. Those instruments used only for training were filled out during the conference.

COMPLETION OF THE SURVEY DESIGN

During the second part of the Commissioner's office and wardens' conference, the demonstration site, the Hilltop institution, was selected. The selection criteria were:

(1) Hilltop is a minimum security institution and the researchers would not be hampered excessively by security restrictions during training and research activity.

(2) Hilltop is a prison for felons rather than a jail (although some transfers from jails were assigned to Hilltop). In a prison, the training and research have wider application to prisons in other states.

(3) There is low staff turnover, so that extended research and training activity might have some continuity.

(4) It is a small enough institution that a large sample of the population could still be easily processed.

(5) Hilltop's position on available survey data is about average for the state institutions; it is not an atypical case.

Most importantly, the Superintendent of Hilltop was eager to host the research activity.[20] The selection of Hilltop rather than another institution was explained to other wardens in the above terms. It was also explained to them that training activity in Hilltop would be a pilot program in which at various times they would be consulted and kept up to date on progress. A second training proposal was formulated in which middle managers and officers trained at Hilltop would then aid in the training of personnel at other institutions.

A question arose about the time lag involved in the policy survey. Top administrators were surveyed in November 1969; middle managers in April 1970; and Hilltop officers and inmates in June 1970. The policy data, in other words, represents different parts of the state's organizations over the good part of a year. However, in that time, each tested hierarchical level received the policy instrument without much advance notice from the levels above. Each level was aware that something was going on in terms of departmental management training, but the managers, fortunately, did not come home to their institutions and brief their subordinates on the impending questionnaire survey. Thus, while the time lag in test administration was not ideal, the advantages along the way seemed to make up for that research disadvantage. Particularly important was the fact that the superiors in each case were instrumental in gaining the cooperation of the next line of personnel. In summary, policy research was gathered from the Department of Correction in the following manner (see Table 5.3).

Table 5.3: Time Schedule of the Administration of the Correctional Policy Inventory in the Department of Corrections

Hierarchical Level	Date	Method	Number of Personnel
Top Managers (Central Office, Wardens, Assistant Wardens)	November 1969	Individually, prior to conference	32
Middle Managers (Selected Captains, Lieutenants, Teachers, Counselors, Supervisors)	April, 1970	Individually, prior to conference	26
Officers Hilltop Minimum Security Prison	June, 1970	Individually, during work shift to all available officers	44
Inmates Hilltop Prison	June, 1970	Group administration to stratified random sample of inmate population	89
		Total	191

POLICY QUESTIONNAIRES AT CORRECTIONAL
OFFICER AND INMATE LEVELS

The Correctional Policy Inventory had to be adapted to be utilized with officers and with inmates. Information desired from officers and inmates was different than that desired from managers. The study of policy as the independent variable in the study of prison organization requires answers to three related questions:

(1) From managers, what is it?

(2) From officers, how do you follow it?

(3) From inmates, how are you affected by it?

Therefore, the questionnaire given to officers asked them to report their actions in specific situations. The questionnaire given to inmates asked them to report their perceptions of how officers and upper staff acted toward them. The object in varying the research question by level was obtaining a three-sided focus of the description of organizational policy. The questionnaire given managers reflected their formulation of program in terms of general change strategy, correctional philosophy, and their perception of the interrelationship of system components. The questionnaire given officers reflected their behavior within an organizational situation shaped by the managerial formulation. The questionnaire given inmates reflected their perception of staff behavior toward them.[21]

Another reason for modifying the questionnaire is that officers and inmates have more limited information to give. They would not have had an informed response about the way in which probation officers should behave, or the way pre-release programs are structured, or about the way the organization handles citizen volunteers, while these concerns are part of the daily concern of managers. Therefore, while the format of four alternative responses to ten problems or situations was maintained, the situations were necessarily chosen to be familiar to officers and inmates.

The questionnaire given to officers and the questionnaire given to inmates were basically the same. Ten different situations concerning custodial or treatment activities were followed by four alternative responses. The officers were asked to rate each of the responses on a scale from 4 (most characteristic of themselves) to 0 (least characteristic of themselves). The inmates were asked to rate each response in terms of the frequency of its occurrence in the behavior of staff. They could rate each item from 3 (happens most of the time) to 1 (happens little or very infrequently). The only difference in the wording of the two forms was that the officers' form read, "I do . . ." while the inmates' form read, "Officers do . . ."

In general, the two questionnaires were very much the same in substance and in the method of their construction. Situations relevant to inmates and officers were selected, and alternative responses to those situations were selected to relate to the four managerial policies. The responses to the questionnaires were then checked for internal consistency by comparing the correlations of items to total scores for each policy. Independence of the four alternatives was checked by correlating the four policy totals. Validity was assessed by comparing questionnaire results to a series of interviews that are reported in Chapter 6.

The item analysis uncovered no weak items on the officer version, and only one weak item of the forty on the inmate version. It was decided then to retain all the times as they were, since modifying the one weak item may have jeopardized strong correlations between the other three items to their respective totals on that item set. The correlation of the four policy totals for each questionnaire showed that there was slightly less independence on the officer and inmate levels than on the management level. The officer version had a negative correlation of - .56 between Restraint and Reintegration and Rehabilitation; while the inmate version had a positive correlation between Rehabilitation and Reintegration of .76. Thus, greater refinement of the questionnaire on these levels is desirable, but it was thought that the versions that we had were usable in order to distinguish between groups. We also thought it possible that inmates might not perceive differences between Reintegration and Rehabilitation at their level because the emphasis on the "individual offender" is high in both policies, and the programmatic distinctions between Reintegration and Rehabilitation on the community dimension might not have been apparent at this stage of correctional development in the department that we were studying.

RELATIONSHIP BETWEEN RELIABILITY AND VALIDITY AND AN ASSESSMENT OF THE QUESTIONNAIRES

Since so much of what one finds out in a research project depends heavily on how one has gone about looking, it is hard to separate a report on the search from a report on the findings. While the search instruments must be dependable if they are to help in obtaining valid information, it is difficult to draw final conclusions about dependability without reference to the information gained. While it would be dangerous to make assertions about the validity of the information gathered if reliability of the instruments is low, the level of reliability necessary for working with data for groups of people may be different from the reliability necessary when the research interest is in the scores of particular individuals. If the final evaluation of research resides in the usefulness of the information obtained, then the policy measurements may have more to offer in their favor than against them.

The emphasis on information utilization is more important to the concepts of reliability and validity than might first appear. The instruments on correctional policy were developed in a process of give and take with the system under study. The managers of that system had invited the research as the beginning of a continuing process of self-study in which results were to be changes in the organization. While it is true that at the point where the policy questionnaires were administered the managers in Hilltop prison were more committed to seeking and using the information than the officers or inmates, these subordinate groups were not isolated from the purpose of the research activity. The original training conference for the Central Office, wardens, and assistant wardens had received considerable coverage in both city and departmental newspapers. While officers and inmates were both skeptical about the effectiveness of a "change program," the aims of the research as part of that program were freely discussed with both groups. The writer was present in the institution approximately eighteen hours a day for a week previous to the questionnaire administration and had free access to managers, officers, and inmates for discussions about the change program, the sincerity of managers, the accuracy of questionnaires and so forth. In addition, systematic interviews were conducted with both officers and inmates in which an assessment was made about their perception of the possibility of change in the system, and the function of the organizational development program in that change.[22] The assessment of the formal as well as the informal coverage of the information is that a majority of persons in the organization answered the questionnaire with hope that the information obtained would be beneficial for the organization and for themselves. As frequently as possible, it was emphasized that the information, to be beneficial, would have to be accurate. All three major groups in the organization—the managers, the officers, and the inmates—were asked several times and in several ways their ideas for goals or procedures of change that might be incorporated into the program. In short, there was a considerable attempt made to reduce the usual autocracy of the research situation and thereby reduce the inaccuracy of the information. While this attempt was by no means completely successful, it is possible that the depth with which the researcher and the research were involved in the organization partially offset weaknesses in its rigorousness. In other words, the research conducted here probably lost where a more detached and traditional approach would have gained, but it probably gained where the traditional approach would have lost. As subsequent uses of the information in the continuing organizational development program have been fairly successful, the information would seem to be valid.[23]

Finally, since there is always greater chance of hitting a target with several shots than with one, it is more likely that valid information will be found with several measures rather than with one. Therefore, the questionnaire findings were compared with interview results and with several measures of behavior, such as disciplinary reports, in order to verify the findings. Whenever possible, both questionnaire and interview findings are compared with other studies of prison policy and organizational structure. These comparisons revealed no glaring differences. The principal difference seemed to be that most of the other studies would stipulate the organizational goal and then go on to differentiate organizational structures. The most admirable of these research projects would be the Street, Vinter, and Perrow work. With their several limitations, the correctional policy instruments were an attempt to replace the stipulations with a measurement.

To review briefly, the chapter began with the recognition that there should be many possible ways of measuring correctional policy. The primary method utilized in this study was a set of questionnaires based upon the correctional policy models developed in Chapter 4.

The management-level version of the Correctional Policy Inventory was the first of the set developed and appears to be the most reliable and valid of the instruments. The officer and inmate versions need work, but demonstrated sufficient reliability and independence that they seemed usable for this research program, within which group rather than individual scores were the basic unit of analysis.

As should be done in all research programs, more than one indicator of each variable has been sought, and in most cases different methodologies have been used. These various indicators of the policy variable are reported in the next chapter.

CHAPTER 6

THE ANALYSIS OF CORRECTIONAL POLICY SCORES

The correctional policy instruments were administered to members of the Department of Correction over a period of eight months, from November 1969 through June 1970. Prior to the use of any questionnaires, a series of interviews was conducted with all Central Office managers, and all institutional heads and their immediate assistants. The interview schedule was a flexible one, in which questions that would produce one- or two-word answers that could be tabulated were alternated with open-ended questions to which the administrator could elaborate on his own ideas. The interview results served as a basis for the original management conference, but since the questions about policy were formulated independently of the questionnaire, the interview responses provide a validity check on questionnaire results and an elaboration of the particular dynamics of the policy interests found in the Department of Correction. In order to gain a different perspective on the managers' views of the department and of themselves, fifty-six correctional officers from the major institutions were also interviewed. The questions asked the officers roughly paralleled the questions asked the managers, but the format of the interview differed considerably. Officers were interviewed in groups as it was convenient for the shift supervisor to relieve men from duty for the interview. In addition to exploratory research, these officer interviews were also used to describe the training program that eventually would reach the officer level, to ask officer suggestions about training, and to solicit officer cooperation with questionnaire administrations that were to follow. With these additional goals in mind, the discussion setting was thought to be advantageous. In the minimum security prison, where the lower-level training and research were to be most extensive, more precise individual interviews were conducted with randomly selected officers and inmates. The interview results in that institution were therefore useful as another independent measure of officer and inmate perception of organizational policy.

CORRECTIONAL POLICY OF THE CENTRAL OFFICE AND CHIEF INSTITUTIONAL MANAGERS

The chief managers in the state consisted of the Commissioner and his special assistants, Deputy Commissioners for Institutions and for Field Services, a Chief Financial Officer and his staff, a Chief of Research and Planning and his staff, parole supervisor, work and education release supervisor, warden and assistant wardens from the maximum security prison, superintendent and assistants from the minimum security prison and the reformatory, wardens from six jails, and the two chief officials from the women's farm and prison complex. The number of managers who scored each policy as the most characteristic of themselves is given in Table 6.1. It can be seen that there is considerable consensus among this group of managers when their scores are taken together. Thirteen reported that Reintegration and fifteen reported that Rehabilitation was most self-characteristic. Only four managers scored either Reform or Restraint highest. These four were the warden and assistant warden from the maximum security prison and two of the jail wardens. In all, twenty-eight of the thirty-two respondents stated that their most characteristic policy emphasized the needs of the individual inmate or the needs of the inmate and community simultaneously.

While the data in Table 6.1 show a general tendency for chief executives to emphasize the individual inmate in their policy decisions, the potential conflict that Table 6.1 suggests between Central Office and institutional personnel is more important than it might first appear. Table 6.1 demonstrates that eleven Central Office managers reported Reintegration as their first preference and six reported Rehabilitation first. Of the wardens and their assistants, only two placed Reintegration first and nine reported Rehabilitation first. The chi-square of 10.04 is significant at the .01 level.

Table 6.1: The Correctional Policy Most Preferred by Each of the Top Thirty-Two Correctional Managers in the Department, Managers Classified by their Location in the Central Office or an Institution

| Manager | Correctional Policy | | | |
	Reintegration	Rehabilitation	Reform and Restraint	Total
Central Office	11	6	0	17
Wardens, Assistants	2	9	4	15
Total	13	15	4	32

Chi-square = 10.04, d.f. = 2, p. = .01

Although the number in the two groups is small, this same sort of conflict was reported among the national sample of Central Office and institution managers studied by the Joint Commission on Correctional Manpower and Training. In that survey, managers of adult institutions, juvenile institutions, probation and parole, and headquarters organizations were asked to rate three "goals" according to how much each was emphasized presently and how much each should be emphasized. The three goals were "Integration," "Treatment," and "Restraint."

Comparisons between those national data and the departmental data must be approached with some caution because the definitions of the three goals and the definitions of the four policies show only a rough correspondence, and the measuring devices were different. One major problem in the comparison is that the short instrument used in the national survey did not require a simultaneous rating of the three goals. Since that instrument did not ask administrators to report their behavior in specific situations, the instrument did not ask the administrators to choose between alternatives, as they do in daily operations. A second problem is that a conservative interpretation of the short definition given for the goals "Treatment" and "Integration" imply that administrators could probably classify some of their Reintegration activity under the goal "Treatment" and some of their Rehabilitation activity under the goal "Integration." The goal "Restraint" is probably an adequate substitute for the two correctional policies of Reform and Restraint.[1]

Nevertheless, a rough comparison would seem possible, if we limit our interest to the relative ranking given the goals by the administration and the headquarters managers. With these cautions in mind, it is interesting that, in that national sample, adult institution and headquarters managers basically agree on the amount of "Treatment" in their organizations presently and on the amount that there ought to be. In regard to "Restraint," the two groups agree on the amount that it is presently emphasized, but institution managers wanted that emphasis to remain stable while headquarters managers wanted it deemphasized. In regard to "Integration," institution managers saw much more in the organization now than did headquarters personnel, but headquarters personnel wanted Integration to become "very strongly" emphasized, while institution managers wanted it emphasized only slightly more than presently.[2]

Since the Correction Policy Inventory asked administrators what policy they emphasized rather than how well that policy was implemented, the most relevant comparison would seem to be between the correctional policy data and the report of the national sample about what should be emphasized. On the level of what is desirable in the organization, the policy preferences of departmental managers appear very much the same as goal perceptions of managers across the country. Institution managers place more importance on Restraint than do Central Office personnel, and they are much more likely to perceive the institutions as a place of treatment of individual problems than as a place preparatory for social reintegration.

While the differences in these two goal complexes are probably too subtle to be distinguished in the organizational analyses of Etzioni or Katz and Kahn, they are likely to have considerable impact on the social interactions within correctional organization. Since correctional policy functions as the model against which the manager measures operations, Central Office managers are likely to be dissatisfied with the behavior of institutions, and institutional managers are likely to be frustrated by the feedback that Central Office executives return to them. The data demonstrate that Central Office personnel have chosen a correctional model in which the capacities of the organization to influence the larger social system are all important. They are interested in changing individual offenders, but they believe that offenders are most likely to change as the organization deemphasizes incarceration and emphasizes the amount of community supervision. With these different orientations, there is bound to be conflict. Central Office personnel will probably view institution managers as short-sighted and crisis-oriented, since they are "overinterested" in the fate of individuals and "underinterested" in integrating community and institutional programming. Institutional managers are likely to perceive the Central Office as naive meddlers, unfamiliar with institutional problems and continually forcing on institutions programs or activities that seem only tangentially related to treatment and custody concerns.

The interviews with the department managers tend to support this interpretation of the data. When the managers were asked, "How do you feel about channels of communications from yourself downward?" the data shown in Table 6.2 were obtained. While nine institutional managers rated communication with subordinates as good or fair and six rated it as bad, only three Central Office personnel saw communication downward as good or fair and twelve saw it as bad.[3] This difference in the perception of the quality of downward communication supports the prediction based on the Inventory data, but it is possible that communication is affected by many factors other than goal perception. More direct verification of the questionnaire data is available through interview questions that asked: "How could institutional programs be improved?" "How would you describe your own primary objective?" and "What kind of training is necessary for line officers?" The responses to each of these questions were classified into three different goal-oriented categories.[4]

While again these goal categories are not exactly the same as those measured by the Inventory, rough comparisons are possible. In Table 6.4, the data from responses to the question about program improvement are reported. While the divergence between the two groups is not as great here as in the Inventory data, it is significant that only institutional managers favored the status quo

Table 6.2: Managers' Rating of Downward Communication Central Office
and Field Personnel Compared from Interviews Conducted
in June, 1969

Managers	Rating				
	Good	Fair	Bad	Don't Know	Total
Central	2	1	12	1	16
Field	5	4	6	0	15
	7	5	18	1	31

Table 6.3: Correctional Office and Institutional Managers Report about the
Way to Improve Institutional Programs, from Interviews
Conducted June, 1969

Managers	Goal to be Emphasized in Program				
	CH (community oriented)	REH (individual treatment)	CUS (custody)	Don't Know	Total
Central Office	8	6	0	2	16
Institutions	2	7	6	0	15
Total	10	13	6	2	31

CH means (1) an awareness of new community-oriented action programs, in which the
deviant-producing community is as much a target for change as the individual offender,
or (2) a call for definite merger of roles, to wipe out the distinction between
rehabilitation and custody.

REH means a vote for treatment of offenders in traditional or new forms, so long as
there was no objection by the respondent to the traditional isolation of the offender in
usual prisons or jails.

CUS means (1) a vote for the status quo, in most instances, or (2) for programs integrally
bound to production in the institution rather than to viable educational training.[4]

or programs that would emphasize custody even more, and that only two institution managers favored programs of joint institution-community action.

In Table 6.4, the interviewed managers were asked to report their own personal objective. These objectives were classified in the same way as were the program improvements. Evident in these data is an even more frequent concern on the part of institutional managers for custody, while there are still eight Central Officer managers favoring community-oriented goals and six favoring traditional rehabilitation.

In Table 6.5, managerial responses to the type of training that they sought for correctional officers are classified in the same way. It is interesting that at this hierarchical level, the Central Office managers' perception of goal-to-be-emphasized changes. Eight thought that officers needed training that emphasized traditional rehabilitation while six thought officers needed training about community-oriented concepts. However, at this level of the organization, a majority of the institutional managers are interested in the custody orientation.

The conclusion seems warranted that both Central Office and top institutional personnel favor a policy that emphasizes inmates' needs rather than custodial precautions. It seems also warranted to conclude that there are significant differences in the model that these officials would use in order to fulfill what they perceive as the needs of inmates. Institutional managers prefer a model of the correctional organization as halfway house and referral agency. While few of the managers speak of correctional goals as those of punishment for a wrongdoing, the disagreement on which kind of

Table 6.4: Central Office and Institutional Managers Report of Their Own Personal Objectives from Interviews Conducted June, 1969

Managers	Goals* of Managers				
	CH (community oriented)	REH (individual treatment)	CUS (custody)	Don't Know	Total
Central Office	8	6	1	1	16
Institutions	3	4	8	0	15
Total	11	10	9	1	31

*For explanation of goals, see Table 6.3.

Table 6.5: Central Office and Institutional Manager Report of the Goal
Orientation of Training for Correctional Officers from
Interviews Conducted June, 1969

Managers	Goal* Orientation of Training				
	CH (community oriented)	REH (individual treatment)	CUS (custody)	Don't Know	Total
Central Office	6	8	0	2	16
Institutions	1	5	9	0	15
Total	7	13	9	2	31

*For explanation of goals, see Table 6.3.

inmate needs to emphasize and what kind of relationship to seek with the community could lead to even further divergencies at lower levels in the organization. Of course, the data at the other organizational levels will reveal which goals the other groups consider primary, but we can anticipate additional conflict. The most direct control that the Central Office policy-makers have over the behavior of the various organizations in the department is the behavior of institutional chief executives. Institutional chiefs, according to all the data, are trying to implement a model in which inmates needs can be met by a relatively isolated and autonomous helping institution. It is extremely unlikely that institutional managers will get their way, since their superiors are only moderately in favor of such a model. But it would also seem highly unlikely that the lower echelons in these institutions will be more responsive to community needs and community change than their wardens, since the top organizational executive is usually the gatekeeper of organizational boundaries.[5] Consequently, the policy preferences of the Central Office executives also seem headed for impartial and faulty implementation.

CORRECTIONAL POLICY OF MIDDLE MANAGERS

The middle managers were a selected group of educators, counselors, and custodial and work supervisors from the various institutions in the department. Much like the upper group, the middle managers were a "mixed bag." There were several counselors with a college education and few years of institutional experience, and there were also prison maintenance supervisors and custodial captains with eighth-grade educations and twenty-five years of experience. It is unfortunate that there was not too much information about the criteria that the wardens used in selecting these managers for the training conference. The institutional managers were told that the middle management conference would cover material similar to that covered in the top-level conference, as such management and correctional concepts were relevant to middle managers. It was also suggested that, in the event that the same kind of training would reach officers, then the middle managers who attended the conference could be instrumental in lower-echelon training.

As presented by the consultants, then, it was to the advantage of the wardens to select managers whom they liked and worked well with and who were perceived to have good rapport with their own subordinates. Quite definitely, then, this was not a random group of middle managers, but a group that as a whole had earned the top managers' approval and support. There may have been some exceptions to this rule, since there were probably some managers selected because of seniority or their strategic location in the organizational social system, regardless of the top managers' approval of them. There may have also been one or two that the warden simply wanted to get rid of for a day or two. That the usual criteria involved the middle managers' effectiveness or success in the eyes of their superiors, rather than some other reason, may be inferred from the promotion rate of members of the group. Within a year of the conference, more than a fifth of the conference attendants had been promoted to the more important middle management or top management positions. The question arises how representative this group is of all middle managers in the department. As a sample, they were probably biased toward "the official view of things." However, this is probably not a significant distortion factor at this level. It is probably true that, if wardens were asked to select inmates for a conference, the group selected would not represent the views of the inmate body in general. But the warden's selection of the middle managers, if it is a rating of the middle managers' power or influence, is probably a good sample, when we are interested in the implementation of policy.

The policy preference of the middle managers, and a comparison of all top managers with all middle managers is given in Table 6.6. It is obvious that there is even more consensus among middle managers than among the top group. Sixteen of the middle managers (or sixty percent) stated that the policy most characteristic of themselves was Rehabilitation. There is no statistically significant difference in the top manager and middle manager policy distribution.

There seems to be slightly more agreement among top and middle managers in the departmental sample than there was in the national Manpower sample. In contrast, the Manpower study found

> a small but significant difference between the perceptions of the second level and the top administrators. The second level managers appeared to feel slightly more strain between what exists and what should be, and they generally rated their organizations' orientation toward the goals of treatment and integration lower than did their superiors.[6]

While this difference did not show up in the department data, some of the conflict is visible in certain interview results. These results do not contradict the policy questionnaire findings, but they suggest that there may be some differences in the depth of commitment and of understanding of top and middle managers. For example, middle managers at Hilltop spoke of good community-institution relations and demonstrated the positive nature of the relationship with examples of "Dale Carnegie" courses and "Guides to Better Living" offered by the local busi-

Table 6.6: Top and Middle Manager Report of the Correctional Policy Most Characteristic of Themselves

		Policy			
Manager	Reintegration	Rehabilitation	Reform	Restraint	Total
Top	13	15	4	0	32
Middle	4	16	4	2	26
Total	17	31	8	2	58

Chi-square not significant

ness groups for Hilltop inmates. The Superintendent asserted that official relationships were good, but lacked depth or productivity. He said, "If anything, outside groups are not aware of how much *we* can contribute to the community. But we are not involved and do not request much from them." His captains, in contrast, complained that it was very difficult to find room to house all the activities that now bring groups to the institution.

Table 6.7 data demonstrate that, as would be expected, there is a significant difference between the policy preferences of Central Office and middle managers in institutions. While middle managers seem to have the same correctional model as their immediate institutional superiors, they do not see relationships with the community or the provision of new social opportunities for offenders as of first importance. This divergence in interest is highlighted by the comments of one of the Hilltop middle managers:

> It is very frustrating now—the lack of communication with the Central Office, it seems that they don't care, even if they do. I know that they don't understand the problems of institutions—they don't have day to day operational experience.

In general, then, middle and top institutional managers seem to agree fairly well on policy, although the difference in imaginativeness and initiative are quite apparent. Middle managers think in terms of set, particular programs; top managers, in terms of principles that are to be applied. It was also borne out that policy of middle managers is even further removed from Central Office policy.

Table 6.7: Central Office and Middle Manager Report of Policy Most Characteristic of Themselves

Managers	Policy			Total
	Reintegration	Rehabilitation	Reform/Restraint	
Central Office	11	6	0	17
Middle	4	16	6	26
Total	15	22	6	43

Chi-square = 11.62, d.f. = 2, p. = .005

THE CORRECTIONAL POLICY OF THE CUSTODIAL OFFICERS
IN THE MINIMUM SECURITY PRISON

The correctional officers, unlike the top and middle managers, were asked how they behave in certain situations and what they perceive as the purposes of certain institutional programs. They were not asked to report their views concerning noninstitutional matters, such as the conduct of probation and parole, since such matters are not directly open to them, while they are of daily concern to managers. The data in Table 6.8 represent the correctional policy model that officers stated they most frequently supported through their behavior. It is a distribution considerably different from either top or middle manager policy distributions. Only four officers supported Reintegration most frequently. Nineteen, nearly half, supported Reform, and the rest were about equally split for Rehabilitation and Restraint.[7]

Just what this emphasis on Reform and Restraint means is highlighted by the interviews conducted at the Hilltop facility. One officer, when asked "What is the goal of Hilltop?" replied: "The main thing now is it is a pre-release institution," referring to the great number of parole-eligible transfers that the institution receives. When he was then asked "Are officers committed to this goal?" he responded: "No, they generally put in eight hours and leave." The next man interviewed, when asked the institutional goal, replied, "More treatment, and better cooperation between departments." When asked if officers were committed to this goal, he said: "Too many have lost interest. The purposes of civil service are a mystery and there is little challenge in our work." Another said, "Rehabilitation itself is a con job, but Hilltop as a whole is trying to convince people it is better to stay in the street." The same man, when asked of officer commitment, said, "Officers as a whole don't know what officers are supposed to be doing."

Table 6.8: The Most Frequently Supported Correctional Policy According to Hilltop Correctional Institution Officers Reporting Their Own Behavior

	Policy Supported				
	Reintegration	Rehabilitation	Reform	Restraint	Total
Officers	4	10	19	11	44

Another man, when asked "What is your own personal goal?" stated: "There is so much to be desired. I'd like to get a position where I could help." Asked the goal of the institution, he replied, "Incarcerating men for a period of time." To this same question, another officer replied, "Right now it seems only to keep the inmate locked up. There is not much rehabilitation in farm work."

Some of the more optimistic answers came not from the officers who supported Rehabilitation as a goal, but from officers who supported Reform and saw Hilltop as the last institutional transfer before the inmates have earned the privilege of parole. A prototype of these responses is demonstrated by the following sequence:

Q.: What is your own personal goal?

A.: Well, it isn't strictly security, or everyone would be locked up. Setting an example is important—not to rehabilitate but to set standards and be the go between with the administration.

Q.: What is the goal of Hilltop?

A.: We are trying to do more than confine. In Winters (the maximum security prison), an inmates' self-respect is gone. Down here we are approaching the street.

Q.: Are the officers committed to this goal?

A.: Some. The problem is with the people who have been here ten to fifteen years. You tell them that the system does not work and expect them to change. A lot of people have adjusted, but it is a big adjustment to ask.

More typical of the officers were the following three sets of responses:

Q.: What is the goal of Hilltop?

A.: I really can't say what the goal is. We don't know.

Q.: Are officers committed to the goal, whatever it is?

A.: Officers follow specifications (e.g., civil service job descriptions). They are expected to waste time.

Q.: What is your personal goal?

A.: I'm retiring next year. And I'd never spend another year here.

Q.: What is the goal of Hilltop?

A.: They are trying. If they reach them, it's a success. Programs here are seen (by the inmates) as an easy out, not as rehabilitation.

Q.: Are officers committed to this goal?

A.: I think we've lost all respect from inmates. On disciplinary reports you don't know who is on trial any more. We don't have the backing we need. And colored people are too much in control.

Q.: What is your personal goal?

A.: Looking forward to my retirement. My family is my interest now.

Q.: What is the goal of Hilltop?

A.: This ain't a farm. It's in between now, and it's high time. It's a step toward getting out.

Q.: Are officers committed to this goal?

A.: Yes, but we don't always know what it is.

Perhaps the most typical of the Hilltop officers as a group were the responses of an officer who was shortly promoted. He was one of the most outspoken and well-respected men in the organization. Shortly after his promotion, he took a leave of absence because of a nervous breakdown. The strain that he felt between the correctional ideal and correctional reality was evident in his interview replies:

Q.: How is communication between officers and captains?

A.: None.

Q.: How is communication to the Superintendent?

A.: None.

Q.: How is communication to the Central Office?

A.: They are more concerned with propaganda.

Q.: Can the average inmate make it when released if he wants to?

A.: No. Frequently we damage inmates.

Q.: What is your primary goal?

A.: Career.

Q.: What is the goal of Hilltop?

A.: Hilltop ideally prepares people for the street. Actually we only hold them.

Q.: Are officers committed to this goal?

A.: Many forget their day when they leave. This is necessary. The pattern here is attributable to years in service. The old guards are disciplinarians.

Q.: Are inmates committed to this goal?

A.: No, they feel conned.

Q.: Is there additional training you would like?

A.: An orientation on what the institution is doing without the endeavor to create a rosy picture. I want to know why we have to destroy an inmate's good work habits. Why make work?

Q.: How is communication with inmates?

A.: The relationship that I have is good and square.

Perhaps it is an adequate summary of the officer level to say that while managers' preferences were also what they were doing, trying to do, or thought that they *were* doing; officers' behavior is frequently not a reflection of what they prefer. Compared with any of the other groups, there is tremendous disagreement among officers about institutional and personal goals. The condition of anomie is evident. Officers who favor a "punitive" or "disciplinarian" stance do not feel supported by their superiors, and officers who favor rehabilitation do not see the opportunity to work for it.

Since middle management and top officials are fairly much in agreement about policy, and officer policy supportive behavior seems rather removed from either group, the relationship of middle managers to officers would appear particularly important. The policy most characteristic of middle managers and the policy most frequently supported by officers is reported in Table 6.9. The chi-square of 12.96 reflects a significant disagreement among the two groups.

The group interview findings conducted in the summer of 1969 highlighted officers' feelings toward middle managers and verify the Hilltop policy and interview results.

[56%] of all managers in the department were dissatisfied with communication to their subordinates. In the institutions, one key area of communication troubles may be the shift supervisor position. This trouble spot should be viewed with caution, however. There is at the present time little direct evidence that shift supervisors themselves are at fault in the subordinate-superior conflict. But information, in the opinion of 18 managers, does not flow past that position with any reliability.[8]

Table 6.9: Policy Most Characteristic of Middle Managers Compared With Policy Most Frequently Supported by Behavior of Correctional Officers

| | Policy | | | | |
Group	Reintegration	Rehabilitation	Reform	Restraint	Total
Middle	4	16	4	2	26
Officers	4	10	19	11	44
Total	8	26	23	13	70

Chi-square of 12.96, d.f. = 3., p. = .005

One problem with the custodial captain or shift supervisor position was evident when considering which group perceived these men as peers. It was the finding of the group interviews that officers considered sergeants and lieutenants as peers but considered captains as part of administration. Administrators, on the other hand, considered captains as part of the custodial force, as men who had come up through the ranks to the top of the bottom class.[9]

The complaint from officers was universal that they had little authority to deal firsthand with problem inmates and inmates' problems. What this complaint actually meant depended on the complainant, who usually fell into one of two categories. Some officers wanted more disciplinary power, while others wanted greater authority in decisions about inmate programs.[10] Similarly, there was one group of officers who wanted stricter adherence to post orders, and there was another group who felt constrained by the idea that they should only follow orders and had no leeway in the structure of their daily activities.

While managers and officers commonly attributed the difference in officer orientation to the age of the officer, or to the years of service, the correlations reported in Table 6.10 show that there are no strong relationships between policy supported by officers and age, years of formal education, years of service, age when hired, days absent, number of jobs held prior to the present one, or the number of dependents. There were no other variables available in the personnel records, but it would seem unlikely that other kinds of background and personal characteristics would influence the behavior of officers more than the variables recorded. Differences in the degree to which officers' behavior supports or does not support the policy of managers would seem most likely to depend on organizational variables such as role requirements or supervisory practices rather than other kinds of variables. In this regard, the organizational analysis of Donald Cressey would seem to be most helpful.

It will be remembered that Cressey suggested that officer behavior is dependent on the sanctioning pattern enforced by administration. In the "treatment-oriented prison," the dominant sanctioning pattern for the control of officer behavior required officers to develop relationships with inmates, to support the

Table 6.10: Product Moment Correlations Between Correctional Officers'
Correctional Policy Total Scores and Variables Found in
Personnel Folder

Variable	Reintegration	Rehabilitation	Reform	Restraint
Age	− .088	.059	.064	.179
Years of Education	− .050	− .030	− .289	.009
Years in Service	.162	.054	.149	.028
Age when Hired	− .278	− .224	− .157	.262
Days Absent Per Year	.104	.002	.092	− .069
Number of Prior Jobs	− .009	− .143	.134	.031
Number of Dependents	− .134	− .075	.065	.047

When r = .30, p. = .05 N = 44 correctional officers

therapeutic atmosphere first, and to enforce custodial regulations second. An officer is successful in the organization if he aids in offender rehabilitation. Harsh sanctions or strict standards for officer misbehavior are contradictory to the Rehabilitation policy of the institution and cannot be applied to improper role behavior by officers. Moreover, there is no standard by which to evaluate officer contributions to Rehabilitation; so whatever they do, within broad limits, is allowable. Often, within the minimum security institution, officers may carry out their concern for Reform without resorting to formal channels. Since they are expected to speak with and to develop relationships with inmates, they may use that area of discretion to apply informal punishments to inmates for behavior they consider inappropriate to Reform values.[11]

Cressey's examination of the comparative consequences for attempting to follow Reform or Rehabilitation policies seems appropriate to the policy stratification in Hilltop. The Hilltop administration operates under a Rehabilitation policy; therefore, the officers are free to develop personal relationships with inmates. Since there are no reliable criteria by which administrators can separate personal relationships that aid offender rehabilitation from relationships that do not, officers have considerable leeway to "innovate" for the accomplishment of Reform or Restraint values under the Rehabilitation policy.[12]

Cressey's description of the treatment-oriented prison included the low-frequency resort to formal disciplinary procedures. Obvious in the officer interviews was the resentment of some officers about the "lenient" approach of the disciplinary court to rule infractions reported by officers. To see how the officers' perceptions of the courts' reaction in disciplinary cases compared to its actual behavior, a study was conducted of all disciplinary infractions reported from January 1, 1969, through June 30, 1970.

There was a low disciplinary report frequency in Hilltop; only ninety reports were filed in the year-and-a-half period. Of these, only thirty-five were accepted and acted upon. In other words, the disciplinary committee did not support reaction to inmate behavior by officers who saw that behavior as wrong. Twenty-nine of the forty-four officers surveyed on the policy questionnaire did not file a single report in that time, even though the resort to formal punishment under the Reform policy is common. Five of the eleven officers who scored high on both Reform policy and Rehabilitation policy filed reports, while only twelve of the thirty-four who were not high on both policies filed reports. Fifty percent of the reports filed by officers high in both policies were accepted, whereas only twenty-seven percent of reports filed by other officers were accepted. It would seem, then, that officers who were high on both policies may have been rewarded. The disciplinary board was more willing to act on reports by officers whose orientation was ambiguous than it was for officers whose orientation was not. In effect, the resort to the Reform pattern (filing reports) in an institution where managers disfavored reports appears to have been more acceptable when the officers also demonstrated at other times a high concern for the individual inmates.

While in all respects the data are slight, Cressey's observational data about the result of sanctioning patterns in Rehabilitation-oriented institutions seems sound. Indeed, it may even have advantages for officers in this type of institution to espouse contradictory policies. What negative effects their Reform behavior brings them from managers who desire Rehabilitation, or from inmates who do not want to be punished, may be cancelled by their equally frequent resort to rehabilitative behavior. And if their personal satisfaction is partially achieved through Reform behavior (e.g., because the compliance pattern clarifies their status or allows them to wield power), this method of gaining satisfaction is protected because they are willing to develop relationships with inmates in other situations.

As Cressey suggests, officers may take advantage of the infrequent use of sanctions against officers in rehabilitative institutions by withholding or giving affection as inmates comply with values held by officers. If officers do so, they have subordinated the goal of improving social relationships (Rehabilitation) to the goal of enforcing community standards (Reform). They are substituting control by identification for control by compliance but they are using informal rather than formal punishments to gain compliance. In an institution such as Hilltop, where officers are encouraged to develop such relationships, but where there is no effective evaluation procedure for the control of that development, the management is essentially at a loss to prohibit or control the use of the rehabilitative method for the achievement of Reform goals. Since the present organizational structure is one in which control patterns and goals do not coincide, there would seem to be no method of achieving the goal of Rehabilitation policy. Since the data show that officers frequently behave in a Reform manner regardless of the policy above, there are evidently few ways in the Hilltop structure that managers can contain this tendency, because they have no effective negative sanctions to apply to Reform behavior on the part of officers. The one *major* control at their disposal is the refusal to legitimate formal compliance control patterns characteristic of Reform. If officers want to continue to behave in a Reform manner, they also must learn to espouse the goals of Rehabilitation and to substitute the face-to-face controls allowed in Rehabilitation policy for the uniform regulations most congruent with a Reform orientation.

While managers have no effective negative sanction for Reform behavior, they also have no set of positive sanctions for Rehabilitative behavior on the part of officers. Managers lack a method of connecting the type of relationships officers develop with inmates with the amount of progress inmates make in the institution. Civil service regulations tend to forbid rewards to officers whose behavior toward inmates is therapeutic. According to these regulations, officers are not qualified to counsel inmates. The actual "therapeutic" work must be done by men who are trained as counselors and who receive pay as counselors. Added to the civil service requirements of a college degree in the appropriate fields, the correctional officers' union forbids management to use officers as counselors because the officers do not receive a salary on par with counselors' salaries. Hence, if an officer really *desires* to behave in a manner congruent with rehabilitative policy, he and the managers who allow him to do so are attacked on two fronts. Officers with strong union affiliations will complain that the officer is a "ratebuster" because he is willing to perform high-priced activity at the lower wage. The Civil Service Commission, on the other hand, will reprimand management for utilizing men who have not passed competitive examinations and are not qualified. Thus, the present Hilltop structure (1) does not negatively sanction Reform behavior and (2) does not positively reward, and may negatively reward, Rehabilitation behavior. Since individuals are more likely to behave in accordance with the organizational sanctioning pattern than with the goals of the institution, where the two are not congruent, officers are more likely to be reformist, or to use rehabilitative discretion for Reform goals than they are to accept and conform to managerial policy.[14]

The two most frequent complaints voiced by officers about the job situation at Hilltop substantiate the disparity between managerial policy and the sanctioning activity to which officers respond. About fifty percent of Hilltop officers interviewed reported that their major complaint involved the unwillingness of administrators to support officers against inmates. They stated that inmates were free to show disrespect and contradict orders because they knew that officers had no power. In essence, these men complained that administrators would not legitimate control by compliance.

Another large group of officers said that the major problem involved the impossibility of their doing anything worthwhile as officers. They thought that the greatest contribution officers could make would be helping inmates to improve their situation in life. They felt that most inmates had a right to be disgruntled and cynical because although managers expressed interest in Rehabilitation, inmates had a small chance of receiving real aid in the present organization. They stated that information which officers had gained in close contact with inmates was not passed on to officials (counselors) who could utilize it and that they were powerless to use it themselves. The development of friendly and open communication with inmates was blocked by civil service regulations and by other officers who would complain to union officials. In essence, they complained that control by identification was not supported.

This lack of structural support for organizational goals was a problem also recognized by the Superintendent. In musing about the effect of imposing a rigid table of organization upon his organization (he did not at the time use one), the Superintendent worried about locking men into set roles:

> One question I would like answered is this: How sure am I that I want a table of organization? Most correctional officers go *only* by the T-O. The problem working with it, is the personnel department who assign specifications to the slots. Those men who really stay to the specifications actively limit other officers and staff.

One attempt by department officials to decrease the disparity between the officer role and the managerial policy was thwarted almost as soon as it began. Shortly after the department was formed in 1967, the Commissioner began suggesting that correctional officers should participate more in the treatment of inmates. Most correctional officers were sincerely glad to hear this suggestion. The officers who had some knowledge of what a therapeutic officer role might entail—in other words, those genuinely desiring to help inmates in some way—were pleased to find that the new Commissioner was on their side. Those officers who did not really understand or care what aid to inmates might entail were also enheartened, for as they interpreted the Commissioner's remarks, he was going to legitimate their Reform orientation, which they, rightly or wrongly, understood as good for inmates. In other words, one group of officers felt that under the new administration officer roles were to be expanded. The other group felt that the role that they were already playing, with or without administrative support, would be strengthened.[15]

Plans for this expansion did not fare well. It was impossible for officers to become involved with rehabilitation of inmates without a proclamation from both civil service and the union regarding which officers under what conditions would participate in the rehabilitation of inmates. The Commissioner's suggestion that officers' roles be expanded so that they would become more involved in the process by which inmates were changed became, almost automatically, an opportunity to set up a new officer position. Approximately two years later, the requirements for a correctional officer III position were published. This new officer was to assist in the counseling of inmates, and would be assigned to a particular dormitory or cell block. He would work closely with the counseling staff, but would report to his lieutenant. He would also have two years of college education. Although he would be an officer, the pay grade was about the same as that for some middle managers. Under the influence of both the union and the civil service, officers learned that the amount of money received symbolizes the amount of authority an official has.[16] Hence, they found it inconceivable that a correctional officer III should report to a lieutenant, who might be receiving less money. And officers did not seem to recognize an increase in responsibility and discretion concerning inmates that should also yield increased status and power within the administrative heirarchy.

As a result, it was difficult for officers to understand what a correctional officer III was, or where he fit into the organization, and the questions of who and where he was in the organization seemed much more important to them than what he did. It did not matter that the correctional officer III would have the kind of discretion with inmates that many officers desired. The additional difficulty arose that no officer had the educational requirement necessary to take the C. O. III examination. Administrators soon saw that the introduction of the C. O. III position had exacerbated the situation because the position as described did not conform to officer expectations about the benefits of an expanded role. Since greater promotional possibilities were necessary, a correctional sergeant position was devised soon after the C. O. III position. This position required several years of correctional experience, but not the additional education. It also promoted the officer into the administrative hierarchy, although it was not intended to bring him closer to inmates, or to utilize his knowledge of and rapport with inmates. This position, however, seemed to make sense to the officers, and sergeant positions were soon filled. At Hilltop, they were filled from among the officer group that the administrators thought would have been the best C. O. IIIs. Thus, while the organizational administrative hierarchy expanded, the officer role remained the same, and some of the officers who seemed best equipped to interact with inmates were promoted out of the officer level. The organization suffered because, on all levels, greater attention was given to how a man would be organizationally defined than to what he might do best.

The overall effect of the original plans for greater officer participation with inmates and the failure of the eventual bureaucratic implementation was damaging to the new department. Whereas the first Commissioner took office with general enthusiasm and support from the officers, after three years they were blaming him for his failure to live up to their expectations. Officers with strong union affiliations anticipated with fervor the possibility of the Commissioner's resignation during the 1970 gubernatorial campaign, and most officers considered his resignation following the election of a governor of another party a victory for the officers. The inability of administrators to structure the organization so that it would be directed by Rehabilitation goals became a political issue, and while officers felt they had been successful in politicizing their dissatisfaction, the political resolution did nothing to change the situation that had generated the dissatisfaction in the first place.

A safe if unstartling conclusion is that correctional officers do not follow the policy of their superiors the majority of the time. In this sample, three-quarters of the men report that their behavior most frequently was consistent with Reform or Restraint policies. An additional finding of both the interview samples is that the officers were definitely dissatisfied with the present work situation. These findings seem to verify what is usually considered common knowledge in prisons. However, the equally common knowledge that the older or less-educated men were more punitive than younger men with less experience and more education is not borne out. Furthermore, there is little interview data that would support the position that officer tendency toward Reform or Restraint was the result of some deep-seated hatred of the inmates, or some really stubborn idea that Reform or Restraint were right. Much more frequent is the idea that Rehabilitation or Treatment was impossible in the present circumstances. Lastly, and perhaps most importantly, the officers have no clear idea what administrative policy of the organization actually was.

To some extent, this lack of knowledge may be attributed to the recent changes in the formal structure of the prison. While the new superintendent of the autonomous Hilltop facility moved quickly to establish the character and goals of his institution (including the training program within which this research was conducted), it was short notice to ask officers to understand changes in policy so quickly, after six years of maximum security administration. In short, part of the anomie among officers about the goals of the institution and the proper behavior patterns for officers may be part of the normal developments of resettling an established institution on a new path.

To some extent, however, the evolution of Hilltop within the new Department of Correction cannot explain this disagreement, dissensus, and dissatisfaction of the officers. Correctional institutions in the second half of this century are always changing. The turnover rate among top managers is higher than among officers. Ten of thirty-two Central Office figures changed in the year of the study, while turnover rate among Hilltop officers was about five percent per year. Programs and projects came and went in abundance, and the city papers were frequently carrying stories about changing departmental goals and changing departmental personnel. In other words, change is rapid in correctional systems now, and it may seem more rapid than it actually is because for years the system changed so little.[17] Also, while a state of change may explain that officers suffered from certain feelings of normlessness, it does not explain why officer behavior drifts toward Restraint rather than Reintegration.

Since correctional top and middle managers have shown considerable agreement on policy, but officers failed to carry that policy out, a key to the working of the prison would seem to be the process of interaction between officers and their immediate supervisors. This relationship is approached in a general fashion by Cressey's analysis of sanction and reward and seems to apply in Hilltop. A more complete examination of this relationship, however, is dependent on the concept of feedback and thus will have to await the measurement of managerial style.

PERCEPTION OF POLICY BY INMATES

Inmates in the Hilltop institution were asked to record how staff members, usually officers, behaved, and they were also asked to infer from that behavior what the purposes of certain staff actions were. If all the managers agreed on policy and all officers behaved in accordance with policy and all inmates were accurate in reporting what they observed, then presumably inmates' and managers' policy scores would be similar. This, of course, was not the case. There were differences between Central Office and institutional managers and differences between institutional managers and officers. It would not be illogical to expect further divergence from the Central Office model at the inmate level.

An important question is whether the inmates were accurate or honest in responding to the questionnaire, or whether they were "out to get the staff." Of course, whether or not the subjects are honest is always a problem with questionnaire research. The researcher usually tries to infer from the responses whether the respondents were serious and accurate in their responses. This type of validity problem is knottier than usual, however, when inmates have been asked to rate the perceived goal-directed behavior of staff, particularly when it is a program goal to act on the information gathered. All levels of staff in Hilltop are covertly and sometimes overtly condemned by inmates every day. They know it happens and expect it. Most of them act as calmly as they can about it, and, as has been shown, few disciplinary tickets are written.

But in this situation, researchers entered Hilltop, gave inmates the opportunity to rate the staff on forty different items, totalled all the scores, and then asked the staff to believe that the result was an accurate picture of the way inmates felt they were treated. By and large, the staff accepted the results as valid to the extent that all the managers in the institution were willing to base an organizational development program on the findings, with the goal of reducing the gap between managerial policy and inmate perception of it. In addition to this action, and the supporting data obtained in the interviews with inmates, one additional procedure was used.

When, after the majority of inmates on the pretest sample had refused to answer the questionnaire, and prior to the administration to the test sample, the inmate editor of the prison paper wrote a report on the purpose of the research. He explained the previous managerial training conferences, reported the failure of the pretest, suggested that accurate results could improve the situation at Hilltop, and urged cooperation. In addition to this announcement, after the sample was selected, it was carefully reviewed by the researcher and a counselor who had attended the middle management conference. The counselor weeded out any inmates who would not be able to take the test because of court appearances, parole hearings, sick call, or absolute illiteracy (could not follow the instructions and the answer sheet in either English or Spanish). After these inmates were replaced from the remaining pool of possible subjects, the counselor selected those inmates whom he felt would not cooperate at all, or whose answers would be extremely biased because of very recent disciplinary problems. Each of the choices that he made (about five in ninety) was discussed with the researcher to make sure that it was simply not anti-staff inmates who were selected out of the sample. When the researcher was satisfied that the inmate was not chosen because he was a known inmate leader or for a similar reason, these inmates were also replaced.

The counselor then contacted each man in the sample on an individual basis and explained that he had been selected for the testing on the luck of the draw. The purposes of the questionnaire were again explained, and every effort was made to answer inmate questions. Nevertheless, it was firmly if politely implied that filling out the questionnaire was mandatory. Few inmates asked directly whether they had an option. On the day of the testing, there were some vocal objections, the major one being that it could not be anonymous since inmates had been called by name to take the test. The method of selection so that each housing unit and work assignment had an equal chance of representation was explained, and it was pointed out that there was no way of identifying answer sheets belonging to particular respondents. This kind of objection quickly subsided largely because the majority of inmates seemed eager to take the test. Again, it was emphasized that the data were to be used in training and reorganizing the prison. In many ways, more effort was expended trying to ensure accurate inmate responses than accurate officer responses.

The results of the policy questionnaire given inmates are reported in Table 6.11. It is obvious that the large majority of inmates perceived the most frequent staff behavior to be consistent with a policy of Restraint.[18]

The data from the questionnaire are supported by the results of the interviews conducted with a random sample of Hilltop inmates. To the question, "What do you think Hilltop is trying to do with inmates?" sixteen responded "nothing," or words to that effect. The other four mentioned some kind of rehabilitation, usually a particular program in which that particular inmate had a vested interest.

Inmate answers to other questions shed light on their perception of a Restraint policy, or, in other words, that the main interest of staff was order maintenance without reference to goals of inmates or the community. For example, one inmate, when asked who he thought "runs the place," responded: "No one, everything runs like a machine." Asked whether security staff "help as much as they can," he stated: "Very few do anything but put in time. That's what they are here for." Representative of the responses seemingly most antagonistic to the prison were the following:

Q.: What do you think Hilltop is trying to do to inmates?
A.: Nothing—to keep them polluted.
Q.: Do you agree with the goals of Hilltop?
A.: I don't know who they are fooling.

Table 6.11: The Policy Most Frequently Supported by Behavior of Staff as Perceived by Inmates of the Hilltop Institution

	Policy				
	Reintegration	Rehabilitation	Reform	Restraint	Total
Inmates	2	3	28	56	89

However, this man's next response about officers was also rather common:

Q.: The security staff says they try to help as much as possible. Do you believe them?

A.: They are regular screws all right. The people I work for are top notch. They'll rap with you.

Apparently the inmates found the organization unproductive, but the staff they found about as good as could be expected:

Q.: What do you think Hilltop is trying to do with inmates?

A.: Not much. There is more going on at the prison [the maximum security unit].

Q.: Do you agree with that goal or not?

A.: Can't see anything they're trying to do.

Q.: The security staff say they try to help as much as possible. Do you believe them?

A.: Some, yes. There are some you can talk to and they will bend over backwards to help you.

The notion that the officers with whom there is greatest contact are most helpful came up several times:

Q.: Security staff say they try to be as helpful as possible. Do you believe them?

A.: Most of them put in eight hours and leave. But there are some exceptions, particularly the ones you work with.

Some of the inmates were rather articulate in their criticism and evidently had thought about such questions:

Q.: What do you think Hilltop is trying to do with inmates?

A.: This place is ass backwards. It should be an industrial center. Programs don't exist for people going out (while training programs do exist at the maximum security unit). Everyone back for parole violation is here because of this setup.

Q.: Do you agree with Hilltop goals or not?

A.: Work release is not open to the reformatory, drugs, and P.V.'s. They don't make selections by the crime of the conviction. Rehabilitation is outside, where addicts can't get to it.

Last, while many were not as precise about it, like the man making the following responses, many inmates demonstrated the ability to separate individual from organizational action:

Q.: What do you think Hilltop is trying to do with inmates?

A.: I don't know. On an individual basis I see nothing. It's an extension of the same idea as the max. Custody and make no waves.

Q.: Do you agree with Hilltop goals or not?

A.: Things are too superficial.

Q.: The security staff say they try to help as much as they can. Do you believe them?

A.: Some are genuinely interested, but they are suppressed by the system.

There is little doubt that inmates found few advantages to their incarceration at Hilltop. It is important that there was no great polarization visible between staff and inmates and no rash accusations from staff about inmates or vice versa. It would be much more accurate to say that the attitude of inmates were quite similar to that of officers. They obviously recognized the possibility of a prison in which, if time was to be served somewhere, it might be put to good use. Inmates, like officers, had stock in the potential of learning in prison sets of behavior that would make reoffending less likely. *Unlike* officers, the inmates were much less frequent to identify this potential but unrealized process as "rehabilitation," or "treatment," with the exception of addicts, who seemed to recognize addition as a problem for a treatment unavailable in prison. The inmates were more likely to emphasize training programs such as work release and vocational education. By and large, they seemed to be job-oriented, did not see seeking job opportunities as rehabilitation or treatment, and did not see Hilltop as a place of opportunity.

ALL LEVELS OF ORGANIZATION ON THE
POLICY OF FIRST PREFERENCE

A summary of the questionnaire data presented to this point is reported in Table 6.12. The policy rated by top and middle managers is compared with officers' reports of the policy they most frequently support with their behavior and with the inmates' perceptions of the policy most frequently implemented. The chi-square of 102.04 demonstrates considerable divergence by hierarchical level concerning what correctional policy is the standard toward which organizational behavior is directed. There is less than one possibility in a thousand that this type of distribution

Table 6.12:　Policy Most Characteristic of Top and Middle Managers Compared With Policy Most Frequently Supported by Officer Behavior and Policy Perceived by Inmates as Most Frequently Implemented

Organizational Level	Policy				
	Reintegration	Rehabilitation	Reform	Restraint	Total
Top Management	13	15	4	0	32
Middle Management	4	16	4	2	26
Officers	4	10	19	11	44
Inmates	2	3	28	56	89
Total	23	44	55	69	191

Chi-square = 102.04, d.f. = 6, p. = .001

would occur by chance. The level of statistical significance is rather inconsequential, however, compared to the significance of the behavior patterns that the data reflect. Importantly, the data should not be taken to suggest that there is a high level of conflict and tension within the prison or that manager, officers, and inmates are at each other's throats because of their disagreement about policy. They are not. There is nothing in the interview data or the informal observation to suggest that the only method managers have of achieving cooperation from officers or from inmates is raw power and threat of punishment.

On the contrary, the policy data reflect a far deeper, more subtle, and less easily resolved problem than the continual crises situations of overt conflict and constant hatred that might exist in some other institutions. The data reflect the fact that in a rather comfortable institution, where staff turnover is very low, where most inmates are selected as good behavior risks, the goals of a therapeutically inclined management are contradicted by the perception of inmates about their situation. To this point, the study of the Hilltop situation would seem to be a verification of Sykes' conclusion that the structural effects of the prison are such that considerable improvement in the basic living conditions and quality of the custodial force will not alter the essential organizational situation.[19] What should probably be considered the most significant consequence of that statement cannot be demonstrated within this study, but it can be inferred from a comparison of the policy frequencies with the attitudes reflected in staff and inmate interviews. And that consequence would be the ultimate effect on those human beings of living continually in a situation that they all consider both absurd and relentless. Such a situation can be changed. But, quite obviously, effective change does not occur by meeting the superficial demands that, in the absurd situation, might seem important. A comparison of the maximum security drudgery in Sykes' account of Trenton with the relative pleasantness of Hilltop raises the conclusion that reformation of the correctional enterprise misses the target when it separates adults from juveniles, pays officers more money, and provides inmates with rooms rather than cells. Such changes may be commensurate with other changes in the larger social system, but they have little to do with correcting corrections.

Furthermore, a comparison with the admittedly custodial goals of Trenton prison[20] with the intendedly therapeutic regime at Hilltop demonstrates that changing the model toward which the prison is supposed to proceed does not seriously alter the situation either. What should seem to make a difference would be to establish criteria for judging the effect of day-to-day behavior upon the accomplishment of long-range goals. As Cressey argues, and as the Hilltop data suggest, officer behavior is generally unrelated to policy above them. In other words, the means of accomplishing the ends have not been established. Much of what officers do seems to happen by accident or by the tendency to drift toward historically familiar but no longer desirable patterns of behavior. Therefore, we must examine the nature of the connection between the manager (or the situation control) and the situation below. How does he read the situation, how does he compare it to his standards, and how does he relay his assessment to alter the situation? In short, how do correctional managers feed back their policy concerns to the people responsible for implementation?

CHAPTER 7

MANAGERIAL STYLE AS AN
ORGANIZATIONAL VARIABLE

It has been argued that officers do not follow the managerial policy of Rehabilitation because they are not rewarded for doing so. The policy of Rehabilitation and the organizational structure that includes manager-officer interaction are not congruent. It is possible that officer behavior follows the sanctioning pattern more closely than it follows the managerial perception of organizational goals. Similarly, it seems likely that inmate perception of staff behavior is more strongly affected by interaction patterns than by the goals that officers believe are being implemented. At all hierarchical interfaces, the behavior of the organizational participants tends to lead the organization further from rather than closer to the achievement of goals intended by the Central Office policy-makers. While at the top of the organization, managers state that organizational goals involve the successful reentry of inmates into the community, or the development of social maturity among inmates, the operant prison goals perceived by inmates are merely those of keeping the organization going, and not those of planned and directed change among inmates.

After analyzing the divergence in goal perception evident in the policy data in the preceding chapter, the conclusion was drawn that more information was needed. The policy data gave an incomplete picture of the organization. The policy data at the different hierarchical levels reflect the outcomes of interaction processes. Managers compare the organizational situation below them to a policy or model. They begin a new organizational action cycle by feedback directed at changing the situation so that the new output is a closer approximation of the model.[1]

An analysis of the data on the perception of outcome has demonstrated that while managers desire the goal of Rehabilitation, the inmates perceive quite a different goal of Restraint as the most frequent outcome. The hierarchical differentiation of the perception of outcomes is not a new finding. Sykes also found that the model that managers intended to implement was not successfully put into operation. In that case, however, the manager's model was one of strict compliance with a host of rules in order to maintain internal order.[2] The divergence from the model led not to a stricter regime, but to an equilibrium between the officers and inmates that reduced the intensity of the demand of the regulations.[3] It is not known, however, how differently the managers, officers, and inmates would have viewed the goals of the organization. It seems likely though, that inmates, while ducking regulations, might have acknowledged obedience to them as the goal of the prison. Sykes is vague whether or not the management intended obedience to the rules to produce any worthwhile effects beyond order in the prison.[4] It is probably safe to suggest that both the staff and the inmates would have agreed that the goal of the Trenton prison was one of Restraint. Hence, the perception of goals and the failure of implementation in Sykes' study have a somewhat different relationship than at Hilltop. In Trenton, all levels might have agreed on the goal, but there were, according to Sykes, structural· defects in the organization that constricted goal achievement.[5] In Hilltop, by way of contrast, it has been demonstrated that there is a disagreement about the goals of the organization, which would certainly lead one to suspect problems in implementation, particularly when a goal such as Rehabilitation would seem to require inmate perception of it before it could take effect.[6]

The Street, Vinter, and Perrow findings are also different. They looked at inmate and staff perceptions and relationships in six different juvenile institutions that they purposely selected for maximum differentiation of goals. In this case, they found greater and more complex interaction among staff and inmates in the Trenton institutions than in the Obedience/Conformity institutions. It is quite possible (and informal observation would make it seem likely) that staff-inmate interactions are more frequent and more complex in Hilltop than at the maximum security prison of

Winters. But to conclude that Hilltop is therefore effective in the achievement of the goal of Rehabilitation would be unwarranted, as we have seen. The comparison of goals among institutions does not help too much with assessing the effectiveness of the goal achievement within one institution.

Finally, while Cressey's analysis of the officer-manager inter-action in the treatment-oriented prisons has been very useful, his emphasis on the contradictory goals of corrections is still unjusti-fied in light of the data so far presented. Cressey argues that the goal of custody or order maintenance and the goal of rehabilita-tion result in conflicting demands on staff that are resolved in the direction congruent with the dominant sanctioning pattern. While treatment is supposedly more important in the treatment-oriented prison than is custody, it is the custodial behaviors that have evaluation criteria attached to them. Therefore, the officers follow the custodial line, albeit more informally than they would in a custody-oriented prison. While security is certainly an important theme at Hilltop, it is true that there is one dominant policy asserted by managers. It is true that officer behavior does not support the Rehabilitation policy, but it is difficult to say that this divergence is caused by officer adherence to another goal set. It is true that many of the officers felt strained between the cor-rectional ideal of rehabilitation and the behavior that they felt was demanded of them by the organization. A study of these out-comes makes it seem quite likely that Cressey's observation of contradictory directives within the prison structure applies in this case. But it would also seem that a good part of the contradictory pressure probably comes from some source other than competitive goals or organizational policies.

In order to locate other sources of conflict, it might be helpful to have a fuller understanding of the managerial role. So far we have only looked at the policy-formulating or model-building portion of that role. The other important aspect of the managerial role is the way in which the manager provides feedback to the organization below. It is this aspect of the role that connects the managerial and lower echelons because it is through feedback that the manager intervenes in the daily activity of the organization. The sets of interpersonal action by which managers perform this task have not been examined, although it has been shown that the officer role as played by the majority of officers does not support managerial policy.

In what way, then, do managers at Hilltop complete their roles as administrators? What is it about the interaction patterns between managers and officers that makes managerial policy ineffective? In what manner is managerial policy transmitted from managers to officers? Is there something inherent in the correctional policy itself that defies transmittal? Have managers failed to feed back information about goal achievement in the proper way (i.e., not as they intended), or is the policy message transmitted accurately and for some other reason rejected by officers?[7]

STUDIES OF MANAGERIAL BEHAVIOR

The importance of supervisory behavior to subordinate performance and satisfaction with the job has been well documented.[8] Employees with evidently the same task requirements can produce with a wide range of quality and quantity, depending upon the supervisor. Likewise, different supervisors with presumably the same goals and the same kind of subordinates can achieve widely varying results. A very important organizational variable is the way in which superiors and subordinates interact. Both parties bring to this interaction their own anticipation of the other's role behavior and their own expectations of their own role behavior. The anticipations and expectations of each person have in common some of the same organizational constraints, and yet both have room to maneuver as they participate in a series of interactions. In other words, the same selective permeability by which the entire organization achieves autonomy from the environment is operative between the organization and its members. They are selectively interdependent, and the pattern of organizational interdependencies forms an organizational matrix.[9] Managers whose role behavior is a conscious effort to strengthen this matrix, rather than to disrupt or to ignore it, may be more successful than other supervisors.

The attempt to order the myriad managerial styles in organizations has been eased somewhat by recent administrative studies that argue that most managers' behavior forms consistent patterns over the long run, as if the manager operated on a theory, although the managers themselves may not articulate those theories.[10] One such attempt to classify the roles of managers was undertaken by Douglas Macgregor, who began by classifying the underlying theories into a Theory X and a Theory Y. Theory X managers use traditional influence and control. They believe that workers are basically lazy and have to be motivated by prods and punishments. Decisions are made at the top and are carried out by authority invested in the decision maker. Theory Y managers use integration and self-control. They believe men are naturally motivated to work, if they are not restrained. Above all, the men are not perceived as or treated as machines.[11]

A similar classification is Likert's division of managers into job-centered or employee-centered groups. He found that there are intangible investments in the organization, such as employee morale and loyalty, that may be liquidated by job-centered management. Employee groups supervised by managers interested in their subordinates' ideas and beliefs were generally more productive, had less turnover, less waste, and less absenteeism.[12] This view of managers was later expanded into System # 1 management, in which the only managerial concern is high productivity; System # 2 management, in which high productivity and keeping employees happy are treated as "two separate and more or less unrelated activities of management"; and System # 3, in which employee satisfaction and high productivity are treated as interdependent concerns.[13]

THE MANAGERIAL GRID

A similar and rather successful way of looking at managerial behavior has been devised by Robert Blake and Jane Mouton and is called the Managerial Grid.[14] The Grid uses some of the same notions in classifying managerial behavior into five modes. There is the assumption that managerial role playing is not haphazard and that there is an underlying consistency in most managerial behavior. Second, there is the assumption that the underlying consistencies may be roughly classified into different combinations of two major managerial activities: (1) activity for achieving high production, and (2) activity centered on employee morale, motivation, and attitudes. They locate and name five managerial styles as the coordinates on a grid (see Table 7.1). Blake and Mouton scale the two axes from 1 (low, but not nonexistent) interest to 9 (high, but not complete) interest. While, in actuality, the infinite differences among managers could be represented by the infinite division of the grid, Blake and Mouton suggest that five main managerial styles appear at the four corners and the middle of the grid.

1/1 managerial style. This style of management is not very common, but it does occur in many organizations and may be the product of conflicts between other managerial styles. The 1/1 manager, as the coordinates on the grid imply, has low concern for both task demands and the needs of employees. He maintains his position by following the organizational rules, and when he must make other people change their behavior, he attempts to do so by invoking the rules or a higher authority. He is not terribly concerned with what subordinates do, as long as they do not demand much from him, or try to pin him down. His general warning to innovative people with suggestions that involve risk is "don't rock the boat." His own personal interest is outside the organization, in hobbies, vacations, retirement plans, and so on.[15]

1/9 managerial style. The 1/9 manager combines a high interest

Table 7.1: Diagram One

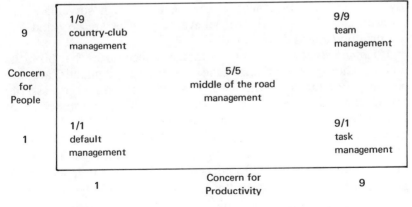

in his personnel and a low apparent interest in production. In other words, his interest in employee morale and social activity appears independent of his workers, or his own responsibilities to organizational tasks. Most of his social activities to improve morale, to keep employees happy, and to make them aware that he is interested in them are not directly tied to the work that subordinates must accomplish. He may, and probably does, operate on the assumption that "a happy crew produces." However, empirical studies in a number of areas have shown that there is no necessary relationship between morale and happiness and employee rate or quality of production.[16] The 1/9 managerial style is usually low-key and low in visibility. Few direct commands are issued. Directives are usually forthcoming as suggestions. The 1/9 manager is likely to reveal little of his own personal feelings and attitudes as he manages. Any of his own concern about production is hidden behind the façade of comradeship.[17]

9/1 managerial style. The 9/1 manager has a high concern for task demands, and a low concern for the individuals and groups that must meet those demands. He does not care how employees feel about him or the job as long as they do the work. He is unwilling to listen to employees, makes most decisions on his own and expects them to be followed. While he may expect subordinates to follow the chain of command rigidly, if they wish to communicate with him, he is likely to cut abruptly across those lines himself if something goes wrong, or if he wants to view operations firsthand. One of the prices he pays for high production from employees without an apparent regard for the sociopsychological consequences is the need for high surveillance of subordinates. He is likely to believe employees are lazy and will not produce unless driven.[18]

5/5 managerial style. The 5/5 manager recognizes that both the sociopsychological variables and production demands are important. But he sees the two sets of activities as necessarily conflicting. He does not strive for an optimum combination of employee-centered and task-centered concerns. Rather, he seeks a balance or compromise, a halfway position. He is the "middle of the road" manager. He will pay attention to employee morale in the same way that the 1/9 manager does, in ways independent of production, but will not go "overboard." In trade, he will ask so much production in the same way that the 9/1 manager does.

Hence, his employee-oriented behavior is unrelated to organizational goals. and his organizational goal-oriented behavior is unrelated to employee goals. He attempts to play the two competing demands against each other.[19]

9/9 managerial style. The 9/9 manager does seek optimum combinations of employee and organizational concerns. In other words, he attempts to integrate the sociopsychological variables in which employees find their reward with the organizational goal of greater production. He does so by organizing the tasks so that employee social groups are involved in the definition and solution of organizational problems. Psychological and social rewards are mediated in terms of task accomplishment. The 9/9 manager sees the basic human work unit as the group rather than the individual. It becomes a group decision what particular individuals will do on specific projects, and the group may make this decision in terms of worker competencies and compatibilities. They are not to be tied down to responsibilities of individual office. The 9/9 manager must be more skilled in coordinating groups and monitoring and moderating information than he need be skilled in the specific technologies of individual jobs.[20]

GRID STYLES AS TYPES OF MANAGERIAL FEEDBACK

The five main grid styles and some major combinations are a satisfactory classification of the several ways that managers complete the managerial role by relating to subordinates. The role concept bridges the psychological and social planes of organizational analysis because it includes the individual's perceptions, expectations, and motivations as well as the organizational constraints within which the individual attempts to implement his personal goals in return for the acceptance of specific organizational responsibilities. Likewise, the concepts of managerial style and correctional policy include, on the one hand, the personal motivations and expectations of the manager and, on the other hand, the behavioral patterns by which the manager seeks to carry out his own organizational responsibilities.

While managers with each style may attempt to implement any of the correctional policy alternatives, the behavioral patterns summarized in the grid format imply a certain set of congruencies between style and policy. It would seem unlikely, for example, that Reintegration policy could be implemented by a 1/1 manager. Policy that demands congruency between environment-organization and internal exchanges will not be supported very well by a manager who, in his personal behavior, is concerned with neither attitudes of his employees nor organizational goals of production. Likewise, a manager with a 9/9 personal style is highly unlikely to espouse a Restraint policy. His high concern for greater production through teamwork will not be very congruent with a correctional policy that calls for low interaction frequencies and low demand for services.

It should also be expected that the dynamics of certain managerial styles, in combination with various policies, may alter the way other managers play out their roles. If a 9/1 warden is responsible for implementing a Reform policy, middle managers below him who personally favor Reintegration or Rehabilitation may, over time, develop 1/1 managerial styles. That is, confronted with a hard-driving, demanding superior who will neither listen to his employees or try to incorporate their values into his organizational administration, employees who do not like their superior's policy may give up all organizational commitment except their office and salary (1/1), or quit. Thus, a 9/1 manager may find that his assistants place few constraints on officers and inmates other than the demand that the situation remain quiet, so that their lack of commitment to the warden's policy is not too observable. Similarly, a middle manager who does not like the severe treatment that employees receive from his 9/1 superior, but who is too committed to his own subordinates to become 1/1, may tend in his own behavior to emphasize concerns for employees and de-emphasize concerns for production. He may play the managerial style in a 1/9 manner and thereby act as a buffer between his men and the warden. In reverse, if the superior manager is 1/9, and his middle manager does not feel that this approach achieves organizational goals, the subordinate may attempt to correct the superior's approach by becoming 9/1. Of course, all these styles may influence the development of similar styles in subordinates, if the subordinates, coincidentally, hold the same policy orientation as the superior. This occurrence might be considered a coincidence, however, in an organization where a high frequency of autocratic feedback patterns from superiors minimizes the discussion of policy differences.

Where policy is not openly discussed, managers on many levels may continue to explain organizational ineffectiveness, or the inability of personnel to agree on policy, as the inopportune combination of personalities. While the personalities of different managers may correlate with different managerial styles, and with different correctional policies, the fact that different managers play out the managerial role in varying fashion has only a partial relation to actual psychological variables that may distinguish individuals. The managerial style as an aspect of role behavior summarizes the way in which individuals relate to the organization by playing a specific part in it. But a manager may change his style, without immediate (if any) change in his personality, if it can be shown (1) that he *is* playing a particular role in a particular way, (2) that there are alternative ways of playing the role, and (3) one or two of the alternate styles may be more effective, for the implementation of his goals, than the one he is playing. If the manager values being effective, he may attempt to change his managerial style upon receipt of this information.

The success of this attempt may depend in part on his personality, in part on the styles of other managers in the organization, in part on the power structure within which he develops his managerial style, and in part on the policy he attempts to implement. While all these variables may be simultaneously present, there is no reason to suspect that the failure of organizational structure to follow policy implications can be attributed to a series of simple personality clashes among managers. Nor should it be expected that collecting managers with the same personality type in the same organization will ensure policy success. Ongoing organizational structure is likely to affect the way managers play their roles in the same way that it affects the way officers play theirs or inmates theirs. The relationship of organizational structure and managerial style should suggest that the full development of the managerial role is partly dependent on opportunity. In a correctional setting, such as Hilltop, 9/1 and 1/1 styles would seem more possible in production and maintenance subsystems where managers deal most of the time with officer and inmate subordinates, and 5/5 and 1/9 styles would seem more possible in boundary subsystems where managers have to deal with peers and people outside the organization. Opportunities for a 9/9 manager would seem small indeed, although the Superintendent and Assistant Superintendent, who by their office are furthest removed from contradictory forces in organizational structure, would be the most likely to behave in the 9/9 style.

STYLES OF MANAGEMENT INVENTORY

Beyond the fact that the Managerial Grid and Correctional Policy classifications arrange and classify types in basically the same fashion (the combination of two underlying dimensions), there are two primary advantages to using the Managerial Grid in the analysis of managerial behavior to be related to correctional policy.

A questionnaire used to measure the managerial styles, called the Styles of Management Inventory[21] has the same format as the Correctional Policy Inventory. Twelve problems common to all managers are stated, followed by five style alternatives. Managers place the alternatives for each item set on a ten-space continuum from most to least characteristic of their own behavior. The scores for each style on each of the twelve problems are added and total style scores ranging from 12 to 120 are obtained. The style totals, taken together, form a managerial style profile for each manager. Since the style and policy scores are generated in the same way, the correlation of the policy and style scores presents few problems.

The second advantage of using the Managerial Grid for managerial behavior analysis is that the Styles of Management Inventory has been given to a national sample of correctional administrators.[22] The strategy of this national survey began by predicting that the current trend in correctional organization was toward the development of Reintegration policy.[23] The hypothesis was stated that, if Reintegration is the trend, then correctional managers will need to be flexible and democratic. The manager must be able to integrate the correctional organization with other service organizations, and he must be able to develop new levels of interactions with the community. The assumption was then made that a 9/9 managerial style would be effective in implementing Reintegration policy, or that a 9/9 manager was the one type who played the managerial role in such a way that changing correctional goals could be carried out. Since the study had the goal of assessing correctional manpower needs, the next step involved a measure of managerial styles presently operant in correctional organizations.[24] A national sample of correctional executives was drawn, and to them the Styles of Management Inventory was administered. Subsequently, the managers were interviewed and additional information about reading habits, professional associations, and so on were gathered.

The survey concluded that there were virtually no professional managers in the correctional field. Most managers had come up through the ranks or had training in academic fields presumably related to crime causation and explanation of inmate behavior. Few had received training in policy formation and arrangement of organizational variables for the accomplishment of specified goals. It was found that the 9/9 style of management was high in the Inventory section that questioned general managerial philosophy, but that most managers implemented policy in a 9/1 manner and had a 5/5 or a 1/1 approach to evaluation or personnel performance or program effectiveness. Most correctional managers were ignorant of integration techniques (of ways to make organizational-environmental and internal interactions congruent), and consequently, most managers were too conscious of the internal system and not conscious enough of external coordination.[25]

Significantly, the grid survey corroborates the open system theory of correctional organization explicated in Chapter 3. It was hypothesized there that split production-maintenance subsystems would entail managerial emphasis on internal control and limit boundary activity to impeding external intervention. The national survey found most prison managers unaware of the need for integration of system components and managing in ways that would tend to reinforce the organizational fragmentation. Thus one empirical investigation of present managerial activity lends considerable support to the effectiveness of the open system perspective. Concomitantly, the development of open system correctional theory gives additional impact to the empirical data by incorporating them in a coherent and logical theoretical framework.

The predictive power of the open system theory can be tested further by (1) comparing departmental managerial style data to the managerial style data of the national sample; (2) locating the various styles within the Hilltop organizational structure; (3) comparing the distribution of styles to the distribution of policy perception; and (4) correlating policy and style scores of the managers surveyed in an effort to judge their actual compatibilities.

MANAGERIAL STYLES IN THE DEPARTMENT
AND IN THE NATIONAL SAMPLE

The national sample of correctional administrators was classified in two ways. The style scores were first compared by the location of the managers in the correctional system: adult institution, juvenile institution, probation-parole, and headquarters personnel. A second comparison was made of top and middle managers across all those organizations. The comparisons of interest to the present study are headquarters and adult institution groups, and top and middle managers. However, the report of the national survey data does not separate top and middle managers by location. Hence, the comparison will have to be made of Hilltop middle managers to a national sample of middle managers who include juvenile institution probation-parole, and headquarter, middle managers in addition to adult institution middle managers. Likewise, the Hilltop top managers are compared to an undifferentiated group of top managers. While this lack of categorization limits the utility of the hierarchical comparison, it may give some impression of the representativeness of the single institution studied.

A second and more frustrating problem is that, in the national survey, an earlier form of the Styles of Management Inventory was used than the one used in Hilltop. The scale used in the national survey consisted of fifteen equal spaces, while the scale used in this study consisted of ten equal spaces. The means of the two groups are therefore not comparable, and we are left with an ordinal comparison of the managerial styles of the department and national samples of correctional administrators.

This comparison of the department and national samples on the managerial style variable is made in Table 7.2. In this table, the means of the five style scores are ranked for four managerial

Table 7.2: Ranks of Means of Managerial Style Scores for Headquarters and Adult Institution Managers in the Department and National Samples

Manager Group	Managerial Style				
	9/9 (team management)	5/5 (middle of the road)	9/1 (task management)	1/9 (country club)	1/1 (default management)
National Headquarters (N=30)	First	Second	Third	Fourth	Last
National Adult Insti. (N=127)	First	Second	Third	Fourth	Last
State Head-quarters (N=17)	First	Second	Third	Fourth	Last
Hilltop Insti. (N=7)	Second	Third	First	Fourth	Last

groups. The national samples from departmental headquarters and adult institutions are compared with the department Central Office and Hilltop manager groups in terms of the way the means for each style were ranked.[26]

It is obvious that for the national headquarters, national adult institution, and department Central Office, the ordering of the style means is in agreement. In each of these three groups of managers, the mean for 9/9 team management was highest, the mean for middle-of-the-road, compromise management was second highest, task management was in the middle, country-club management was fourth, and management by default ranked last. In light of the agreement on the ordering of styles of those three groups, the rank of the 9/1 task-management for Hilltop managers seems a departure worth noting. Among the seven Hilltop managers who were most active in the first two years of the program, there is a very heavy emphasis on the managerial style that places high concern on productivity (or goals of the organization) and low concern for the goals of the people within the organization.

Table 7.3 carries us farther into this matter by making a comparison of the ranking of means for the styles of top and

Table 7.3: Ranks of Means of Managerial Style Scores for Top and Middle Managers From the Hilltop Institution and the National Sample

Manager Group	9/9 (team management)	5/5 (middle of the road)	9/1 (task management)	1/9 (country club)	1/1 (default management)
National Top (N=133)	First	Second	Fourth	Third	Last
National Middle (N=258)	First	Second	Third	Fourth	Last
Hilltop Top (N=2)	First	Third	Second	Fourth	Last
Hilltop Middle (N=5)	Second	Third	First	Fourth	Last

middle managers. It is important to remember that the top and middle management groups in the national sample are for all four settings studied in that survey. Consequently, these are rather heterogeneous groups while the Hilltop managers all work together. Nevertheless, it would seem worth noting the heavy emphasis placed on 9/1 management by both the top and middle managers in Hilltop. For the Superintendent and Assistant Superintendent of Hilltop, the 9/9 style was ranked first and 9/1 second. For the five Hilltop middle managers, 9/1 ranked first and 9/9 second. In contrast, for the top managers of the national sample, the 9/9 mean ranked first, 5/5 second, 1/9 third and 9/1 was only fourth. For the national sample of middle managers, the 9/1 mean was slightly higher, ranking third.

Thus, while no statistical comparisons are possible, it could be important that the Hilltop managers depend on a 9/1 style considerably more of the time than a fairly representative sample of correctional managers across the country. It would also be significant that the heaviest emphasis on 9/1 management occurs among the middle managers. In the last chapter, it seemed evident from the policy data that managerial consensus about goals was not passed down to officers. Since the middle managers are the ones directly responsible for officer perception of managerial policy, the way in which they pass on policy to officers may be at least one explanation of the divergence in managerial policy and goals supported by officer behavior. According to the policy data, the middle managers attempt to implement the policy of Rehabilitation through the way in which they structure the officer-inmate situation below them. The policy of Rehabilitation would require, within the prison, an easy-going and informal relationship between officers and inmates so that officers could have the discretionary opportunities to act as a referral to the proper treatment source or so that the officer himself could help the inmate to work out simple problems. It is a policy that requires considerable trust by supervisors and considerable freedom for the officers. The managers should act as consultants in different problems but otherwise administer to the needs of the officer in relating to the client-patient.

The analogy, of course, is the hospital, in which the administrators trust the doctor's judgment about medical matters but manage the situation to help the doctor best serve the patient. The analogy breaks down rather rapidly in a prison, but it is possible that the 9/1 style of middle managers makes the analogy fall apart more quickly than it otherwise might.

A 9/1 manager has a high concern for production, for the satisfaction of organizational goals, but a quite low concern for the individuals within the organization. While planning and goal-setting, he is not likely to confer with subordinates and, while implementing, he is likely to supervise quite closely and strictly. While evaluating, he is not likely to seek feedback about his own behavior or about the subordinates' explanations of problems. Rather, he is likely merely to tell the subordinates what mistakes have been made. None of this kind of behavior seems consistent with the notion of subordinates as treaters. On the contrary, the subordinates confronted with 9/1 supervision are likely to adhere quite closely to rules and regulations, and, consequently, to allow in their own subordinates (the inmates) little of the freedom of expression that could make them "clients." These kinds of relationships, at this point, are assumptions. It is possible to test them out to some extent by finding the "normal" or most common associational trends between managerial styles and correctional policies. Prior to doing that, however, it is possible to obtain a more precise look at the managerial behavior in Hilltop through the interviews conducted in the department and at the prison.

THE GENERAL PICTURE OF MANAGERIAL STYLES FROM DEPARTMENTAL INTERVIEWS

The first round of interviews, conducted in the summer of 1969, concentrated largely on perception of goals and quality of communication. The behavior patterns of managers were not frequently a direct issue, although they came up more frequently in the group interviews with the fifty-six officers than in the individual interviews with managers. The clearest picture of managerial style in this first round of interviews was generated by four different questions.

The first two questions involved the managers' assessments of upward and downward communication. Two different findings were important here. First, Central Office managers were dissatisfied with both upward and downward communication. The Central Office staff thought the way in which information traveled down from themselves to subordinates in the field was deficient, as was the way in which information returned to them from below. Although Central Office managers rated 9/9 as most characteristic of their behavior, the amount of teamwork was evidently still not satisfactory. In contrast, the managers in institutions were satisfied with downward communication, but not with information flowing in the opposite direction. They thought they had established satisfactory channels for telling subordinates what they wanted done, but they did not seem able to gather accurate feedback from subordinates about the results of operations below. While there may be several explanations of this situation, inaccurate upward communication is one typical characteristic of 9/1 management. The 9/1 manager very forcefully influences the levels below him, but his apparent lack of interest in his subordinates' viewpoints and his frequently punitive reaction to their failures tends to make subordinates reserved about the information that they relay to their superior.

This kind of relationship between correctional officers and their superiors was demonstrated in somewhat exaggerated fashion in one of the correctional centers. In response to the two questions discussed above, the warden of the jail stated:

Communications are excellent. I keep three copies of all communications. And the guards get ten minutes of instruction at roll call. We have staff meetings on all levels once or twice a month and I get reports from all of them.

This response of a manager whose highest score was 9/1 on the style inventory and Reform on the policy inventory is a little more regimental than the response of some of his peers, but it does serve to illustrate a dependence on a quasi-military process of communication and an emphasis on the formalities of the process rather than the reaction of the subordinates.

His officers' reaction to this stylistic vertical communication is clearly apparent in their response to the question about vertical communication in the officer interview schedule. The following statement was made by one of the six officers in the group and loud vocal agreement followed from the other officers.

We need answers from [the warden] that we never get. We don't think he is really interested in the running of the place. So—we learn to lie a lot, to the inmates, to ourselves, and to him. Anytime he wants to know what is going on, we say everything is okay, because he won't do anything anyway.

Similar results were obtained at larger institutions where there was a greater buffer between the warden and the officers. In these larger places, the officers complained about the intractableness of the middle managers. In general, the officers who demonstrated a more custodial orientation used their lack of discretion and harsh, but sometimes inconsistent, supervision as the reason for their lackluster performance as officers. They said it did not pay off to stick one's neck out, regardless of the importance of Rehabilitation, because they always found themselves in the wrong. Given the kind of supervisors that they had, the only safe way of operating was the rule book way.

Another group of officers was less vindictive in their feelings about the superiors' rigorous enforcement of rules and regulations.

They stated that the purpose of such rules was to limit the possibilities of corrupt relationships developing between the custodial force and the inmates.

> They insisted [to the other group of officers] that these directives were not meant to undermine an officer's earnest attempt to calm people down in crisis situations or to treat inmates as individuals.

> These officers were aware of the Department rationale for keeping officer-inmate contact closely supervised. However, they suggested almost en bloc that the present inmate-officer relations were also unsatisfactory and that it was the present captor-captive norms which produced the wrong kind of informal, underground relationships. [27]

In other words, these officers were not objecting to the need for supervision, but they felt that the kind of supervision that they were receiving tended to generate the very behavior that the managers wanted to discourage. In essence, these men were reporting the very same communication processes that Sykes observed in Trenton prison twenty years earlier. A militaristic regime that gave little discretion to officers only drove discretionary acts underground where they were harder to observe and control. [28]

The officers' felt need for above-board discretion is reinforced by the officers' response to the last relevant question, concerning the kinds of additional training that they would like to have. A majority of the fifty-six officers were strongly in favor of in-service training rather than outside training that might be available, for example, in community colleges. To some degree, this insistence on the service program was obviously a reaction against the added time, expense, and initiative that off-the-job training would require from the officers. However, much of the desire for in-service training was also due to their past experience that the kinds of information and skills that they might learn on the outside were not easily employable on the job, if the organization itself remained unchanged. To these officers, in-service training implied active intervention in the kinds of behavior patterns that made up the organizational structure. [29]

Many officers recognized on a "gut level," if not on an intellectual one, that training of individuals outside the organizational environment does not necessarily affect the role performance required within the organization. The failure of outside training to influence the variables of organizational structure has been documented several times.[30]

The last comment of relevance in the department-wide interviews was the general attitude of officers toward any training, no matter where it was located in relation to the organization. Most officers stated that until the officer role was substantially modified, most training was useless. The aim of training usually seemed to be increasing the officer's ability to relate to inmates in order to make decisions himself, and to appreciate the complexities of treatment as opposed to custodial goals. Most of the knowledge and skills obtained in training were not employed when training was completed. Consequently, as the officers felt competent for more complex assignments because of their additional training, they also felt considerably more strain and conflict in the performance of the officer role.[31]

The conclusion from the general interviews would be that where there is close supervision, the subordinate does not perceive the possibility of and therefore does not attempt to influence the decisions made above him. As a consequence, managers are hard-pressed to monitor the implementation of their plans and the perceived need for 9/1 supervision is reinforced. Finally, where the cycle of 9/1 supervision and ritualistic response of subordinates is operating, efforts at change in the organization are also retarded.[32]

MANAGER-OFFICER RELATIONS APPARENT IN HILLTOP INTERVIEW RESULTS

The relationship between officers and managers in Hilltop is not very different from the relationship in other institutions in the department. There is in the investigation of those relationships the added dimension that the inmates were asked their perception of officer-manager interaction. In addition, the Hilltop managers responded to a series of questions on the history of the institution that allow us to see the development over time of the 9/1 supervision and the bureaucratic response from officers.

THE HISTORY OF THE INSTITUTION

The captain serving in the institution longest had begun his career in the old minimum security farm that had been located much closer to the city. When he was asked what he perceived as the major changes in Hilltop, he did not respond as the interviewer expected. Instead of mentioning the quick changes that had occurred since the formation of the Department in 1967, the captain recounted his view of the development of the Hilltop institution since 1961. Particularly important to him were the physical and social contrasts with the old farm. Because the history does much to explain the development of a rather strict regime at Hilltop, his words are worth quoting at length.

> The first big change was the introduction of classification people, which we had at the old max but not at the old farm. There was a big fight between custody and classification, because they were taking away some operations from custody like job assignments. This was hard to take by guys who had been making these decisions for years.

> Therefore, all things that went wrong at Hilltop were blamed on classification, the whipping boys. I know other classification people suffered, but some, especially (X) made their own trouble here. Since [the present counselors] came, things have been better. They were officers for a while. They have bent since they've been here.

> Classification now sees the custody picture much more than they used to. They used to be trained at college, but not familiar with prisons. [The present counselors] were both officers.

> The other big change is in the prison itself. At the old farm, inmates requested transfer. At the new farm inmates were told. Also, up here the family is much harder to see. Inmates had things more personalized at the old farm. At the new farm, the new staff and equipment made personal possessions unnecessary. So this seemed more like a prison. Consequently, custody at the new place had to be tougher. The old place was con-run, but we broke up that leadership. There was little real security at the old farm. Farmers were hired to farm. Post orders were determined by what the first man did.

An additional comment of the Superintendent carries this development further, as it relates to the behavior of middle managers.

> The single largest problem under [the past warden of the maximum security prison] was no information passing down. Even on this kind of

thing—notice for laundry supervisor tests would sit on his desk and people could not apply for the test.

I've noticed a difference in the attitude of supervisors since the separation [of Hilltop from the maximum]. Their attention to duty is better now. In the last ten months the man in the middle has come a long way. But how far down this spirit goes, I don't know.

Evidently, the Superintendent recognized the behavior of middle managers as problematic in the past, but he attributed much of their rule-boundness and lack of initiative to patterns that had been established under a maximum security administration.

To a large extent, this might be true, but two of the captains, in their own way, demonstrated the difficulties yet to come. One, making an after-the-interview comment about training said:

In training, you have to get down to the officers. All the captains here will be retired in five years. Your young officers should get the training. It's the officers who make the shift. *No one tells me information, I have to go get it.* It is the officers who have the contact [italics added].

This captain had doubts that the present middle managers would change. A comment by the captain who remembered the old farm may underscore this problem. When asked what changes had occurred since the inception of the Department, he said, "I haven't seen much change as far as custody. We had big anticipations. Custody is still custody. Other departments felt changes."

One man is aware that the future belongs to the men below him, and inadvertently points out the difficulty with vertical communication is still very much alive. The other captain mentions another characteristic typical of nonsystematic management. Each department has rather clear and distinct boundaries. Custody and classification are separate entities without too much in common. As long as custody is still custody, as long as the largest part of a fragmented organization is characterized by the kind of relationships we have here, it seems very unlikely that prisons as organizations will change.

COMMUNICATION FROM THE OFFICERS' PERSPECTIVE

The most constant theme in the officers' description of vertical communications was the dearth of information coming down. Officers complained that they were constantly surprised by the announcement of changes in the routine. They stated that their opinions were never solicited about rule or procedure changes, and no one ever inquired after their opinion about an inmate's behavior or progress.

In Table 7.4, the officers' responses about vertical communication are classified as good, bad, or don't know. Although it provides only a very rough guide to the manager-officer relationship, the issue of communication was the key one according to most officers. Five officers said that they were satisfied with communication patterns the way they were. Included were two officers whose reason for satisfaction apparently was the strict supervision they received and the minimal number of decisions they were required to make. Fourteen officers were dissatisfied with present vertical communication and usually stated their lack of participation or inclusion in decisions as the reason. Two officers did not have an opinion.

A lieutenant in the sample said, "I wonder at times why things are so often kept secret. But officers don't always ask for explanations." About the most neutral response was, "Management could inform the men more frequently, but things are better now than they used to be." A more negative response series was this:

Q.: How is communication with captains?
A.: There isn't any. There are no reasons given for decisions and no results of plans are reported. There are no explanations; we are supposed to operate on loyalty only.

While the total lack of explanation from above was a frequent complaint, the reality of the situation was somewhat different. Officers were given notice of changes at roll call and sometimes in mimeographed sheets handed out with paychecks. These sheets were frequently discarded immediately and ignored completely. It is quite true that explanations, when given, were not often re-

Table 7.4: Officer Interview Responses to the Question "How Are Communications From Officers to Captains?" From Hilltop Interviews June, 1970

	Response			
	Good	Bad	Don't Know	Total
Officers	5	14	2	21

ceived with complete attention. The lack of communication, as the lieutenant observed, was an interactive, mutually reinforced situation.

A slightly different twist to the communication problem was given by another officer who felt that managers dominated their men, not to achieve goals, but to stay in power:

> There is a supervisory incapability. There are no attempts to assess the ability of officers. Management is on top to stay there.... This information lack hurts the officers. The inmates don't see us as loyal to the administration.

One of the officers who thought communication was satisfactory because it was militaristic in nature gave this response:

> I was in the army. An order is an order and we follow it. The supervisors can be very helpful in personal problems.... I have been taught chain of command. I relay information.... Nothing has been so important that I have to go above [the immediate supervisor].

Another officer who was satisfied with communications also implied in his answers that officer opinions are infrequently sought by superiors.

> Communications are tremendous. They [captains] are always available and there is no delay in answers. Any decisions that come down is properly thought out, but I've never been included in making decisions [sic].

Much more typical was the last response: "Communications are fair. We are surprised very often. We have no say. We should have. Our suggestions are never followed."

Probably the most important thing to note is that officers were more likely to say that they were surprised by new commands or were not included in decisions much more often than they complained of no information at all. This kind of complaint reflects a different manager-officer relationship than was evident in matters of policy. The officers' typical response about managerial goals and objectives concerned a lack of information. Officers did not know what goals were supposed to be. On a day-to-day basis, however, officers are evidently told what to do, but they are not consulted. Making unilateral decisions and keeping decisions unannounced until the point of implementation are characteristic of

9/1 management. The subordinates are treated much like non-human parts of the organization. It is assumed that giving the correct order will achieve the desired response without concern for the ways in which officers would prefer to do the job.

Another marked contrast with the officers' perception of goals was the willingness of officers to follow the lead of their superiors. In terms of policy, officers genuinely seemed interested in knowing what goals they were helping to accomplish. While there is no way to be sure, it appeared that officers would agree with managerial policy if they knew it. On the other hand, it did not seem likely that officers would easily accept the managerial inattention to officers' feelings and attitudes in the matter of daily communication. In other words, the officers may have accepted a Rehabilitation policy, but they were not about to accept 9/1 management.

This possibility raises the most interesting point about managerial style and correctional policy. Are there styles that are naturally more congruent with certain policies than other styles might be? Are there other styles that are not so effective for the implementation of certain policies? It would seem so at this point, because the 9/1 managerial style used by Hilltop middle managers did not seem to supply Hilltop officers with enough information about policy that the officers could share in the judgment of it. Furthermore, the officers did not seem to have the room to maneuver under the 9/1 supervisory style that they could effectively carry out their part of a Rehabilitation model.

THE ASSOCIATION OF CORRECTIONAL POLICY
AND MANAGERIAL STYLE

Using the Styles of Management Inventory and the Correctional Policy Inventory, one can set up a matrix between managerial grid styles and correctional policy. This matrix will provide a measure of congruence or conflict between the correctional model of a manager and the behavior that he uses to move his organization toward that model.

Twenty relationships between correctional policy and managerial feedback techniques are listed in the matrix of policy and managerial style. Some of these twenty relationships would seem to be fairly unimportant for our considerations. We should, however, be able to predict the important relationships from the theory of open system management. The predicted associations are symbolized by the use of + signs in Table 7.5.

Table 7.5 is constructed from the following hypotheses:

(1) Reintegration and 9/9 will have a strong positive relationship. It would seem to take a highly flexible manager who was interested in maximizing both organization and organizational members' goals in order to implement a model of complex internal and environmental interactions.

(2) Rehabilitation will have a positive relationship to both 5/5 and 1/9 policy. The Rehabilitation policy, which is closed to community variables while open to inmate personality variables, should correlate with the nonassertive, but supportive 1/9 style, which is a traditional style of therapists. On the other hand, Rehabilitation in a custodial institution is really a balancing act between sincere interest in offenders and the coercive nature of the correctional environment. Therefore, Rehabilitation should correlate strongly with the 5/5 compromising style.

(3) Reform will have a positive correlation with 5/5 and 9/1. Reform is open to community influence but not to influence from subordinates and inmates. A 5/5 style may prove effective in allowing staff to ventilate feelings without altering decisions. A 9/1 style would seem most compatible, however. A manager in this model needs to be insensitive to demands from below, since inmates are not perceived in the Reform model to possess legitimate demands.

(4) Restraint will correlate with 1/1 and 9/1. If Restraint is really a model by default, it may correlate with management by default. However, it is hard to think of a 1/1 manager initiating policy. Hence, if Restraint is an official operating policy, it should prove most compatible with the 9/1 style. A 9/1 manager can demand loyalty to the organization and high production in chores of organizational maintenance.

Table 7.5: Management Style and Correctional Policy, Predicted Correlations

Policy	Managerial Style				
	9/9	5/5	9/1	1/9	1/1
Reintegration	+				
Rehabilitation		+		+	
Reform		+	+		
Restraint			+		+

In order to have as large a number of correctional managers as possible from as widely varying organizational situations as possible, in addition to Inventory administrations in conjunction with the Central Office and middle management conferences, the same material was administered in a similar way at a Correctional Management Institute for correctional administrators in the northeastern states.

The correlations of the policy and style scores for the fifty-six managers is shown in Table 7.6. Four of the seven hypothesized associations seem very clearly to be true; 9/9 management and Reintegration policy correlate at r. = .498. Rehabilitation correlates with 5/5 management at .4619. Reform correlates with 9/1 management at .3986, and Restraint correlates with the same style at .4307. The suggested associations between Rehabilitation and 1/9 and between Restraint and 1/1 are definitely not supported by the data. The association hypothesized between Reform and 5/5 is somewhat stronger, but could have occurred by chance. Specific management styles do appear related to specific correctional policies. The data suggest, for example, that a Reintegration model is most likely to be successfully implemented if managers relate to staff via a 9/9 style. A Rehabilitation policy would most likely be implemented by a manager who relied heavily on a 5/5 style. The 9/1 style is congruent with both Restraint and Reform models. All of this is not to say that a compatible managerial style is sufficient to attain a given policy. But styles that are not well matched to the desired policy may well explain the discrepancy found between goals and outcome.

Table 7.6: Product-Moment Correlation Matrix, Correctional Policy Scores by Their Managerial Style Scores for 56 Correctional Managers in the Northeastern United States

Policy	Managerial Style				
	9/9	5/5	9/1	1/9	1/1
Reintegration	.4980*	.1517	− .2533	.1842	− .1300
Rehabilitation	.2242	.4619*	.1316	.1360	.2291
Reform	.1874	.2540	.3986*	− .0395	.0883
Restraint	.1883	.0877	.4307*	− .0037	.1926

*when r. = .303, p. = .01, N=56

If the organization were effective, the managerial policy would be reflected in officer behavior and perceived by inmates. This has been found not to be the case in Hilltop. The suggestion has been made that one reason for ineffectiveness may be the way in which managers attempt to transmit policy to officers. Policy is transmitted by the way in which managers relate to subordinates. The addition of this intervening variable may explain the lack of similarity in the comparison of managerial policy, officer behavior, and inmate perception of goals. It was suggested that officer behavior would be more predictable in terms of managerial style than managerial policy, because officers are more likely to follow managerial behavioral cues as to where sanctions lie than they are to follow managerial formulation of policy.

It is apparent that the Hilltop managers, who seek as a group to implement Rehabilitation policy, have not chosen the appropriate style by which to do so. They implement policy in a 9/1 style, which is congruent with Reform or Restraint. Officers report that their own behavior most frequently supports Reform policy, and inmates perceive officer behavior most frequently supportive of Restraint. Significantly, Hilltop managers ranked the 5/5 style, which is congruent with their policy choice, only third. Hence, those ten officers who reported that their most frequent behavior pattern did support Rehabilitation were most likely responding to the official managerial policy in spite of the intervening managerial styles. Most officers in the daily performance of their role attempt to create a matrix of congruent interaction patterns. Their first reaction in the process of reducing conflict is to ignore policy and behave in ways consistent with managerial style. Their second reaction is to attempt to support the policy of Rehabilitation, although managers do not interact with them in ways that make this an easy task. Officers, in other words, are far from insensitive to the organizational policy, or the goals of administrators. In most cases, however, they react first to the variable that mediates policy formulation and their reception of it. In the case of Hilltop, this intervening variable, the managerial style, will tend to dissuade officers from following organizational policy.

In summary, the last four chapters have described in depth the two crucial aspects of the correctional management role. First, a correctional policy typology was developed in an attempt to categorize and measure the ways in which correctional executives formulate the standards against which the output of the correctional organization will be evaluated, or toward which it should be directed. The data from the statewide interviews and questionnaire administrations suggest that different executive levels do not prefer the same policy, and, moreover, that officers and inmates do not see the policies preferred by executives to be implemented.

Then, in an effort to examine why the policy implementation was ineffective, a second model was involved, concerning managerial style, or the ways in which managers interact on a daily basis with their staff. The data show that middle managers depend rather heavily on a 9/1, task-oriented style, and interviews corroborate and elaborate on this finding. The managerial feedback pattern most dominant in Hilltop does not support very well the kinds of staff behavior that would appear most clearly related to executive policy. Lastly, a correlation of style and policy scores for a number of correctional executives in the northeastern states demonstrates that there generally is a congruent policy-style combination, one predictable from the open system theory developed in Chapter 3 and the characteristics of the policies described in Chapter 4.

CHAPTER 8

MEASURES OF THE CORRECTIONAL SITUATION

The data on correctional policy and the data on managerial style "surround" the correctional situation that the manager is trying to control. The situation itself exists between the manager's manipulation of input (or the managerial style) and the manager's demand for output (or the manager's correctional policy). The correctional situation, in other words, is all the activity within the organization that is important to the accomplishment of goals. The situation is the "throughput" of the correctional system, the area in which the inputs are transformed in order to become outputs. It is this part of correctional activity that has for many years been treated as a "black box." We have frequently studied the inputs to it and frequently studied outputs from it. Very few observations of the processes between those two viewing points have helped to alter the output significantly.

THE SITUATION AS STRUCTURED BY POLICY AND STYLE

The internal situation for which we seek a measurement has not been frequently studied, probably because it is difficult to define. It is much easier to talk about the prison in its entirety, or to talk about one segment of the prison at a time. The situation we want to look at here, however, is *not* the externally visible prison, or is it "what it feels like to be an inmate," or "what it feels like to be an officer." Our situation is the social interactions among all the people, including managers, as they are affected by managerial strategies.

One definition of this situation has been called the "character" of the organization.[1] This was one attempt to explicate the felt differences between the internal atmospheres of different juvenile institutions. Trying to raise to a rational level the reasons for these usually intuitive and emotional assessments of institutions was difficult. The argument was made that, analogous to individuals, organizations may have "character," which is an overall effect of the organization upon any particular observer or participant. The major variables influencing character are relationships with the environment, organizational goals, staff-staff relations, and staff-inmate relations.

A similar description of the organizational situation is given by Street, Vinter, and Perrow. They speak not of character but of organizational "climate."[2] They suggest that each institution has a unique climate, while each institution may not have unique goals or unique executive strategies for the implementation of goals.[3] The climate is not only the result of executive action, but also of staff and inmate responses to executive directives, action initiated by staff or inmates, and executive responses to these actions. The climate might be called the total effect of living and working within the organization. It is important to distinguish the concept of climate from any particular activity or set of activities (such as a managerial style) because the climate is the accumulation over time of these activities and is thus a variable in its own right.

The claim that an organizational climate is "unique" will be modified as the study of climate progresses. In order to treat climate as a variable, it obviously must become known as having a set of values that can be specified.[4]

One attempt to quantify the organizational climate variable has been Rudolph Moos' work with the "environmental press" of an institution.[5] According to Moos, the analysis and prediction of behavior has too often emphasized personality factors and too infrequently studied the environmental factors that affect behavior. Recent psychological studies, particularly concerning institutional behavior

all . . . strongly indicate the importance of the setting and the person's interaction with the setting in accounting for the behavioral variance [and] suggest that systematic assessment of environments might greatly increase the accuracy of behavioral predictions.[6]

In the formulation of the Social Climate Scale, Moos presented himself with the following kind of problem:

Which of the items identifies what might be characteristic of an environment which exerts a press toward affiliation or toward autonomy, etc.? What might there be in an institutional environment which could be satisfying to, or would tend to reinforce or reward, an individual who had a high need for affiliation or for autonomy, or spontaneity, etc.? [7]

In other words, Moos was seeking to measure the ways in which the social environment of an institution may press an individual toward certain kinds of perceptions and certain kinds of behaviors. He was concerned that correctional officials too frequently consider that inmate behavior is explained in terms of the individual's psychological characteristics. He made the counter-suggestion that much behavior in a prison may be socially induced by pressures that affect all organizational members.

The existence of such an environmental press toward particular kinds of human interaction would be crucial to the formulation of correctional policy. Reform, Rehabilitation, and Reintegration policies all seek to change inmate behavior in one way or another. Either the behavior is a direct target of change, or alterations in behavior are treated as indications of variation in an internal change-target such as an "attitude." Since the correctional goal is implemented through policy and managerial style, or through structuring the internal situation in certain ways, that situation of structured interaction is the medium in which plans for inmates unfold and also the medium in which inmate reactions take place and are observed. A measurement of a consensus from organizational members about such a medium or climate would support the policy of Reintegration as a correctional goal, since it is this policy that attempts to change the interactions among inmates and staff rather than change something within inmates. In contrast, Reform and Rehabilitation policies that focus on internal attitudes or conditions rather than on interconnections between people would be less viable alternatives to the extent that the environment is a determinant of behavior.

This kind of consideration is beyond the scope of this study. We are not presently concerned with the consequences of particular climates, although this is obviously an important problem for future investigations. Presently, we want to study climate as a consequence of the two major aspects of the managerial role. If it is possible to show that changes in managerial behavior are accompanied by changes in the social climates of institutions, then our system model may really provide us with methods of altering the "throughput" of an organization and hence the effectiveness of prisons in changing inmate behavior.

CLIMATE AS THE INTEGRATING CONCEPT IN THE STUDY OF PRISONS AS ORGANIZATIONS

If the social climate is really a variable of cumulative interactions in an organization, then this environment should differ as the interaction patterns differ. In particular, we would expect that the environment should press toward social health or harmony when style and policy indicate managerial concern for organizational congruence, and the environment should press toward social ill health and discord when style and policy indicate managerial lack of concern for congruence in organizational life. For example, if an institution had a managerial policy of Reintegration and a managerial style of 9/9, the climate should be relatively healthy. The 9/9 managerial style indicates simultaneous concern for goals of organizational members and goals of the organization itself, while the policy of Reintegration indicates a simultaneous concern for offenders and community. At the opposite extreme, an institution with a managerial style of 9/1 and a policy of Restraint should be relatively unhealthy. The 9/1 style would indicate that managers are not willing to consider employee goals while they are trying to achieve organizational goals, and the Restraint policy would indicate lack of concern for both offender and community. The first example demonstrates maximum concern for congruence in the organizational matrix, while the second example demonstrates minimal concern for congruence in the organizational matrix.

In the last chapter, it was demonstrated that both of these combinations of policy and style are effective. That is, the 9/9 style is the feedback technique most likely to be effective in the implementation of Reintegration policy. Likewise, the 9/1 style is most likely to be effective in the implementation of the Restraint policy. While, in this sense, both pairs are examples of "congruent" or consistent style and policy, only the first example should produce a healthy organizational climate, because only the first pair (of 9/9 and Reintegration) indicates on the part of the manager a *conscious* use of the tendency of organizational members to achieve congruence. Or, as it was stated in the third chapter, only certain system managers understand their role as one of system management.

It may also help to understand that the organizational climate is *not* a desired end product of the prison organization, but is only a means to that end. Some prison goals require a healthy climate while some other prison goals require an unhealthy one. To carry through, the goal in the first example is, by definition, returning changed offenders to the changed community. The organizational environment or the medium in which that goal is achieved is one of harmonious social interactions. The goal in the second example is, by definition, maintaining the organization for its own sake, or holding offenders out of an unchanging society. The social climate or organizational medium in which that goal is effected is one of discord and disharmony.

By adding one more stipulation to this model, we can attempt to explain with it the difficulty of social control in a prison such as the one Sykes studied. We can also resolve some theoretical difficulties, such as the contradictions between Katz and Kahn's theory of people-processing organizations and their subsequent description of educational and political prisons. This additional stipulation is that human beings would prefer healthy or harmonious climates to unhealthy ones. Or, stating this idea in terms of its managerial implications, it will be more difficult to maintain an unhealthy social climate as a means to an end than it will be to maintain a healthy social climate as a means to an end.

If this is true, we can restate Sykes' political principle about fundamental limitations of the total regime so that it conforms to the system model. Sykes termed the interaction between inmates and officers in the Trenton prison a "corruption" of the totalitarian regime because officers made concessions to inmates in order to gain some semblance of order. Utilizing the concept of climate, we can suggest that an "uncorrupted" total regime would have resulted in a far more repressive regime, and a far more psychologically and socially unpleasant climate than the one that, in fact, existed. As inmates and staff in Trenton interacted, their interaction tended to modify the climate toward one of social health. In other words, a homeostatic process between captors and captives evolved in which there was some mutual responsibility for what took place. The organizational participants struggled for some interdependence in spite of the official goals which would have had both groups acting as automatons.

In conclusion, the concept of organizational climate may be used to clarify the subsystem interactions that were predicted in Chapter 3. During the discussion of the system model, it was suggested that, in an integrated organization, the production subsystem would be emphasized, the maintenance subsystem would generate varying structures as production tasks varied, and that the boundary subsystem would tend to make the organization interdependent with the environment. In the fragmented organization, by way of contrast, production is deemphasized, maintenance is primary, and the boundary subsystem acts to close off the organizational maintenance work from outside influences. In terms of the climate concept, it may now be stated that an integrated organization, or one with a healthy climate, increases the probability of achieving organizational goals, while the fragmented organization, or one with an unhealthy climate, decreases the probability of achieving goals. The integrated organization would possess the characteristics of a learning system. It would be able to change its internal structure in order to achieve goals. The fragmented organization would, in the long run, seem to be an unstable system. It would not be able to change its structure in order to achieve its goals.

THE SOCIAL CLIMATE SCALE

Moos decided to measure twelve separate dimensions of the environmental press.

(1) *The Dimension of Spontaneity.* Ten questions on the Social Climate Scale ask organizational members whether or not they can do what they feel like doing in the organization. How often do people do

spur-of-the-moment things? How often are there ulterior motives and hidden agendas behind activities? Presumably we would not find much spontaneity among officers or inmates in a Reform institution. We would probably find much more in a Rehabilitation institution. We would expect spontaneity where there is an emphasis on developing and expressing feelings. Likewise, managerial styles of 1/9 and 9/9 and to a lesser degree 5/5 should encourage spontaneous behavior, but 1/1 and 9/1 managerial styles would not.

(2) *The Dimension of Support.* Ten questions on the scale measure the amount of encouragement and positive reinforcement or lack of challenge one feels in the organization. How often does one feel confidence in oneself, trusting that someone else is not waiting to betray or punish? Rehabilitation policy should generate a supportive atmosphere, as would 1/9 and 5/5 management. In contrast, Reform and Restraint policies and 9/1 and 1/1 management would tend to create defensive behaviors and aggressive, nonsupportive climates.

(3) *The Dimension of Practicality.* Ten questions on the scale deal with the degree to which the organization or people in it deal with problems or have goals that appear to have payoff for the respondent. Were prison programs make-time or useful? Would the prison leave an inmate hanging when released or would he be prepared to start parole on solid footing? The two policies that would generate practicality would be Reintegration and Reform. There is a heavy concern in either of those policies for the completion of tasks and for the pragmatic consequences of those tasks. For inmates, there is a heavy emphasis on vocational training in both policies. Practicality should also be influenced by 9/9 and 9/1 management, since there is heavy emphasis by either upon the usefulness of activity in the accomplishment of goals.

There may, however, be a somewhat surprising show of practicality in institutions with a rehabilitative policy, if the ideology of treatment is, to use Etzioni's term, particularly pervasive. To the extent that such an ideology is an accepted principle by staff and inmates, then the "therapeutic" atmosphere would seem practical, since people would perceive changes in internal attitudes as a reduction in criminality.

(4) *The Dimension of Affiliation.* Ten questions asked how many friends one had in the institution. Were there many forces tending to keep people apart, or was comradeship rewarded? This environmental dimension should be positively influenced by Reintegration policy and by 9/9 management. It is a goal of that policy to

facilitate intergroup communication, and it is a technique of that style to work through groups in order to accomplish goals. Rehabilitation policy that emphasizes the milieu approach and change via identification should also strengthen this dimension.

(5) *The Dimension of Order.* Ten questions asked about physical order. Were rooms neat or messy? Did people keep appointments or were they constantly cancelling out? How much of the daily activity was predictable? This dimension did not ask about relative regimentation. It was possible for an institution to maintain order and remain fairly flexible, and it was possible for an institution with emphasis on mass treatment of people to be disorderly. Nevertheless, order should correlate with Reform policy, since neatness and punctuality are treated as virtues to be instilled in inmates.

(6) *The Dimension of Insight.* Ten questions asked how often people looked for motivation and reasons behind another's or their own behavior. How superficial were relationships, or how deep? Insight obviously should be characteristic of an environment structured by Rehabilitation policy. It is in this policy that the motivations and reasons for behavior are emphasized.

(7) *The Dimension of Involvement.* Ten questions asked to what degree people were committed or involved in the events of the prison. Did they participate in decision-making or not? Did they carry out orders in the letter or the spirit? There is most likely a press toward involvement in an environment structured by 9/9 management and Reintegration policy; 9/9 management requires that the group responsible for a task assign roles to its members as they analyze the problem presented to them. The activity of the group binds them to the goal and makes them interdependent. Reintegration policy demands that various information sources be pooled together and the various skills possessed by the members of the organization be integrated.

(8) *The Dimension of Aggression.* Ten questions asked how much open conflict and visible anger were present in the environment. Were people always shouting? Were there many fights or threats of them? Did people cooperate with each other, or were group tasks disrupted and hard to manage?

It is difficult to predict which policies will correlate with a press toward aggression. While Moos' subscales demonstrated a fair degree of independence, it is hard to say that more aggression will be felt when a policy such as Rehabilitation encourages spontaneity or a policy such as Reform represses it. Rehabilitation and Reintegration policies work to resolve aggressions and therefore deal with conflict openly. Reform and Restraint forbid expression of aggression and therefore alter the ways in which it is expressed.

The managerial style that probably increases a press toward aggression is the 9/1 style, which makes a high demand for production and uses manipulation of rewards in order to achieve it.

(9) *The Dimension of Variety.* Ten questions asked how many different kinds of things there were to do in the organization. Was organizational life tedious and monotonous or varied and complex?

Variety should be increased by policies that treat change as a complex activity and by the 9/9 management style that uses a variety of maintenance structures in order to support production. It is the Reintegration policy that views human behavior as most complex. Therefore, the Reintegration strategy calls for an increase in opportunities for inmates. As these opportunities increase, the alternatives open to staff should also increase.

(10) *The Dimension of Clarity.* Ten questions asked how clear and understandable the organizational goals were. Did things make sense in the organizational scheme or were reasons for orders, activities, etc., hidden?

As we have seen from the Hilltop officer and inmate policy interviews, organizational goals were rather unclear in that institution. There was a conflict between the policy and the style in which it was implemented. Clarity, in other words, may be a product of consistency between policy and style. Ignoring these possible interactions for the time being, it would seem that the Reform policy should influence a press toward clarity because the rules and regulations are constantly emphasized. Likewise, a 9/1 management style may influence the clarity dimension because 9/1 managers set out their rules, rewards, and punishments in advance. On the other hand, this kind of manager is not so open about his goals, and he may produce some confusion about the reasons for the sanctioning pattern that he enforces. In this sense, Reintegration policy and 9/9 management should produce a higher press toward clarity.

(11) *The Dimension of Submission.* The ten questions about submission asked how frequently people were forced to do things one way, how often they knuckled under and had no method by which to appeal decisions.

The press toward submission should be produced by managerial strategies that limit the behavioral alternatives. Reform and Restraint policies offer staff and inmates the fewest choices to make on their own and the fewest opportunities to exercise discretion.

The managerial styles that should press toward submission are

9/1 and, to a lesser extent, 1/1. A 1/1 style is probably a symptom rather than a major cause of submission, but a 1/1 style asks others to submit to the regulations, and it does not reward innovation.

(12) *The Dimension of Autonomy.* The last dimension was measured by the ten questions about the amount of activity one could do on one's own. How much self-determination is present? How many times must someone ask for advice or permission?

The Rehabilitation policy emphasizes self-expression and may to some extent press toward autonomy. But the kinds of decisions that the Rehabilitation policy would allow a client to make on his own are limited. The Reintegration policy obviously should press toward autonomy in the environment because change via internalization asks the inmate to adopt behaviors that he personally values. The 9/9 managerial style should also increase a press toward autonomy, since this style operates to include subordinates in planning and decision-making.

In addition to these twelve main dimensions, two scales of the questionnaire were included to locate "halo" effects. A positive halo scale identified persons answering in extremely laudatory terms about all aspects of the institution. A negative halo scale identified people answering in extremely negative terms to all aspects of the institution. In all, the questionnaire consists of 140 items to which the individual answers true or false, as he feels the items are characteristic or uncharacteristic of the institution.

Moos tested his scale in sixteen California Youth Authority institutions with small resident and staff populations. He found little correlation between the climate dimensions and background characteristics of inmates (such as age and length of stay), relative lack of correlation among the scale dimensions themselves, and predictable correlations with objective data (resident/staff ratio, frequency of aggressive behavior) and certain dimensions of the scale.[8] Results of the questionnaire administration distinguished institutions from each other, whether inmate and staff scores for each institution were compared separately or combined. Moos concludes that the dimensions measured by this questionnaire may be at least as important as the more readily available objective indices such as number of residents, number of staff, types of security and custody precautions, or amount of physical space available.

The results of this study suggest that there is a range of other dimensions which differentiate between units and must be taken into account in unit descriptions. These other institutional dimensions thus far have been most clearly brought out in the vignettes and "clinical" descriptions prepared by trained observers or participants. . . . The SCS may provide investigators with relevant and important additional dimensions on which units can be assessed systematically.[9]

ADMINISTRATION OF THE SOCIAL CLIMATE SCALE

The administration of the Social Climate Scale in large, adult institutions took place in the department after the first training conference for Department of Correction Central Office and top institutional staff. In the hiatus between the first and second conferences for top managers, the trainers and administrators were looking for a way of demonstrating the effects of policy and style as they had been measured at the first conference. Although the wardens, particularly, were somewhat anxious of the probable results, the group agreed that seeking such data was important. Administering the Social Climate Scale in the Department was a crucial decision for the managers. Their decision was an indication of their willingness to use information for evaluation rather than for punitive attacks on certain managers or institutional staff.[10]

Twenty percent samples of inmate and staff were selected by pulling every fifth personnel and inmate file within each of the seven largest institutions in the state. These seven were as follows.

(1) The Winters Prison. It was built in 1961 with a capacity of 1,000 inmates. At the time of the survey, the inmate population was 900. It is a maximum security operation, and until 1969 it was the only formally recognized prison, since Hilltop was a satellite, managed by the Winters' warden and his assistants. Relative to other maximum security prisons, living conditions in Winters are quite comfortable.

(2) The Hilltop Prison. Hilltop was recently separated from Winters. It is called a minimum security institution in the Department, but it might be classified as medium security in other states. It has a capacity of 400, and the population has fluctuated wildly, probably because of changes in classification of minimum security inmates and because of the change in its status to a separate institution.

(3) Carrollville Reformatory. This institution was built in 1911 for offen-

ders from age sixteen to age twenty-one. It is basically a maximum security unit with a variety of school and vocational programs. There were several administrative changes in rapid succession at Carrollville, and there was general consensus at the beginning of the study that Carrollville had had for years an overly punitive regime.

(4) Newtown Correctional Center. This is a large, local jail taken over by the Department when counties were abolished in the state. The building was in disrepair at the time of the study; and, with roughly 200 convicted and detained inmates, it was probably overcrowded.

(5) Shipburg Correctional Center. A large jail, holding roughly 300 inmates and detainees. The facility had one modern wing, although even the addition was built without toilet facilities in the cells.

(6) Centerville Correctional Center. The largest jail, holding about 350 inmates and detainees. The Centerville Center was also the site of the first work-release program, which operated out of the abandoned sheriff's quarters. This institution was dropped from the test sample because of a poor staff return rate. The poor rate was apparently related to the Centerville warden's absence from the top management training conference and thus his lack of understanding and commitment to the project.

(7) Oceanview. This is a complex of institutions for approximately 125 women. There are maximum, minimum, and jail units on the grounds. Oceanview is organized on a cottage-counselor principle like traditional training schools, rather than along traditional prison lines.

All the state institutions have a high Spanish-speaking population and the inmate population is roughly thirty percent illiterate in English. Because of the high rate of illiteracy, the Social Climate questionnaire was tape recorded in both English and Spanish. The inmates of each institution were asked to check a True or False answer sheet as the recording was played. The administration felt that staff would object if the test were administered to them in the same manner. The staff in the sample were therefore given coded questionnaires which they filled out at home and returned. Since the questionnaires returned were checked against a master list, nearly all staff filed returns, but twenty-six percent of the questionnaires were filled out incorrectly, or were left blank. The poorest return rate occurred at the Centerville jail (fourteen percent). Since Centerville was one of three correctional centers in the study, and the only obvious difference between it and the other two was that its warden had not attended the first training conference, Centerville was dropped from the study. The overall return rate for the remaining six institutions was eighty-three percent, with a range from seventy-six percent at Newtown to ninety-nine percent at Shipburg.

CLIMATE SCALE AND BACKGROUND CHARACTERISTICS

Because inmates completed the Social Climate Scale under conditions of complete anonymity, it was not possible to study the background characteristics of individual inmates in relation to the Social Climate Scale. Moos, facing the same conditions, substituted the correlation of background characteristic averages for the whole institution with dimension averages for the whole unit. The largest inmate population that Moos confronted, however, was twenty-seven. With over one hundred inmates in three of the samples, and with an institution population of only six, no such correlations seemed reasonable.

The background variables of sex, age, and length of years in correctional service were available on staff responses. Correlations of the age and length of service with climate scores substantiated Moos' findings of little association (see Table 8.1). The only significant finding was a positive association of .2967 between age and the dimensions of support. The lack of association is important because Moos was trying to construct a measure of environmental press in an organization, not an idiosyncratic press of individuals.

. Since the important hypotheses about fragmented organization concern the existence of significant differences among groups, these variables and sex were also used as the independent variables in an analysis of variance. If these variables successfully differentiated social climate groups within the organization, the hypotheses about the impact of policy and managerial style on the situation would be suspect, since age and length of service and sex should not be dominant structural principles. Age and length of service proved to be poor variables for classification. Staff groups delineated by age were significantly different only on the Social Climate Dimensions of Support (p = .01), affiliation (p = .01), and involvement (p = .01). Staff groups separated by years employed

Table 8.1: Product Moment Correlations of Social Climate Dimensions With Age and Length of Service For All Staff

Dimension	Age	Length of Service
Spontaneity	.0812	.0138
Support	.2967*	.1108
Practicality	.1826	.1163
Affiliation	.2473	.1024
Order	.1280	.0978
Insight	.0832	.0357
Involvement	.2304	.0767
Aggression	− .0889	− .0366
Variety	− .0814	− .0311
Clarity	.1199	.0425
Submission	− .0292	.0998
Autonomy	.0169	− .1156
Positive Halo	.1684	− .0033
Negative Halo	− .0837	− .0448

*when r = .254, p. = .01   N=274

were significantly different only on Social Climate Dimensions of Support (p = .05), order (p = .05), and involvement (p = .05). When staff were grouped by sex, there were significant differences on eight of the fourteen subscales. However, there were only 34 females and 237 males, and most of the females were members of the Oceanview institution. It therefore seems wise to withhold judgment of the impact of sex, pending an evaluation of the Oceanview institution. In sum, Moos' scale seemed fairly independent of the two individual characteristics that we could account for.

THE SOCIAL CLIMATE OF THE HILLTOP INSTITUTION

In the other institutions, the Correctional Policy Inventory and the Styles of Management Inventory could not be extensively used. The top managers in the other institutions responded to both inventories in conjunction with the first training conference. There were some middle managers from each institution present at the middle management training conference where the inventories were also used. But only from Hilltop was a large enough delegation of middle managers selected that their scores on policy and style could represent the entire middle level for the institution. From other institutions, no more than two or three managers were sent to the conference. Hence, only at Hilltop is the picture of managerial strategy in terms of policy and style inventories very complete.[11] Therefore, before examining the climate data for all institutions, it may be helpful to examine the Hilltop climate in light of the greater amount of information we have about that institution.

We know that the Hilltop managers have a Rehabilitation policy, but we have seen that the policy is not effectively implemented. We have also seen that the middle managers, particularly, depend very heavily on a 9/1 managerial style. While it has not been called their "managerial style" to this point, officers reported that their behavior most frequently supported a Reform policy. Officer behavior that does this should be very similar to a 9/1 style from a manager.

In terms of climate, there is an initial emphasis on Rehabilitation that may affect somewhat the environmental press dimensions such as spontaneity, support, and insight. However, most of the effect of the Rehabilitation policy of managers must surely be negated by the 9/1 style of the same managers and, at the lower levels of the organization, by the shift in policy to Reform and Restraint.

As Moos' subscales run from a low of 1 to a high of 10, we would expect relatively high scores (over 5) on the aggression and submission dimensions, and relatively low scores (under 5) on all the other dimensions. We know from interviews that officers, particularly, complain of close supervision and lack of goal definition. We might then expect particularly low scores on the dimensions of clarity and autonomy. In general, we should expect the climate to be relatively "unhealthy," in the sense that someone choosing a social environment to live in would probably desire aggression and submission to approach 1, and the other dimensions to approach 10. Furthermore, as the policy data distinctly demonstrated a low perceived concern for the inmate, we should expect that the environmental press at the top of the Hilltop organization should be much healthier than the press at the bottom of the organization.

The data in Table 8.2 tend to bear out these expectations. The two highest dimensions are Aggression (6.74) and Submission (8.20). Clarity (3.12) is rather low and Autonomy (2.39) is the lowest of the twelve means. Spontaneity (2.62) is also rather low. The dimensions of Practicality and Order have means both over five, which may indicate the strength of 9/1 management and the de facto Reform policy in the institution. It is also important to note that the social climate is considerably healthier toward the top of the institution than it is toward the bottom. Managers do not feel the same environmental press as inmates do or even as officers do. Under these circumstances, managers may have difficulty understanding officer and inmate behaviors that are affected by an unhealthier climate.

Table 8.2: The Social Climate of the Hilltop Institution Reported as an Average for the Entire Sample and Separately for Managers, Officers, and Inmates

	Social Climate Dimension					
Level	Spontaneity	Support	Practicality	Affiliation	Order	Insight
Manager (N=6)	4.50	5.50	7.50	7.83	8.00	5.00
Officer (N=40)	3.67	5.55	5.83	6.45	7.20	4.63
Inmate (N=88)	2.02	2.65	5.03	3.42	4.01	3.11
Grand Mean (N=134)	2.62	3.56	5.38	4.51	5.06	3.64

	Social Climate Dimension					
Level	Involvement	Aggression	Variety	Clarity	Submission	Autonomy
Manager (N=6)	5.80	6.18	5.83	6.83	7.17	3.17
Officer (N=40)	3.43	6.15	5.27	4.98	7.18	3.25
Inmate (N=88)	3.48	7.04	4.53	2.03	8.74	1.94
Grand Mean (N=134)	3.56	6.74	4.73	3.12	8.20	2.39

THE RELATIONSHIP OF SOCIAL CLIMATE
TO OTHER VARIABLES MEASURED

If the Social Climate Scale is at all useful, it should be able to discriminate among prisons. The variance of Social Climate scores among institutions should be greater than the variance for individuals within institutions. If this is not true, then the scale does not measure social or organizational environments. If the scale does highlight among prison differences, then it would seem to be sensitive to something about organizations. Since we have argued that correctional policy and managerial style are important determinants of organizational behavior, these variables should go a long way toward explaining organizational differences.

Unfortunately, it was not possible to use managerial style and correctional policy inventories in all institutions. Therefore, it is necessary to divide the Social Climate Scale scores on other variables that are known to have certain associations with the policy and style variables. One variable that is known to vary with policy is hierarchical level in the organization. A variable that varies with managerial style is the amount of choice a man perceives himself to have in decision-making. Another is how frequently his opinions are sought by decision-makers, and another is the accuracy of records kept, since the more autocratic the management, the more inaccurate the information seems to be. It was possible to pool some of these variables together into an "organizational profile" questionnaire that was administered to all staff with the Social Climate Scale. Therefore, after investigating the usefulness of the Climate Scale for distinguishing organizations, it is possible to see whether the organizational variables we have deemed important do make a difference on the internal situation as measured by the Social Climate Scale.

THE SOCIAL CLIMATES ANALYZED IN TERMS OF
THE PRISONS AND THE GOALS OF THE PRISONS

Table 8.3 provides a summary of the analysis of variance performed on the twelve climate dimension scores for the six institutions. In all cases but on the dimension of Aggression, the scores vary significantly from institution to institution. Thus the Climate

Table 8.3: One-Way Analysis of Variance Summary, Social Climate
Dimensions for Six Correctional Institutions From a Survey
Conducted in November, 1969

Social Climate Dimensions	D.F.	Variations Among Levels Mean Square	D.F.	Residual Mean Square	Variance Ratio	P
Spontaneity	5	33.65	698	6.51	5.16	.01
Support	5	47.58	698	9.63	5.08	.01
Practicality	5	136.80	698	12.49	10.95	.01
Affiliation	5	50.03	698	12.13	4.12	.01
Order	5	51.97	698	9.52	5.42	.01
Insight	5	32.73	698	6.48	4.12	.01
Involvement	5	39.90	698	10.10	3.95	.01
Aggression	5	20.58	698	22.97	.90	.01
Variety	5	45.49	698	7.08	6.42	.01
Clarity	5	34.06	698	7.77	4.38	.01
Submission	5	75.88	698	23.86	3.18	.01
Autonomy	5	34.43	698	4.80	7.17	.01

Scale would seem to be sensitive to *something* about differences among institutions.

The usefulness of the Social Climate Scale will depend on our ability to predict the ordering of the prisons as they are differentiated by their Social Climate dimension means. One could make this prediction based upon a clinical assessment of the climate in the institution. Moos suggests that his scale is a quantification of the vignettes and informal observations about organizational character. If it is, there should be a general agreement between the Moos' subscale scores and the general assessment of climate by a trained observer. This approach, however, is not as useful for our purposes as a prediction based upon types of managerial strategy.

Because there was no questionnaire by which to measure goals in five of the institutions, an assessment of policy will have to be made from the policy questionnaires of the top managers, interviews with the top managers and officers, and the writer's informal observations about the structure of the organizations as it was influenced by goals. Assessing policy in this manner, one is likely to rate two institutions as Rehabilitation-oriented, two as Reform-oriented, and two as Restraint-oriented.

The *Oceanview* institution had a *Rehabilitation* policy. The top two officials at Oceanview both reported Rehabilitation as their first choice. Interviews in the institution demonstrated a high concern for inmates, and considerably less concern for changing the community. Most importantly, the Oceanview institution was structured along the lines of a traditional training school. The institution was organized into cottages and most decisions about inmates were made by the professional staff in charge of each cottage. The Treatment staff at Oceanview equalled the custodial staff in number, and nearly twice as much money was spent yearly on each inmate at Oceanview as at Winters. Oceanview probably came as close as we can find to a prototype Rehabilitation institution.

Carrollville Reformatory also had a *Rehabilitation* policy. Carrollville was a maximum security institution, which certainly detracted from the strength of the rehabilitative atmosphere. But the two top executives at Carrollville reported that rehabilitation was their first choice of policy. Interviews in the institution underscored the fact that Carrollville had not always been a Rehabilitation institution. A very harsh regime was reduced quickly by the first Commissioner of Corrections, and the Commissioner's newly appointed Superintendent had, in his first six months of office, impressed many people. Structural changes were also visible. The school program and vocational training program had been expanded and between June and December 1969, a dozen new counselors were hired. With a long-term adult population, these changes may not have made too much difference, but with a short-term youthful offender population, the change in policy should have been reflected in climate.

The *Hilltop* institution had a *Reform* policy. We knew much more about Hilltop than about the other institutions. Judging from questionnaires, interviews, and daily operating patterns, Reform was probably a fair compromise when balancing the Rehabilitative policy of managers against the perceptions of Restraint by the inmates.

The *Winters* institution had a *Reform* policy. The warden at Winters was almost a personification of the Reform policy. When he was appointed, the departmental paper claimed that he was "firm but fair." Three of the four top managers of the Winters institution preferred Reform policy, according to the Inventory results. The interviews at Winters underscored the closeness of the supervision and the strict adherence to rules and regulations. To bolster the intended policy, which was to instill accepted community attitudes in the inmates, there were many vocational training and work programs at the maximum security institution.

The *Shipburg* Correctional Center had a *Restraint* policy. The warden of Shipburg preferred a Reform policy according to the Inventory results, but interviews in the institution quickly highlighted despair and deceit on the part of the officers and concern for image rather than substance on the part of the warden. In addition, there were no programs or possibilities for training that would suggest anything but the goals of Restraint.

The *Newtown* Correctional Center had a *Restraint* policy. This institution, much like the other jail, had no social or physical facilities to boast about. Unlike Shipburg, the warden's position at Newtown had changed hands three times in 1969. While the third of these wardens was to prove one of the more capable administrators in the department, the climate at Newtown was probably affected by changes in leadership and two riots as much as by the newest warden. The general attitude from the interviews was that, for the present, officers merely seemed glad still to have jobs and an institution in which to do them.

In Table 8.4, the twelve Social Climate dimension means for the six institutions are presented. The institutions are listed in the order in which they were described. Oceanview, with the most rehabilitative policy is listed first and Newtown, with the most Restraint-oriented policy, is listed last. If climate is affected by goals, all dimension means except Aggression and Submission should descend in value from Oceanview to Newtown. Aggression and Submission should ascend in value from Oceanview to Newtown.

It is clear that the prediction of means in terms of institutional goals was fairly successful. The extremes were correctly predicted. Oceanview seems to have the healthiest climate and Carrollville the second healthiest. The Newtown climate is the least satisfactory. The dimensions of Aggression and Submission do not conform to the prediction at all. It would seem from the data on those two

Table 8.4: Social Climate Scale Means for Six Correctional Institutions

Social Climate Dimension

Institution	Spontaneity	Support	Practicality	Affiliation	Order	Insight
Oceanview (N=75)	4.23	5.32	6.04	6.09	5.43	5.21
Carrollville (N=130)	3.53	4.49	6.36	4.89	4.80	3.90
Hilltop (N=135)	2.62	3.56	5.38	4.51	5.06	3.64
Winters (N=167)	2.88	3.70	5.07	4.66	5.03	3.61
Shipburg (N=102)	3.37	3.62	4.07	4.23	3.85	3.75
Newtown (N=95)	2.86	3.53	3.35	3.82	3.62	4.23

Social Climate Dimension

Institution	Involvement	Aggression	Variety	Clarity	Submission	Autonomy
Oceanview (N=75)	5.17	6.53	5.21	4.07	5.89	4.07
Carrollville (N=130)	4.04	7.28	4.53	4.11	6.68	2.75
Hilltop (N=135)	3.56	6.74	4.73	3.12	6.32	2.39
Winters (N=167)	3.64	7.34	5.42	3.41	8.13	2.53
Shipburg (N=102)	3.80	6.39	4.10	2.77	6.92	2.97
Newtown (N=95)	3.16	6.54	3.78	2.93	7.03	2.01

dimensions that the maximum security factor rather than goals increases the aggressiveness and submissiveness felt in the institution. It is also obvious that, where it was difficult to distinguish, with the methods available, the policies of the institutions, the prediction was less successful. Hilltop, Winters, and Shipburg are occasionally misordered, as on the dimension of Spontaneity, and sometimes correctly ordered, as on the dimension of Practicality. But, in all the cases, the means of these institutions are rather close together. In general, it would be fair to say that the social climate differs as expected, being relatively healthy in institutions with a Rehabilitation policy and relatively unhealthy in institutions with a Restraint policy, while climates in institutions with a Reform policy fall between these extremes.

THE SOCIAL CLIMATE ANALYZED IN TERMS OF THE "OPENNESS" OF MANAGEMENT

The preceding chapters on correctional policy and managerial style attempt to draw out the consequences of decision alternatives that range from the preset and predetermined to the undetermined and nonjudgmental. Taken together, the Hilltop data have shown that a policy of Rehabilitation implemented in a 9/1, task-oriented managerial style can be associated on lower organizational levels with increasing interpersonal polarization and increasing divergence from a recognition of the original policy. If the Hilltop data are similar to policy-style relationships in the other prisons, then the differentiation on Social Climate dimensions may be seen as the end result of progressive polarization in the playing of organizational roles. As the organizational members rate their own roles, managerial positions should be more open to others than officer positions, officer positions more open to others than inmate positions.

In order to test this hypothesis, an "organizational profile" questionnaire was devised and administered to staff with the Social Climate Scale. The questionnaire was originally designed as a "reversed managerial grid," by which employees would rate their supervisors on the two dimensions of concern for employees and concern for production. However, the fifteen questions for each dimension did not prove independent; there was a high intercorrelation between items supposedly demonstrating concern for employees and items supposedly demonstrating concern for work. Therefore, the Blake-Mouton grid format was discarded, and a simple continuum was substituted.[12] While the questionnaire does not measure concern for personnel and concern for organizations separately, it does seem to measure the perception by personnel of their manager's tendency to achieve goal congruence or to maintain a fragmented structure.

The original questionnaire consisted of thirty items. When it was seen that the two-dimensionality was not achievable, the decision was also made to choose the ten items of the thirty with the highest correlation to the total score. Each item consists of two statements about a specific organizational activity, separated by a five-space scale. The respondents were asked to check the space that they felt represented the behavior of their organization on that activity:

1. The records which are kept on the organization fail to reflect the real work which is being done.

    Records which are kept in the organization really measure how well the job is getting done.

    : _____ : _____ : _____ : _____ : _____ :

The items were scored from zero at the item extreme that represented the perception of organizational insensitivity, inaccuracy, and closure, to four at the item extreme that represented the perception of organizational sensitivity, accuracy, and openness. The scores on the ten-item questionnaire then ranged from zero (or completely closed) to forty (or completely open).

Upon reflection, it would seem that the questionnaire could have been given to inmates as well as to staff, since there are no questions that refer strictly to management or staff, but only to subordination and superordination. Unfortunately, inmates were not tested. At the time that the questionnaires were administered, asking for staff responses on two questionnaires and inmate responses on one seemed to be taxing organizational cooperation. While important data are therefore missing, the persistent trends toward fragmentation in Hilltop on policy and style questionnaires and in the Department on climate questionnaires, leads to the rather safe assumption that inmate scores on the organizational questionnaire would be the farthest removed from management responses.

Table 8.5 shows that the managerial level is, indeed, perceived as the most open by the role incumbents, and the officer level is perceived as the most closed by the role incumbents. The organizational profile mean for managers is 22.29, while the mean for officers is 16.91.

The hypothesis that the perception of individual or the distance from other organizational members increases at lower organizational levels is therefore supported. Table 8.6 shows that the profile differences between hierarchical levels are significant at considerably better than .05.

Table 8.5: Organizational Profile Means for Four Prison Hierarchical Levels From Prison Survey, November, 1969

	Group	N	Mean
1.	Managers	31	22.29
2.	Counselors, etc.	45	20.07
3.	Supportive service	14	20.71
4.	Officers	181	16.91

Table 8.6: Analysis of Variance for Organizational Profile Scores of Prison Staff Classified by Hierarchical Level, From 1969 Survey

Variance Among	Degrees of Freedom	Mean Square
Staff Levels	3	354.60
Residual	267	105.43

Variance Ratio 3.36 significant at .05.

SOCIAL CLIMATE DIMENSIONS ANALYZED BY ORGANIZATIONAL PROFILE

Since the organizational profile questionnaire seemed to distinguish democratic from autocratic feedback patterns, it seemed usable as a substitute for the managerial style questionnaire. In order to see if the profile would delineate distinct Social Climates, employee groups were classified by their organizational profile scores. The groups were separated by whether they were within or outside two standard deviations from the organizational profile mean. Three employee groups were thereby distinguished:

(1) a group perceiving the organization as very open (scores of 28.5+);

(2) a middle group perceiving the organization as average (scores from 7.5-28);

(3) a group perceiving the organization as very closed (scores of less than 7).[13]

The analysis of variance performed on the Social Climate dimensions for these profile groups yielded significant differences on all dimensions but aggression and submission (see Table 8.7).

In all cases where there is a difference of significance, the comparison of Social Climate means demonstrates the impact of

Table 8.7: Social Climate Dimensions as Reported by Staff Classified by Response on Organizational Profile Questionnaire

Dimension	Variation Among Profile Score Levels (high, low, avg.)		Residual		Variance Ratio	P.
	Degrees of Freedom	Mean Square	Degrees of Freedom	Mean Square		
Spontaneity	2	15.18	268	3.52	4.31	.05
Support	2	136.90	268	4.00	34.20	.01
Practicality	2	157.49	268	5.25	28.54	.01
Affiliation	2	107.70	268	4.13	26.06	.01
Order	2	53.77	268	6.45	8.34	.01
Insight	2	12.91	268	3.90	3.30	.05
Involvement	2	123.31	268	6.18	19.97	.01
Aggression	2	27.31	268	30.14	.91	.20
Variety	2	31.47	268	10.15	3.10	.05
Clarity	2	190.00	268	7.30	26.02	.01
Submission	2	4.10	268	3.36	1.22	.20
Autonomy	2	41.32	268	3.87	10.68	.01

open system management (see Table 8.8). For example, personnel who felt that they were managed in an open manner had a mean support score of 7.15, while the average group had a mean of 5.95, and the group that felt they were managed in a closed manner had a mean of 3.92. The open group had a Practicality mean of 7.60, as opposed to 4.18 for the closed group. In other words, the group that felt they were managed openly also felt that the prison Social Climate included a consideration for the accomplishment of specific practical goals. Personnel who were managed in a closed fashion felt that the prison had little of practical value. In the same way, the group managed openly felt it was easier to make friends on the job (Affiliation mean of 7.77) than the group managed in a closed fashion (Affiliation mean of 4.94). Likewise, the open group felt more Spontaneity, Order, Involvement, Variety, Clarity, and Autonomy in the prison climate.

It seems clear that the way in which men perceive themselves to be managed had considerable effect on the kind of social situation that they found themselves in. In general terms, the openly managed group lived in a healthy atmosphere, and the closed group lived in an unhealthy and strained one. The effects then that management can have on the probability that personnel will act in an open and considerate way with inmates are certainly great. It would seem much more likely for officers, for example, who feel great amounts of Spontaneity, Support, and Practicality in their work situation, to extend the much greater effort that is needed in order to make inmates perceive and react to Reintegration and Rehabilitation behavioral patterns rather than Reform and Restraint patterns.

SOCIAL CLIMATE SCORES BY HIERARCHY

The Social Climate data analyzed by prison demonstrated that prison Social Climates do indeed seem to differ. Where the college-educated counseling staff of "treatment" personnel were obviously superordinate and where Rehabilitation ideology had evidently had some structural effects, the environmental dimensions such as Spontaneity, Support, Affiliation, Clarity, and Autonomy were relatively high, and the dimension of Submission

Table 8.8: Social Climate Means for Three Organizational Profile Levels
for Staff in Six Prisons

Social Climate Dimension	Profile Group		
	Low (Closed); N=51	Medium N=168	High (Open); N=52
Spontaneity	3.65	4.36	4.69
Support	3.92	5.95	7.15
Practicality	4.18	6.37	7.60
Affiliation	4.94	6.80	7.75
Order	5.73	6.76	7.77
Insight	4.27	4.91	5.25
Involvement	2.75	4.48	5.83
Aggression	6.90	5.94	6.83
Variety	4.75	5.57	6.31
Clarity	3.45	5.27	7.29
Submission	6.63	6.58	6.15
Autonomy	2.84	3.74	4.63

was relatively low. In prisons with a lower concern for the inmate, the reverse is true. Using general information about the policies of the prisons, it was possible to predict, roughly, the ranking of means on the Social Climate Scale. Ranking staff by their scores on the organizational profile questionnaire, one was able to distinguish Social Climates across prisons.

A variable that would seem to differentiate both the correctional policy and the organizational profile would be the one of hierarchical level. We have seen in Hilltop that the policy intended by managers becomes increasingly less recognizable until, at the inmate level, a totally different policy is perceived. We have also seen that the organizational profile scores are higher at the top of the organization and lower at the officer level. As we descend toward the inmate level, the behavior of the immediate supervisor seems to increase the amount of conflict the subordinates feel and the amount of fragmentation in the organization. A separate advantage of using heirarchical level as an independent variable in the analysis of variance, is that we can include inmate scores. In general, the higher organizational levels should have the higher social climate means and the lower organizational levels should have the lower means, except in the cases of Submission and Aggression, where the reverse should be true.

To test this hypothesis, the respondents to the Social Climate questionnaire were divided into five groups: (1) wardens down through lieutenants; (2) counselors, supervisors, and teachers; (3) supportive services such as clerical or secretarial; (4) officers; and (5) inmates. The means on each of the twelve climate dimensions are presented in Table 8.10. Divided into status positions (from 1 to 5), the groups report rather different Social Climates. However, unless the custody positions are compared separately, a U-curve appears in the comparison of group means. In many cases, group two (counselors, supervisors, and teachers) and group three (supportive services) are higher than group one (wardens through lieutenants). On the Submission and Aggression dimensions, groups two and three are considerably lower than the managerial group (compare the means in Table 8.9). By eliminating these two groups and comparing the means of managers, officers, and inmates, the U-curve disappears except on the dimensions of Spontaneity and Submission. There are probably two related reasons

Table 8.9: Social Climate Dimension Means for Five Prison
              Hierarchical Levels

Dimension	Warden-Lieutenant N=32	Counselors Teachers N=46	Clerical N=14	Officers N=182	Inmates N=430
Spontaneity	4.03	5.02	4.50	4.13	2.45
Support	5.84	6.87	7.07	5.41	2.79
Practicality	6.44	7.22	6.64	5.88	4.38
Affiliation	6.69	7.35	7.29	6.39	3.39
Order	6.94	7.63	7.29	6.51	3.33
Insight	5.09	5.46	5.21	4.65	3.36
Involvement	4.62	6.09	5.93	3.84	3.44
Aggression	6.13	5.46	5.50	6.62	7.24
Variety	5.97	5.13	5.57	5.59	4.13
Clarity	5.41	6.33	5.93	5.02	2.16
Submission	7.16	5.67	5.93	6.66	7.23
Autonomy	3.56	4.39	4.86	3.52	2.13

why the managerial group feels less Spontaneity, Support, Practicality, Affiliation (etc.), and more Aggression and Submission than groups two and three. First, the managers must feel a subordination to their superiors (lieutenant to captain, warden to deputy commissioner) that the two staff groups do not feel. Second, both groups two and three are perceived in all institutions with the exception of Oceanview as having limited scope and responsibility in the prisons. They, above all, do not have direct responsibility for keeping order in the institution. Thus it is very likely that these groups may feel less pressure, and less of the effects of fragmentation than the managers who have responsibility for maintaining proper internal order. On the dimensions that might be associated with an integrated climate, inmates do have the lowest of the five means; and, on the dimensions associated with a fragmented climate, inmates do have the highest of the five means. That the scores differ significantly by hierarchical level is demonstrated in Table 8.10. Except on the dimensions of Sub-

Table 8.10: Analysis of Variance Summary for Social Climate Dimensions for All Respondents (Staff and Inmates) of Six Institutions, Respondent Classified by Level in Hierarchical Structure as Listed in Table 8.9

Dimension	Variation Among Levels		Residual		Variance Ratio	P
	Degrees of Freedom	Mean Square	Degrees of Freedom	Mean Square		
Spontaneity	4	149.07	699	5.89	25.31	.01
Support	4	403.13	699	7.38	54.63	.01
Practicality	4	156.97	699	12.56	12.50	.01
Affiliation	4	449.48	699	9.90	45.40	.01
Order	4	513.70	699	6.95	73.95	.01
Insight	4	102.65	699	6.12	16.77	.01
Involvement	4	95.24	699	9.83	9.68	.01
Aggression	4	51.97	699	22.79	2.28	.01
Variety	4	88.29	699	6.89	12.81	.01
Clarity	4	436.48	699	5.51	79.28	.01
Submission	4	35.14	699	24.17	1.45	.01
Autonomy	4	120.13	699	4.35	27.59	.01

mission and Aggression, the among-level variance would be very unlikely to occur by chance.

The analysis of Social Climate scores by hierarchical level suggests very strongly that the Social Climates of the institutions in the state differ rather significantly from position to position. The traditional break between inmates and staff is certainly visible; the greatest difference in means in most cases occurs between officers and inmates. Nevertheless, there are also differences among staff groups. While the inmate-staff split may be an exacerbated hierarchical break, it is not a unique one. Officers' scores are usually closer to inmates' scores than to managerial scores. While many critics of prison organization claim that the major hindrance to rehabilitation is the formation and maintenance of the inmate counter culture, the Social Climate data suggest that the problem is essentially an organizational one. The positive feedback loops in the fragmented prison generate a number of different climates. Over time, these climates may lead to different perceptions of reality.[14] As a consequence, the communication of information for joint problem-solving breaks down. Different organizational groups emerge with group-specific methods of problem definition and solution. Problem-solving and reward systems of one group may be irrelevant or in conflict with the problem-solving and reward systems of other groups. In the long run, about the only things that these structurally bound groups value in common are the competition against each other by which each group reinforces its own identity, and the physical space of the facility itself, which becomes a playing field for the system of amplified misunderstandings.

Perceptions about organizational integration can be affected. The seemingly unwieldy and unyielding prison organization may be changed. The internal social situation will vary as management alters goals and changes the way in which it relates to lower levels of the organization. The dimensions of Social Climate that would presumably measure organizational health will be felt more strongly when management is democratic than when it is autocratic, when it involves people in decision-making rather than treats people like means to an end. Altering the patterns of management in a prison is a large undertaking, but it can be more optimistically addressed if we know that not all prisons must have the characteristics of total institutions.

Indeed, we could conclude that the concept of "total institution" lacks validity, where we are comparing one prison to another. These organizations may be quite different internally, and it may well be these internal differences that allow us to change them so that they more effectively achieve the change goals that are now commonly espoused by correctional executives, legislatures, and the public alike. Key variables in the creation of change would appear to be managerial policy and managerial style, which, taken together, apparently explain to a great degree the internal differences between correctional organizations.

CHAPTER 9

CHANGE STRATEGIES IMPLIED BY AN
ORGANIZATIONAL THEORY OF PRISONS

POLICY, STYLE, AND CLIMATE AS A
NETWORK OF SYSTEM VARIABLES

An emergent goal of prison research and prison administration is to change prisons so that these organizations manifest more completely the model of people-processing organizations. In order to attack this change problem, considerably more knowledge is needed about the present organization of prisons. As we gather data about prison structure and operational consequences, we can make decisions about which of these structures more closely approximates the model. If we can then study the ways in which these more desirable structures are generated, vary, and disintegrate, it may be possible to influence the conditions that tend to increase the frequency of desirable structures.

This research has focused on one particular set of variables that may add to our knowledge of organizational behavior of prisons. The three main variables analyzed in this research, when they are taken together, may help to set some of the ground rules that can become strategies of organizational change within prisons.

Correctional poliçy, managerial style, and social climate data form a network of system variables. It has been shown that policy and style are related to each other and that both of these aspects of the managerial role influence the social climate of the entire organization. The research has demonstrated the applicability of a general systems model to the analysis of interpersonal behavior and group perceptions in a minimum security prison.

Policy was treated as the standards set by the manager against which he evaluates the behavior of the organization. Managerial style was treated as the method of feedback from the manager to the situation by which he planned to alter behavior in the situation so that situational output would more closely approximate policy. The social climate was treated as the situation itself—that is, the cumulative interactions of all levels of the organization that are under managerial control. It was shown that both policy and style can distinguish climates from each other. Therefore, policy, style, and climate would seem to be viable representations of the key components in the general system model as that model was described in Chapter 3.

Some additional variables not investigated in this research would be other kinds of inputs to the organizational situation and the varieties of ways in which the manager may compare organizational output to his policy. A third set of variables, which has only been represented here in terms of the warden's relation with the central office, would be the set in which the manager is not the controller, but part of the situation being controlled. Obviously not all the variance in social climate is accounted for by policy and style. Other portions of this variance may be accounted for in terms of these or some other variables.

Some additional methodological techniques that have not been utilized here would include more complex data analyses that could account for interaction effects between the variables and some more complex classifying and counting techniques that could treat the entire policy or style profile as variables, rather than the first preferences of policy or style, which were the variables emphasized within research.

Because this primary utilization of the general system model generated data that were basically supportive of the individual hypotheses and therefore of the model, these additional investigations with more sophisticated methodologies can be recommended. If this line of research is continued, an additional advantage of operations research and the general systems model is likely to appear. That advantage would be that analytic techniques related to general systems theory will decrease the dependence upon questionnaire and interview procedures. The disadvantages of questionnaire and interview as a means of gathering data were acceptable in this research because most of the research energy was expended in developing the conceptual framework. Furthermore, the opportunity to do any research at all hinged on the commitment of administrators to a program of action during which the research instruments also served training and developmental purposes. If this kind of training continues, both research knowledge and administrative commitment should increase to levels where more rigorous investigations can begin.

MANAGERS OF SYSTEMS AND SYSTEM MANAGEMENT

In Chapter 3 it was suggested that not all managers treat their organizations as systems, but that all correctional management could be studied as the management of systems. In other words, while not all managers understand their role as the control in a system model, the consequences of their role behavior in the organization can be predicted from hypotheses based on the system model.

The consequences of making or not making this kind of distinction may be fairly academic until researchers actually desire to influence the behavior of prisons. Research, whether it has been called basic or applied, has always been conducted because of its usefulness. Presently, the uses that are valued do seem to be shifting from ones such as increasing the researcher's status in the research or university community to ones such as changing the phenomena that have been studied.

Probably one major reason for this shift is the perception by administrators of precisely the distinction we have been making. Prison managers have begun to perceive their roles as those of control of the situation. Managers have not always perceived their roles in this way, nor have their supervisors always demanded it of them.

For example, when it was socially acceptable for the goal of invoking the criminal sanction to be retribution, the prison manager was less pressed to be an agent of control (or an agent of change). The prison manager, when he was the chief keeper, was responsible for keeping the castoffs of a social control process that had already been completed. Retribution is a reflexive process that looks back to an act already completed. It is morally right to punish the morally wrong. In that situation, the warden is not responsible for the future behavior of inmates or for any effects that his prison may have on that behavior.

Currently, society seems to desire not only that something go into a prison, but also that something else come out of a prison.

In order to accomplish goals when the use of the criminal sanction is forward-looking, the warden must perceive his role as quite different from that of chief keeper. Processing rather than keeping people requires of the manager new ways of relating to people, whether they be staff or inmates, and new ways of putting these people together. Or, to state it more precisely, the chief keeper's problem was one of separating people (i.e., making prisoners and society independent), while the contemporary warden's problem is one of integrating people (i.e., making prisoners and society interdependent).

In a sense, then, the keeper had no goal to achieve, or needed no production subsystem. He was in charge of a stable maintenance structure and was responsible for boundary activity that was supposed to keep community and prison from influencing each other. Since it does not make much sense to talk about a system that is not productive, it makes more sense to treat a retributive prison as a component in another, larger system, the productive activity of which is supported by the stability given it by the retributive prison. The political organization of society may be such a system and could be used to explain, for example, why keepers used to be political appointees.

The contemporary warden, in contrast, is definitely saddled with a production goal, although he may not have developed the techniques by which to achieve it. One of his difficulties, as we have seen, is that his prison has usually adopted the boundary and maintenance structures that were effective in the retributive prison.

The correctional policies of Restraint, Reform, and Rehabilitation, it was argued in Chapter 4, all have some basic inconsistencies that will have dysfunctional consequences when organizations are structured upon them. It may be possible to understand these policies as rationalizations for the continued utilization of these outmoded structures. New support structures could be generated by the tasks of people-processing, but the outlines of these tasks remain vague themselves when they must be invented in organizations where restrictions on change are very strong.

Faced with this dilemma, the correctional manager has begun to turn to researchers for consultation. Perhaps it is this seeking for information, more than anything else, that identifies the qualitative shift in correctional organizations. It is through this seeking for information that the manager takes on the role required for system management. It is in terms of gathering and analyzing information about the organization that the manager can compare output with goals and react to the difference.

INEFFECTIVE CHANGE STRATEGIES

Many attempts to improve prisons, to make them more capable of changing inmate behavior, are too recent to receive anything but very tentative evaluations. There are some change attempts, however, that have been instituted frequently enough so that we can attempt to analyze why they have been ineffective. Based on this analysis, predictions can be made about which more recent but similar change attempts will also be ineffective.

As the comparison between the goal-achievements of Trenton prison and Hilltop prison seemed to indicate, there are numerous characteristics of prisons that can change without altering the perceptions of inmates about their condition. The salaries of prison workers relative to the general financial distribution in society can increase; the educational requirements for correctional staff can increase; the physical living conditions for inmates can improve; the frequency of parole can increase, or, in general, prison policy can change from Restraint to Rehabilitation without changing the inmates' understanding of their condition as prisoners or their understanding of the intentions of staff.

Some of the contrasts in this comparison of institutions are drastic enough that one might conclude that effective change is impossible. Inmates respond to incarceration as such an overwhelmingly negative experience that variations in the nature of incarceration can draw forth no distinctive responses. While despair may be a normal reaction to our comparison, the conclusion that change is impossible flies in the face of the facts. Inmates *do* distinguish between hard time and easy time, or good time and bad time. Moreover, even inmates as resolutely opposed to the present regime as the late George Jackson believe in the possibility of a correctional experience that would be beneficial to the inmates from the inmates' point of view. Furthermore, while the policy change between Trenton and Hilltop was considerable, it seems unlikely that style or climate differences were very great. A policy change may bring some changes on such as those that we have listed, but unless the policy change is mediated by changes in the feedback loop, the basic control of the situation has not altered, and the climate itself will remain about the same. While there is no way to verify this by studying Sykes' prison with the style and climate questionnaires, the analogous differences between Hilltop and Winters did demonstrate that those two institutions had similar managerial styles and similar climates.

This kind of change we can call ineffective because it is incomplete. If only one aspect of the manager's role changes, the correctional improvements actually resemble a name-changing process in which the basic structure of the thing renamed has remained unchanged. There would seem to be two basic reasons for the incompleteness of the attempted change. Either the manager has not understood the interdependence of the two aspects of his role, or he has been unable to achieve such interdependence.

The failure to understand the interdependence has been covered in some detail. Part of the failure may simply be the newness of the idea of system management. This new concept of management is delineated over time. It is a developmental, evolutionary process. If, as Emery and Trist have suggested,[1] the "causal texture" of organizations has *evolved* to a new stage of "turbulence," the correctional manager lacks role models on which to base his new behavior in the more complex environment.

In support of this evolutionary assumption, a general history of the humanities and philosophy is relevant. The traditions of Western philosophy and social thought have emphasized analysis considerably more than synthesis.[2] In the literary realm, for example, the social system model constructed by William Blake was long regarded as "visionary" and "apocalyptic" rather than as a realistic appraisal of urbanization, industrialism, and capitalism.[3] Religiously, Western man long focused on salvation of individual souls rather than on the reorganization of social structure.[4] Constrained by these broad trends that retarded synthetic and integrative approaches to the resolution of social problems, the role of system management is part of a cultural revolution. It may take considerable time for a prison manager, for example, to begin thinking of his role as an integration of an organization rather than the balancing of its separate parts.[5]

If, however, it is the case that a manager understands both aspects of the system management role, then a major problem of fulfilling the role is the number of secondary reactions[6] that occur in a system that has traditionally been treated as an aggregate of parts. For example, correctional officers, who have for years been managed as if their custody function could be isolated from "treatment" of the inmate, learn to react in certain ways to managers and inmates. They will tend to reject suggestions that they should interact socially with inmates because increased social interaction, while necessary to people-processing is detrimental to guarding.

The manager's initial attempts at increasing the frequency and complexity of staff-inmate interaction will meet with resistance, even if these overtures are made through a style congruent with more democratic decision-making and greater use of discretion at lower organizational levels. These changes in style of feedback will be threatening to well-established methods of officer evaluation.

It might be contended that unionization of the guard force can be attributed to the autocratic managerial styles that were compatible with retributive goals.[7] Nevertheless, the initial reaction to more democratic styles that are compatible with people-processing goals will be a strengthening of unionization around such issues as specifications of the custodial position, and fairness of evaluation. It has also been demonstrated that inmates will react similarly to the new request that they be interactors in an organization rather than captives in a large social conspiracy. Inmates accustomed to being evaluated in terms of "keeping in line" will react to the changing managerial role as a new ploy in that conspiracy.[8] Thus, even a manager who understands his role as the one of system management, will have considerable difficulties with his role performance.

These kinds of general trends may highlight the causes of ineffectiveness of a great amount of correctional policy change. Some more recent and more specific change attempts that seem to conform to these broad trends and may also be ineffective are the following:

(1) Higher educational requirements for correctional personnel, particularly for officers. There is little evidence in this study that amount of formal education correlates with any particular correctional behavior. There is some evidence that, as officers receive college-level training, their commitment to the job decreases. Higher educational requirements themselves would not seem to influence behavior in the desired directions. There must first be some decisions about organizational design, about the goals to be achieved through that design. Then we might begin thinking about the educational prerequisites of people expected to interact in that design. Presently, much of this planning activity seems to be bypassed in the rush to educate personnel. Improvements in individuals may not bring improvements in organization.

(2) Increased in-service training. Several states at this point have opened training academies for their correctional personnel. Many of the same problems that pertain to higher educational requirements pertain here. The training academy usually runs a one- or two-week session for all entering personnel, or for all working personnel as they can be relieved from duty. The actual training frequently resembles lower-level college courses, with an emphasis on lecture followed by some discussion. Other than the fact that personnel can be required to attend in-service training more easily than they can be required to attend an outside college, the value of this form of training is rather doubtful. The academy curriculum usually consists of one- or two-hour guest lectures by relevant state officials. There is little opportunity for the examination of the training information under actual working conditions.

(3) Training conferences and training laboratories. A setting that usually does offer new information in ways that promote adoption of the information by the trainees is the conference or laboratory setting. Lecturing in this setting is usually held to a minimum, and questionnaires, simulations, and seminars on problems suggested in the work situation are used to help the trainee examine his own operating assumptions and compare his ideas with those of his peers. There is considerable value in this training in an atmosphere that is remote from the pressures of daily work. Competent trainers can also provide a valuable experience in group process. On the negative side, it would seem difficult to schedule these training experiences at regular intervals, and it is usually difficult or impossible for the trainers to follow

up the behavior of trainees back on the job. A related difficulty is that the expense of these conferences and the need to keep the organizations running during a conference prevents training all members of the organization at the same time.

(4) Inmate governments. Recently, there have been some experiments with elected inmate councils or governing bodies that make some important decisions about inmate welfare. This kind of approach to increase inmate responsibility may tend to highlight the caste-like separations between staff and inmates.

A variety of other innovations aimed at the improvement of correctional institutions could also be mentioned, but these four are sufficient as examples. While there are considerable differences in aim, and probably in outcome, of these change attempts, they would all appear to address the secondary reactions to fragmented organizational life. As such, they may function to mask difficulties in the basic organizational structure by legitimating the perception by staff and inmates that problems in prison life lie within an individual or a certain set of individuals rather than in the way in which these sets of people interact.

THE STRUCTURE OF A LEARNING SYSTEM

In contrast with these kinds of change strategies, the strategy implied by this research involves rebuilding the organization rather than adding pieces as new problems appear. Rebuilding should begin with the development of new models of organization that have a more logical relationship to the kinds of goals correctional organizations are now trying to achieve. It is obvious that once such models are constructed, a major problem is one of implementation. In order to implement a new model, existing structures and personnel will have to be changed rather than discarded. Thus, the models that are developed should include methods of transition from the existing organization structures to the new ones.

We have concluded that existing structures emphasize maintenance activity and de-emphasize production. The performance of certain specified roles in the organization has been substituted for behaving in ways that achieve a desirable external output. The existing boundary activities lower the visibility of internal operations by doing such things as demanding autonomy from external influence so that custody precautions or professional relationships are not disrupted. The existing boundary subsystem also questions the legitimacy and devalues the reliability of external validation measures, such as recidivism rates.

These present activities are not conscious efforts by correctional administrators to avoid evaluation of their procedures. Rather, these activities are more accurately described as a functional statement that the fragmented organization cannot withstand much external influence. The tremendous amount of energy that goes into maintaining an unhealthy climate requires that the organization take a defensive stance toward the environment. Since correctional production is integrally bound up with increasing the flow of information and resources between the organization and the environment, maintenance of a set social structure obviously decreases the ability to develop productive techniques of change that might withstand the rigor of an external validation process. The existing structure might be summarized as a vicious cycle from low goal attainment to a defensive organizational posture to the inability to develop the kind of environmental relationships that could improve goal attainment.

While this is a vicious cycle, it is also a rather stable one. Violence within the prison and the occasional burst of riots demonstrate the dysfunctional aspects of the cycle only when it reaches extreme proportions. But the information about internal violence and about riots usually feed back into the system in a way that validates the felt need for high overt control and only secondary attention to the dynamics of change.

In other words, this vicious structural cycle is a homeostatic process: the system responds to changes in input in order to return the system to its original operating state. For example, inmate and officer roles in the Trenton prison formed a homeostatic system. Each party had negotiated with the other a state of interaction in which both sides were satisfied.

In a correctional model that emphasizes production rather than maintenance, the manager must use rather than ignore the process of homeostasis. Organizational goals and organizational structure must utilize the tendency of human participants to be interactive rather than utilizing organizational authority to keep such interactions from occurring. A manager who accommodates the principle of homeostasis in his organization will be one who increases the capacity of his organization to facilitate interaction. However, this manager would want not only to facilitate inter-action, but also to select from a variety of interactions those that are most likely to have desired outcomes. In other words, he would want to have as many of these interactions programmed so that he can predict outcomes and so that he can rechannel inter-actions that are leading away from program goals. He also needs structures that can react to new problems to which responses have not been programmed so that an effective search can begin for new paths of action.

One could say that, under this kind of management, organiza-tional change and organizational control are synonymous. The organization is under control to the degree that it is free to change internally in order to meet any specific problems that are brought to it. This kind of organization could be called a learning system because it responds to newly presented problems in terms of past experience with similar problems, or it begins to study novel problems by applying processes of problem solution that have been effective in the past. As the organization continues to con-front problems, its store of useful information increases. An on-going evaluation process weeds out programs that are no longer usable.

In the correctional area, this kind of organization might be approximated if the correctional ideal, "Treat each inmate as an individual," became a structural principle rather than grist for a cynic's mill. Internally, such a prison would have to provide for the inmate an organizational structure that reacts to the inmate's viewpoint. Externally such a prison would have to provide for the community an organizational structure based upon the com-munity definition of the inmate as a problem. Or, to state these requirements another way, the prison must serve two client de-mands simultaneously, one from the community and one from the inmate. These problems are probably not the same, but they are obviously related and may be reciprocal. For example, the in-mate's problem may be lack of a job or lack of the training in order to obtain a job. The community problem may be its in-ability to provide jobs, to provide the training for them, or to handle within itself the people who have neither job nor training.

If the problems presented by either client were even that

simple, the correctional task would be relatively easy. A major confounding factor in the presentation of either problem is that both clients have reduced the problem-solving alternatives through coercive actions (commission of a crime and prosecution) long before service from the correctional organization is demanded. Thus, a major correctional task is the redefinition of the problems for either client prior to selecting channels of action.

If this is the general outline for the construction of a productive correctional organization, the key structural principles should involve: (1) goal definition, or identification of problems; and (2) information flow, or the accuracy and frequency of communication. The internal organizational structure suggested by these two points is one of small, fairly autonomous teams who have large, centrally stored resources available upon which to draw as the team members define problems. The structural relationship to the environment suggested is one of small, geographically dispersed units, located close to the source of the original problem identification by both clients, but that are linked to other units by a central information system that can facilitate the learning process in all units.

The staff of these small units should probably have backgrounds and skills that are very mixed. The mix should change in relation to the kind of community and individual problems that are brought to the particular unit. Although it may not always be the case, the variety of problems brought to any particular unit should be smaller than the range of resources that can be called upon for solutions.

In order to facilitate the accuracy of information, the communication within units should be democratic. Anyone who has information, or other kinds of resources that impinge upon the solution of a problem, might be part of staff for the solution of that problem. In other words, each unit should have very flexible boundaries. Members of the community should be sought and included in unit operations for the duration of particular projects.

There would seem to be two major prerequisites to this kind of communication and flexibility of structure. The team members must be skilled in problem-directed communication, rather than in communication that is protective, defensive, or built around hidden agendas. In order for boundaries to be flexible, there must not be too many legal restrictions upon the physical movement of the staff or clients.

In order to increase the accuracy of problem definitions, these units will be effective to the degree that they can be located not only in spatial but also in temporal proximity. In other words, as little additional activity as possible should intervene between the presentation of the clients' problems and the response of correctional units. The longer the distance between problem and correctional response, the more work must be done by the unit to redefine the problem in its original terms. If too long a time has intervened, this redefinition becomes impossible because either client has undergone significant change. Ideally, these units would be pre-conviction, problem-solving centers dispersed throughout a community in proportion to frequency and type of problems presented in different parts of the community.

Behind these small units should be an information network with centralized storage. This center would constantly monitor the activity in any of the action units in order to provide feedback to the units based on information about similar activity in the past. Furthermore, the central data analysis center must coordinate the problem-solving activity of all the units. In order to do this coordinating activity, it must be able to synthesize data on all the particular problems in terms of patterns that are presented. By doing so, this central agency will enable the prediction of specific problems before particular units are confronted with them. Also, the study of these patterns of problems will enable the development of new problem-solving strategies. In addition, the analysis of problem patterns can facilitate problem solution at a higher level than can occur at any of the smaller units. The central information agency can treat these patterns themselves as problems and begin problem solution in higher governmental and organizational levels. For example, it is on this level that problems of impoverished individuals can be related to the economic structure of the entire community.

UNRESOLVED ISSUES IN THE CHANGE OF PRISON STRUCTURE

One issue that is beyond the scope of this study is the strategy of change required to move from our present organizational structures to the new model. It is considerably easier to build a model that would increase the probability of goal achievement than it is to suggest how we can move from one model to another. The data in this study would suggest some guidelines from which a systematic strategy might emerge.

Organizational climates seem healthier when staff perceive management as more democratic, and when the prison policy places higher concern on needs of inmates. It would seem likely that present structures can be changed to emphasize these two aspects of management when decision-making is decentralized and goal attainment is openly discussed with staff and inmates. This trend may be encouraged when the prison is organized into small work teams who are allowed to decide their own roles for the duration of particular tasks. Teams might be staffed differently depending on the range of problems which will be brought to it, but, as a general principle, it would seem beneficial if the staff members were heterogeneous in skills and interests. In this way, the teams might avoid the identification of staff with like groups of staff and instead emphasize identification with the problems that have to be solved. As staff members become competent as team members, teams might be enlarged to include inmates as problem-solvers.

Management must take a risk in beginning the team-building process. Managers must turn over some authority to these groups in order that the teams may define problems and define their roles in terms of problem solution. The manager has to take the risk that men who have been closely supervised and have shown little initiative and creativity will behave differently when the situation is changed. The men who begin the teams must take the risk that the manager will not undercut their assumption of responsibility and utilization of discretion. Outside intervention may be helpful in this process, as it has been helpful in changes implemented in the Hilltop prison.[9]

Teams within the prison must be coordinated just as units in a community need to be coordinated. If the team is working successfully internally, there remains the possibility that they will conflict as they compete in the prison for scarce resources and for different uses of the same information. Careful attention must be given to the system of interrelationships between teams and to the way in which the accomplishment of their individual goals will contribute to the overall goals of the prison.

If the prison can make the shift from centralized to decentralized decision-making and from goal definition by the top of the organization to goal definition by work teams, then the manager becomes the coordinator. Just how far a manager of a prison can go in this direction is not known. It would seem likely, however, that there are limitations on the decentralization of power in a prison, beyond the obvious one that inmates have been convicted, and that parameters are being set for him by external agents much more than would be true for the community-based units described in the new model. He cannot be simply a coordinator, but he must approach the work teams with much of policy decided and a considerable number of problems already defined. He can probably take a consultative role, but at just what point between the autocratic role and the coordinator's role he will find viable balance for his organization is unknown.

If the prison is to become a more democratic organization internally, it will also need to become more integrated with the surrounding community. Prison teams will eventually work on problems that carry the team out of the prison and into the community. One example would be if a small team of staff members accompanied a group of inmates from prison to a halfway house setting or to a parole setting. Another way of accomplishing this interchange would be to have prison teams work on the problem of creating suitable employment or in other ways acting as advocates for prisoners. Concomitantly, these teams should also begin the task of helping to solve community problems. As the community perceives the prison as a resource in some areas, it may be less willing to withhold aid to the prison in other areas.

This process of restructuring may be valuable in its own right, depending upon the goals of the prison, but it probably makes more sense to reorganize a prison in this way if this restructuring process is a transition to the new correctional model. If the aim of restructuring is the implementation of the new model, the process might be seen as a large retraining program. It would actually be much more valuable than that. This transition stage would not only serve as a training period but as a testing period, in which different kinds of staff-inmate team combinations may be studied. The new model could be modified in terms of an ongoing evaluation of the transition period.

There are some factors that are very likely to retard this change process, and, therefore, deserve considerably more study in relation to organizational change in prisons. Many of these factors may be invisible now and will only emerge when the actual change process begins. Some other difficulties, however, can probably be predicted.

The unions to which correctional officers belong are likely to offer some resistance to change. The growth of the unions has been built around union success at objecting to particular demands of the fragmented prison organization upon its uniformed members. The union may react to prison change as a threat, if the changes are sweeping enough to undercut the organizational facts of life within which the union has found its strength. The nature of the union as an organization and the peculiar legal restrictions on unions of government workers should be studied.

In addition, the trend toward unionization of inmates should be studied. The new model, and the transition to the new model, would seem to address through structural change many of the problems that a union of inmates would address as grievances. However, whether or not there is an inmate union where such change takes place, there may be the social forces present among inmates that could generate a union and could also generate objections to change in the prison organization.

In studying either type of union, research should include the study of functions a union could serve if prison structure changes. While much of union activity focuses on objections to certain demands of the work organization, the union might also serve other functions that should be considered in relation to the new correctional model.

A second source of objection may come from the new political activities of minority groups. The issue here may be similar to the one with the unions: changes in the present structure of prisons may do harm to the maintenance structure of other organizations even if the change in the prisons is in the directions preferred by these organizations. Militant black politics, for example, may need the prison as something against which to rally.

A likely complaint by such political groups, or, for that matter, officer or inmate unions, will be that the new changes are just additional ploys by the establishment to fool the underdog and gain his cooperation. An ethical issue is raised by this kind of complaint that is really too deep and important to be addressed in this volume. That issue is the difficulty in differentiating an engulfing and confining super-system from an enabling and facilitating one. The dilemma has frequently been pointed out that rehabilitation is brainwashing. There may be many ways of masking the coerciveness of supposedly helping activity. The mask may even fool the supposed helper. Similarly, if organizational change techniques really become effective, these may be little more than the razor's edge separating changes that are socially beneficial from vast plots of political sabotage. Increased effectiveness in social system change will increase the chances of detrimental as well as beneficial change.

The only way in which this kind of problem has been addressed in this study has been the smaller but similar problem of the relationship between the researcher and the administrator. This relationship itself deserves considerably more study. More effective ways for these two people to communicate must be found if the transition period between models is to be successful. If a new model of corrections is to be implemented, then it is likely that a correctional administrator will have to be a researcher. It will be his task to gather information about community organization and make decisions about that information so that communities are less frequently disorganized.

There are obviously many other issues such as local-state-federal governmental relations, alternative funding methods, and the relationship between funding continuity and the effectiveness of program that should be investigated for their effect upon prison change. Perhaps two of the most important issues are the adaptability of the proposed change strategies to different kinds of prisons, and the effect of this kind of change upon the other components in the criminal justice system.

One might question, for example, whether the data collected in this study and the new correctional model based upon that data would be valid for a maximum security rather than a minimum security prison. Obviously there is no way of answering such a question without attempting the same kind of research in maximum security prisons. The data in Chapter 8 concerning the Winters Prison and the Carrollville Reformatory suggest that the general system model is equally applicable in maximum security prisons. That is to say, the behavior in present maximum security prisons can be predicted by using the general systems model.

That maximum security prisons might be described in the same way, however, does not mean that maximum security prisons are equally open to change. It is probably much more likely that productive teams can be built in minimum security prisons than in maximum security prisons. It is probably much easier to carry on research in minimum security prisons than in more secure ones. It may also be more likely that the people in minimum security prisons see more reason to change. Some of the differences between minimum and maximum security prisons have not been addressed in this study, because they have not been relevant. Some of these differences, such as size of the population and dangerousness of the population, are going to make a difference to somebody, when the issue becomes one of prison change.

If the thoroughgoing change represented by the new model is desired, then one way of beginning change in maximum security prisons would be to phase them out slowly after minimum security prisons had considerable experience in the methods of change. If we can think of a present correctional system slowly changing into a community-based system, it might be possible to time the transition so that maximum security prisons do not really need to change. Rather than change, the maximum security prison, its personnel, and inmates might be gradually transferred to less secure facilities after the community-based centers were already operational.

Last, we can also anticipate rather mind-boggling problems concerning police and court organization adjustments to a new correctional model. The majority of correctional work would be handled by community units on a pre-conviction basis, in order to avoid the redefinitions of the problem that would occur if there were intermediate processing by other agencies. Police organizations would need, in this case, to act as referral agencies to the correctional units, and criminal prosecution would be replaced in many instances by informal, pre-conviction adjustments. The forerunner of this kind of court process might be the juvenile court referral to different social agencies. This may not be a good model, however, since this referral system seems to be based on the lack of desirable post-conviction alternatives, rather than any desirable pre-conviction services, at least in many instances. The kind of correctional center suggested by this research is a social welfare center, if we could learn to understand welfare as a quality of life rather than a method of income. Community units would be problem adjustment centers, particularly for an urban population. It is unclear what kind of post-conviction alternatives might be needed to back up such a system. But it is clear that the primary function of the new correctional model would be to retain people in the community rather than to keep them out.

The basic function of such a system, if one function can be stated, would be the reverse of the basic function of our present system. Urban societies presently seem to amplify deviance by formalizing the reaction to deviance and by cutting deviant actors out of the social system. Centralized in small groups, deviants tend to be perceived as, and to behave as, increasingly deviant people. In the long run, this kind of reaction to deviance tends to make the social system unstable because it creates subsystems with conflicting values, the needs of which cannot be met within the existing social system. The new correctional model would focus on *deviance* rather than *deviants,* by treating both the community and the individual as clients with resolvable problems. We could accurately call this a model of a *correctional* system because the system would provide negative feedback to the community so that community structure could be continually reorganized to meet the needs of a greater proportion of its people.

POSTSCRIPT

This book has dealt with an area of social science inquiry that is of particular concern to administrators of correctional organizations, as well as to the social scientists who study them. The theoretical conceptualization of prisons as organizations means little to an administrator except as he or she can use the theory to manage the organization. This is *not* a statement against "theory." As this study points out, I am aware of managing by using certain principles or theories about the administration of my staff and facilities, and inmates. But the point is that administrators frequently leave these principles unstated and change them slowly. When social scientists actually stepped into my prison with fairly well-articulated goals of changing certain administrative activities and responsibilities, it suddenly became an urgent concern of mine as to how this new group "would work out," and what would happen when they left. I would like to address some of an administrator's concerns with such a project, in terms of a series of questions.

(1) *What prompted me to play host to a training and research project?* I guess I was mostly concerned with the amount of information and expertise which were available in the institution that was not being utilized or gathered. It appeared to me that something was wrong; that we had so much effort, interest, knowledge, which was dormant, which was not being used in the direction of assistance to the redirection of our inmate population. I guess I felt that in some ways we needed assistance in terms of ferreting out this information and in applying what we had ferreted out to meaningful purpose.

(2) *What conflicts occurred between prison administration and the requirements of the administration of a research project?* Conflicts were initially staggering. In retrospect, it appeared to me

that I had permitted the institution to be turned inside out and thoughts came into my mind such as, "My God, what have I done?" I guess the major conflict which seemed to arise constantly was not so much between the administration of the research project and the administrator, but between the administrator and the employees; they're wondering, "Why go through all the agony when we know what the answer is going to be?" I think it came as a shock to all of us when the research project pointed out to us, with some hard facts and data, that we really didn't know what the answers were; in fact, in some instances we didn't even know what the questions were.

(3) *Were there any practical changes caused by or commensurate with the findings and concepts involved in the training and research?* I imagine the change that is most pronounced was one of opening communication among all employees and between the inmate population and employees. In years prior to these research projects, communications were in a feudal age: Who are these serfs who question we landlords? We have long experience, know what is best for all of our charges; there is no need for communication because communication only brings with it questions, answers, confrontation, problems.

Ten years ago, no officer was charged with explaining policies, rules and regulations, or the reason for change. As I imagine any administrator knows, with the opening of communication, however, does come a greater possibility and probability of verbal confrontation and yet these positive changes outweigh the negativeness that accompanies the change.

(4) *What problems were caused by the researchers leaving Connecticut?* When the projects were over and the longhairs left our institution, I guess the inmate population felt, "Well, somebody else has been in and gone, somebody else has made money and gone, somebody else has satisfied their academic requirements and gone; it's another passing fancy." I am not so sure that initially the staff didn't have somewhat the same reaction: "Flash-in-the-pan, it's all over with." I am convinced that the population and the employees were quite surprised and even amazed that we were going to continue and we were going to put to action the information that was gleaned from the studies and the work, and that we were going to make it work.

(5) *What are the future plans for Enfield relevant to this research?* Changes in the national attitude, the correctional attitude, the inmate expectation, the staff's feelings, and possibly my own feelings will have to be weighed in terms of where we go from here. We read constantly the quotes of Saxby, Martinson, Fogel, etc., and we wonder how what they are saying will impact on projects such as the ones described in this study. But since the research conducted between 1969 and 1972, my prison has not been inactive. Commensurate with the conclusions in Chapters 6 on policy, 7 on managerial style, and particularly 9 on system change, several things have happened.

(1) We have decentralized classification decisions at Enfield, assigning caseloads to teams that include correctional officers, work supervisors, and counselors.

(2) We have instituted inmate discussion groups, led by correctional officers. These groups have two functions: (a) identifying problems and specific practical objectives for each inmate in a group and working with him on progress toward objectives specified in contracts negotiated with the classification or "treatment teams"; (b) identifying problems in institutional administration that should be brought to the attention of administrators.

(3) By using these two kinds of teams in coordination, we have tried to expand both the number and kinds of people—including officers and inmates—who have a say in institutional policy and practice.

(4) We would like to investigate in the near future extending the concept of contracts between the treatment teams and the inmates into the area of parole programming. In other words, we would like to see better continuity in case planning achieved by having correctional staff and inmates working very early on on specific plans for post-institutional experiences.

(5) Lastly, the Connecticut Department itself is now emphasizing a new utilization of its community correctional centers (the former state jails) by increasing substantially the proportion of offenders on various types of community release status.

It seems clear to me that all these steps, particularly 4 and 5, follow on, or can be theoretically justified on, the kinds of system changes that flow from the data of this study. Key administrative and political issues that go beyond a book such as this, however, include whether these new steps can be integrated into an effective programmatic unity given present public attitudes and the present turn in the economy.

—Richard M. Steinert
Superintendent, Connecticut Correctional
Institution—Enfield

NOTES

CHAPTER 1

1. Frederick Winslow Taylor, *The Principles of Scientific Management* (New York: Harper, 1911).

2. F. O. Roethlisberger, *Management and Morale* (Cambridge: Harvard University Press, 1956).

3. With the possible exception of the work of Chris Argyris, who seeks an optimal balance of individual and organizational need fulfillment. *Personality and Organization* (New York: Harper and Row, 1957); and *Integrating the Individual and the Organization* (New York: Wiley, 1964).

4. Robert Blake and Jane Mouton, *The Managerial Grid* (Houston: Gulf, 1964); Rensis Likert, *New Patterns of Management* (New York: McGraw-Hill, 1961); and *The Human Organization* (New York: McGraw-Hill, 1967).

5. Donald Clemmer, *The Prison Community* (New York: Holt, Rinehart, and Winston, 1958); Gresham Sykes, *The Society of Captives* (Princeton: Princeton University Press, 1957); and Erving Goffman, *Asylums* (Garden City: Doubleday, 1961).

6. Goffman, ibid.; Donald Cressey, "Social Psychological Foundation for Using Criminals in the Rehabilitation of Criminals," Journal of Research in Crime and Delinquency, vol. 2, 1965, pp. 49-59; Thomas Mathiesen, "A Functional Equivalent to Inmate Cohesion," Human Organization, vol. 27, no. 2, Summer, 1968, pp 117-124.

7. David Street, Robert Vinter, and Charles Perrow, *Organization for Treatment* (New York: Free Press, 1966); David Street, "Inmates in Custodial and Treatment Settings," American Sociological Review, vol. 30, 1965, pp. 40-55; Thomas Wilson, "Patterns of Management and Adaptations to Organizational Roles: A Study of Prison Inmates," American Journal of Sociology, vol. 74, no. 2, September, 1968, pp. 146-157.

8. Roy King and Norma Raynes, "An Operational Measure of Inmate Management in Residential Institutions," Social Science and Medicine, vol. 2, 1968, pp. 41-53.

9. Elmer K. Nelson and Catherine Lovell, *Developing Correctional Administrators*, Research Report of the Joint Commission on Correctional Manpower and Training (Washington, D.C.: Government Printing Office, November, 1969).

10. Nelson uses the Managerial Grid, note 4, above, as operationalized in Jay Hall; Jerry Harvey, and Martha Williams, *Styles of Management Inventory* (Austin: Teleometrics, 1964).

11. Street, Vinter, and Perrow, note 7, above. This landmark study is reviewed rather completely in Chapter 2.

12. I.e., Peter Garabedian, "Social Organization in a Correctional Residence," Social Problems, vol. 11, Fall, 1963, pp. 139-152; and June Morrison, "The Inmate Volunteer, a Study of Paradoxical Assumptions," Journal of Research in Crime and Delinquency, vol. 4, no. 2, July, 1967, pp. 263-268.

13. Robert Wallace, "Ecological Implications of a Custody Institution," Issues in Criminology, vol. 2, no. 1, Spring, 1966, pp. 47-60.

14. For example, there are several packaged management training programs that are sold to correctional agencies. Some of these training programs gloss over the difference between inmates and automobiles when listing the skills needed by managers.

15. Argyris, *Integrating the Individual and the Organization,* note 3, above.

16. Phillip Selznick, *T.V.A. and the Grass Roots* (New York: Harper and Row, 1948). The more complete breakdown of these different kinds of organizational activity occurs in Daniel Katz and Robert Kahn, *The Social Psychology of Organizations* (New York: Wiley, 1966) as discussed in Chapters 2 and 3.

17. Michael Crozier, *The Bureaucratic Phenomenon* (Chicago: Chicago University Press, 1967), pp. 195-198.

18. I.e., Abraham Blumberg, *Criminal Justice* (Chicago: Quadrangle Books, 1970), pp. 149-155; Donald Cressey "The Nature and Effectiveness of Correctional Techniques," in Lawrence Hazelrigg, *Prison Within Society* (Garden City: Doubleday, 1969), pp. 349-362; both speak about explanations of activity that are either meaningless or mean too many things to be useful.

19. Cressey, ibid., p. 353.

20. Blumberg, note 18, above, pp. 145-146; Thurmond Arnold, "Law Enforcement— An Attempt at Social Dissection," 42 Yale Law Journal, 1 (1932).

21. See Selznick's use of cooptation, note 16, above, pp. 13-16.

22. Attempts have been made. Cressey, note 6, above; Hans Toch, *Violent Men* (Chicago: Aldine, 1969), pp. 246-247; and see U.S. Department of H.E.W., *Experiment in Culture Expansion,* Report of proceedings of a conference called, "The Use of Products of a Social Problem in Coping with the Problem," (California Rehabilitation Center, Norco, California, July 10, 11, and 12, 1963).

23. Nelson, note 9, above, p. 4, forecasts such a correctional trend, merely through the evolutionary process of organizations.

24. See ibid., pp. 85-86.

25. F. E. Emery and E. L. Trist, "The Causal Texture of Organizational Environments," Human Relations, vol. 18, 1965, pp. 21-31.

26. Shirley Terryberry, "The Evaluation of Organizational Environments," Administrative Science Quarterly, vol. 12, no. 4, March, 1968, pp. 590-613.

27. See Nelson, note 9, above, pp. 79-81.

28. On the uses of vagueness to avoid evaluation see Selznick, note 16, above, pp. 59-64.

29. Keith Warner and Eugene Havens, "Goal Displacement and the Intangibility of Goals," Administrative Science Quarterly, vol. 12, no. 4, March, 1968, pp. 539-555. For the application of simple cause-effect evaluation techniques and their unintended consequences in police work, see the discussion of clearance rates in Jerome Skolnick, *Justice Without Trial* (New York, Wiley, 1967), pp. 164-181.

30. Nelson, note 9, above, pp. 23-32 and 48-54.

31. All names of institutions and towns are fictitious.

32. The social climate of seven institutions in the state were measured using an instrument developed and described by Rudolph Moos, "The Assessment of the Social Climates and Correctional Institutions," Journal of Research in Crime and Delinquency, vol. 5, no. 2, July, 1968, pp. 174-188. Results are reported in Chapter 8.

33. Leslie Wilkins, *Social Deviance* (Englewood Cliffs: Prentice-Hall, 1965), pp. 22-25.

CHAPTER 2

1. The classic in this tradition is Donald Clemmer, *The Prison Community* (New York: Holt, Rinehart, and Winston, 1958).

2. Ibid., p. 316.

3. Ibid.

4. Daniel Katz and Robert Kahn, *The Social Psychology of Organizations* (New York: Wiley, 1966). The present study, particularly Chapter 3, borrows heavily on their analysis of organizations as open systems. Their mention of prisons preceded their full treatment of the organization in general, and the attempt has been made here to withhold the subject of open systems for later discussion.

5. Ibid., p. 16.

6. Ibid.

7. Ibid. It must be emphasized that the view of prisons attributed to Katz and Kahn in this section is at times an extrapolation of characteristics that they discuss only in a general way that pertain to organizations with which they classify prisons. It is possible to view parolees as an exportable product, the acceptance of which is very dependent on community reaction. However, a negative community reaction to parolees usually does not change prison structure while commercial concerns treat negative response to their products as a cue to restructure internal operations (and to change products). Prisons do not act in an economically rational manner. Katz and Kahn hypothesize that the difference lies in the fact that parolees as output are capable of acting on their own. Prisons usually attribute output failure to parolees, while commerical concerns do not have that escape. In other words, feedback is diffused in people-processing organizations.

8. Ibid., pp. 211-212.

9. Gresham Sykes, *The Society of Captives* (Princeton: Princeton University Press, 1958). Donald Cressey, "Contradictory Directives in Complex Organizations: The Case of the Prison," in Lawrence Hazelrigg (ed.) *Prison Within Society* (Garden City: Doubleday, 1969), p. 482, offers this speech from chief custodial officer to his new guards: "So don't fail to enforce a rule, even if you think it is nonsense. It is there for a reason. Don't blow hot and cold; enforce the same rule in the same way every day. Come in and see me or see a lieutenant if you think the rule doesn't make sense. But if it is there, enforce it."

10. Katz and Kahn, note 4, above, p. 114.

11. Ibid., p. 134. It should be noted that inmates in so-called rehabilitative or educational prisons often claim that the goals of these prisons are still fundamentally political, but that psychological punishments have replaced the physical ones.

12. Ibid., p. 114.

13. Amitai Etzioni, *A Comparative Analysis of Complex Organizations,* (New York: Free Press, 1961).

14. Ibid., pp. xiv-xv.

15. Ibid., pp. 28-31.

16. Ibid., pp. 74-75.

17. Ibid., p. 75.

18. Ibid., pp. 84-86.

19. Ibid., pp. 96-101.

20. Ibid., p. 131.

21. Ibid., pp. 139-140.

22. Ibid., pp. 142-144.

23. In later chapters, the prison atmosphere will be measured by the Social Climate Scale, that works on the concept of "environmental press." See Rudolph Moos, "The Assessment of Social Climates in Correctional Institutions," Journal of Research in Crime and Delinquency, vol. 5, no. 2, July, 1968, pp. 174-188. Moos uses twelve specific climate dimensions, to which Etzioni's more general variables of scope and pervasiveness could have important theoretical relevance.

24. Etzioni, note 13, above, pp. 163-164.

25. Ibid., p. 165.

26. Ibid., p. 64.

27. Ibid., pp. 293-295. In reality, this does not seem quite true, and is becoming less true. Certain correctional systems now make use of "halfway in" houses as well as "halfway out" houses, so that parolees who are perceived by officials as needing more intensive work may be called back into an organizational setting periodically. Work release programs in which prisoners are free during the day and locked up at night have similar characteristics.

28. Ibid., pp. 310-311.

29. Perhaps the most widely known are "Contradictory Directives in Complex Organizations: The Case of the Prison," note 9, above; "The Achievement of an Unstated Correctional Goal," in Hazelrigg (ed.) *Prison Within Society* (Garden City: Doubleday, 1967), pp. 50-67 and "Limitations on Organization of Treatment in the Modern Prison," *Theoretical Studies in the Organization of the Prison* (New York: Social Science Research Council, pamphlet 15, 1960), pp. 78-110.

30. Peter M. Blau, *Bureaucracy in Modern Society* (New York: Random House, 1956); Alvin W. Gouldner, *Patterns of Industrial Bureaucracy* (Glencoe: Free Press, 1954); Robert Merton, *Social Theory and Social Structure* (Glencoe: Free Press, 1949), pp. 151-160.

31. The generalization of the individual research studies is given by James March and Herbert Simon, *Organizations* (New York: Wiley, 1958), pp. 36-47.

32. Merton, note 30, above, pp. 151-160.

33. Cressey, note 9, above, pp. 486, and 491-493.

34. Donald Cressey, "Achievement of an Unstated Organizational Goal," note 29, above, p. 61.

35. See Ibid., p. 62; Cressey, note 9, above, p. 489.

36. Cressey, "The Achievement of an Unstated Correctional Goal," note 29, above.

37. David Street, Robert Vinter, and Charles Perrow, *Organization for Treatment* (New York: Free Press, 1966).

38. Ibid., p. 17.

39. As does Talcott Parsons, *The Social System* (New York: Free Press, 1951). Both Katz and Kahn and Etzioni voice indebtedness to the Parsonian format. On the disadvantages and contradictions in Parsons' framework, particularly as a basis for the analysis of open systems, see Walter Buckley, *Sociology and Modern Systems Theory* (Englewood Cliffs: Prentice-Hall, 1967).

40. See Richard McCleery, "Correctional Administration and Political Change," in Hazelrigg (ed.) *Prison Within Society* (Garden City: Doubleday, 1969), p. 117.

41. Street, Vinter, and Perrow, note 37, above, p. 18.

42. This is the perspective suggested and used with great success by Phillip Selznick, *T.V.A. and the Grass Roots* (New York: Harper and Row, 1948). Goals of TVA, in Selznick's view, were formulated with the policy of the agency to work cooperatively with local groups. Structure was elaborated in terms of agency-community liaison and so on, and most activity was patterned by cooptation and delegation that the policy implied.

43. Street, Vinter, and Perrow, note 37, above, p. 48.

44. Ibid., p. 21.

45. Ibid., p. 21.

46. Ibid., p. 22.

47. In addition to these research findings summarized in *Organization for Treatment,* many of these findings and others are discussed at greater length in the many articles and papers generated during the course of the study. These materials are listed in ibid., pp. 325-326. Of particular interest are the works of Grusky on role conflict, Zald on power structure, and Street on inmate social structure.

CHAPTER 3

1. Alfred Kuhn, *The Study of Society* (Homewood: Irwin, Dorsey, 1965), p. 51.

2. Donald Clemmer, *The Prison Community* (New York: Holt, Rinehart, and Winston, 1958).

3. Gresham Sykes, *The Society of Captives* (Princeton: Princeton University Press, 1958).

4. I.e., see Claude Brown, *Manchild in the Promised Land* (New York: Signet, 1965).

5. John Irwin, *The Felon* (Englewood Cliffs: Prentice-Hall, 1970), p. 63.

6. Daniel Glaser, *The Effectiveness of a Prison and Parole System* (Indianapolis: Bobbs Merrill, 1969), pp. 9-14.

7. Richard Cloward, "Social Control in the Prison" in *Theoretical Studies in Social Organization of the Prison* (New York: Social Science Research Council, pamphlet 15, March, 1960), pp. 20-48.

8. Richard McCleery, "Correctional Administration and Political Change" in Hazelrigg (ed.) *Prison Within Society* (Garden City: Doubleday, 1969), pp. 113-149.

9. John F. Galliher, "Change in a Correctional Institution," Crime and Delinquency, vol. 18, no. 3, July, 1972, pp. 263-270.

10. Warren G. Bennis, *Changing Organizations* (New York: Wiley, 1966), p. 133; for examples of organizational variables that were deliberately changed, see F. E. Emery and E. L. Trist, "Socio-Technical Systems," in F. E. Emery, *Systems Thinking* (Baltimore: Penguin, 1969), pp. 281-296.

11. Daniel Katz and Robert Kahn, *The Social Psychology of Organizations* (New York: Wiley, 1966), p. 451.

12. It is obvious that the process is simplified to make a point. It is impossible for Etzioni to mean that the trend toward less coercion is external to all organizations, since the environment of one organization includes many other organizations. Hence, less coercion in organizations affects the environment, which in turn affects the organization.

13. Cloward, note 7, above.

14. Donald Cressey, "Limitations on Organization of Treatment in the Modern Prison," in *Theoretical Studies in Social Organization of the Prison* (New York: Social Science Research Council, pamphlet 15, March 1960), pp. 78-110.

15. Donald Cressey, "Achievement of an Unstated Organizational Goal," in Lawrence Hazelrigg, *Prison Within Society* (Garden City: Doubleday, 1969), pp. 50-67.

16. *Newsweek,* September 27, 1971, p. 32.

17. Harold Bradley, "Designing for Change: Problems of Planned Innovations in Corrections," Annals, vol. 381, January, 1969, p. 90.

18. Ibid.

19. Ibid., p. 91.

20. See Allen Schick, "From Analysis to Evaluation," Annals, vol. 394, March, 1971, pp. 57-71; and Warren G. Bennis, note 10, above, pp. 10-14.

21. For one of the earliest articles that really recognized the differences between punishment for crime and change in offenders in terms of the changes that the new goals would demand of criminal justice administration, see George Dession, "Psychiatry and the Conditioning of Criminal Justice," 47 Yale Law Journal 319 (1933).

22. See Herman Mannheim and Leslie Wilkins, *Prediction Methods in Relation to Borstal Training* (London: H.M.S.O., 1955), pp. 105-111. One of the few predictive pieces of information about the prison experience itself was whether the boy had been allocated to an open or to a closed Borstal. In contrast to the relatively successful actuarial prediction obtained, the judgments of Borstal heads and cottage leaders about success of the paroled boy were worse than chance. In all fairness, of course, part of the

differential in predictive effectiveness must be attributed to the different technique used—the statistical method should be expected to be more accurate. See Paul Meehl, *Statistical vs. Clinical Prediction* (Minneapolis: University of Minnesota Press, 1966). Assuming, however, that Borstal officials are fairly capable judges of human character, we must conclude that part of the differential can be attributed to the fact that prison behavior is not as predictive of parole behavior as is preprison behavior. To this extent, we could understand the prison not as a black box through which offenders travel, but as a vacuum.

23. F. E. Emery and E. L. Trist, "The Causal Texture of Organizational Environments," in F. E. Emery, *Systems Thinking* (Baltimore: Penguin, 1969), pp. 241-257.

24. Shirley Terryberry, "The Evolution of Organizational Environments," Administrative Science Quarterly, vol. 12, no. 4, March 1968, pp. 590-613.

25. See Elmer K. Nelson and Catherine Lovell, *Developing Correctional Administrators* (Washington, D.C.: Final Research Report, Joint Commission on Correctional Manpower and Training, November, 1969), pp. 23-32; and see Bradley, note 17, above, p. 90.

26. Nelson, ibid., p. 79.

27. Douglas MacGregor, *The Human Side of Enterprise* (New York: McGraw-Hill, 1961), pp. 6-10. In the following discussion, the term "controlling" should not be confused with the meaning that word may have taken on in the analysis of administrative behavior in schools of public administration, where the manager's role is broken into phases of goal-setting, planning, implementing or controlling, and evaluating. In the next few paragraphs, "controlling" is used generically to stand for all of these activities as the manager stands between the environment and the internal structure of the organization.

28. This task is admirably performed by Kuhn, note 1, above, for society as a system, and by Stafford Beer, *Decision and Control* (New York: Wiley, 1966), for business and other profitable enterprises.

29. See Chris Argyris, *Integrating the Individual and the Organization* (New York: Wiley, 1964), pp. 173-175.

30. Ibid.

31. Daniel Katz and Robert Kahn, note 11, above. For very similar but briefer models, see Philip Selznick, *T.V.A. and the Grass Roots* (New York: Harper and Row, 1948); and Argyris, note 29, above.

32. The argument could be made, and probably in many cases substantiated, that the primary transformation does not involve inmates but the image that the outside public has and desires to keep about inmates. In this case, inmates and what happened to inmates would be secondary to prison officials and to the rest of government. While following up this tack might produce a considerably different model, it is not chosen here because it is not the primary objective intended by correctional staff or stated by the legislatures. In the model described above, the stated goal of changing inmates is taken at face value. If the subsequent analysis of prisons based on this assertion of goals forces some unpopular conclusions about the current prison system, there are two alternatives open: (1) to reject the present goals in favor of another model (such as producing images of punishment for society) or (2) to strive to correct the present goal-achievement disparity.

33. Katz and Kahn, note 11, above, p. 30.

34. This argument can only be carried so far, of course, particularly as change techniques become more sophisticated, correctional planners begin to take physical plant into consideration when constructing the organization. In this transitional period in correctional history, however, it is true that many prisons or jails that have similar physical trappings are used quite differently.

35. W. Keith Warner and A. Eugene Havens, "Goal Displacement and the Intangibility of Organizational Goals," Administrative Science Quarterly, vol. 12, no. 4, March, 1968, pp. 539-555.

36. Bradley, note 17, above, pp. 97-98.

37. Post Orders for forestry detail, in the Hilltop institution, undated. This detail was recently abandoned.

38. See Herbert Packer, "Two Models of the Criminal Process," 113 University of Pennsylvania Law Review 1 (1964); and John Griffiths, "Ideology in Criminal Process or a 'Third Model' of the Criminal Process," 79 Yale Law Journal 359 (1970).

CHAPTER 4

1. See the Governor's Special Committee on Criminal Offenders, *Preliminary Report* (New York: State of New York, 1968), pp. 29-30.

2. See George A. Shipman, "Role of the Administrator–Policymaking as Part of the Administrative Process," in Fremont J. Lyden, George A. Shipman, and Morton Kroll (eds.) *Policies, Decisions and Organization* (New York: Appleton-Century-Crofts, 1969), pp. 122-123.

3. Ibid. It is the general policy or legislative goals by which Etzioni classifies organizations, rather than by operational or organizational policy.

4. An example is the statutory parole board mandate that the board release from incarceration inmates who are already rehabilitated, while in operation, the board is sensitive to many other factors, such as length of time to mandatory release. See Remington et al., *Criminal Justice Administration* (Indianapolis: Bobbs Merrill, 1969), pp. 883-896.

5. Robert Katz and Robert Kahn, *The Social Psychology of Organizations* (New York: Wiley, 1966), p. 259.

6. See Chapter 2, above. For an excellent extended discussion on the variety of goal definitions and their empirical relationships, see Mayer Zald, "Comparative Analysis and Measurement of Organizational Goals: The Case of Correctional Institutions for Delinquents," Sociological Quarterly, vol. 4, no. 3, Summer, 1963, pp. 206-230.

7. A. Angyal, "A Logic of Systems," In F. E. Emery, *Systems Thinking* (Baltimore: Penguin, 1969), p. 28.

8. James March and Herbert Simon, *Organizations* (New York: Wiley, 1958), p. 185.

9. Katz and Kahn, note 3, above, p. 270.

10. Jerome Skolnick, *Justice Without Trial* (New York: Wiley, 1967), pp. 13-15.

11. Lon Fuller, *The Morality of Law* (New Haven: Yale University Press, 1964), pp. 157-158.

12. Skolnick, note 8, above, p. 14, and see Donald Cressey, "Achievement of an Unstated Organizational Goal," in Lawrence Hazelrigg, *Prison Within Society* (Garden City: Doubleday, 1969), p. 56, that following different policies, prisons relate to the public differently, with consequent differences for the inmates.

13. On the combination of outside and inside concerns that become organizational policy, see Shipman, note 1, above, pp. 121-125.

14. John Irwin, *The Felon* (Englewood Cliffs: Prentice-Hall, 1970), p. 158.

15. Robert P. Schenrell, "Valuation and Decision Making in Correctional Social Work," Issues in Criminology, vol. 4, no. 2, Fall, 1969, p. 101.

16. Don Gottfredson, *Measuring Attitudes Toward Juvenile Detention* (New York: National Council on Crime and Delinquency, 1968).

17. Cressey, note 12, above, pp. 50-54.

18. Sheldon Messinger, "Issues in the Study of the Social System of Prison Inmates," Issues in Criminology, vol. 4, no. 2, Fall, 1969, p. 138.

19. On the idea that most people and most organizations are generally more effective or "healthy" when treated as open systems in the requirements for the achievement of goal congruency, see Chris Argyris, *Personality and Organization* (New York: Harper and Row, 1957), pp. 76-122.

20. Katz and Kahn, note 5, above, p. 341. That these patterns and values are internalized is inferred from the amount of initiative demonstrated by the individual and by the lack of external control prompting the behavior in question.

21. Similar policy constructs in studies of different organizations include the following: F. E. Emery and E. L. Trist, "Socio-technical Systems" in Emery, *Systems Thinking,* note 5, above, pp. 281-296, textile mills and coal mining; R. Likert, *New Patterns of Management* (New York: McGraw-Hill, 1961) industrial companies; Charles Perrow, "The Analysis of Goals in Complex Organizations," American Sociological Review, vol. 26, no. 6, 1961, pp. 854-866, medical hospitals; Roy D. King and Norma Raynes "Operational Measure of Inmate Management in Residential Institutions," Social Science and Medicine, vol. 2, 1968, pp. 41-53, mental hospitals for retarded youth; Lloyd Warner and J. O. Low, *The Social System of the Modern Factory* (New Haven: Yale University Press, 1947), shoe factories; Robert Blake and Jane Mouton, *The Managerial Grid* (Houston: Gulf, 1964), commercial concerns.

22. Herbert Kelman, "Processes of Opinion Change," Public Opinion Quarterly, vol. 25, Spring, 1961, pp. 57-78; and "Compliance, Identification, and Internalization: Three Processes of Attitude Change," Journal of Conflict Resolution, vol. 2, 1958, pp. 51-60.

23. Some of the policy denotations have appeared in previous descriptions of correctional behavior and predictions of correctional trends; see Clarence Schrag, "Contemporary Corrections: An Analytical Model," paper presented for the President's Commission on Law Enforcement and Administration of Justice, mimeographed 1966; Daniel Glaser, "The Prospect for Corrections," paper prepared for the Arden House Conference on Manpower Needs in Corrections, mimeograph, 1964, and see notes 21 and 25.

24. This method of identification has both advantages and detractions. On the positive side, several of the labels have been used, independently of each other, in previous descriptions of policy. See ibid. and Kim Nelson and Catherine Lovell, *Developing Corrections Administrators* (Research Report of the Joint Commission on Correctional Manpower and Training, November, 1969), pp. 77-78. Other observers have noticed the same general policy classifications; hence, the use of these tags provides linkage with a tradition of policy study. However, the terms are used in the general vocabulary, with the exception of Restraint, as synonyms. Therefore it must be emphasized that, from this point in the paper, Rehabilitation refers not to all change-efforts, but to a particular mode and Reform does not refer to changing the entire system, but change-efforts conducted in another mode. See also note 25, below.

25. A preliminary description of some of the elements of the models is found in Vincent O'Leary, "Correctional Assumptions and Their Program Implications," Proceedings of the National Conference on Pre-release (Huntsville, Texas: Institute of Contemporary Corrections and the Behavioral Sciences, November, 1967). O'Leary developed the models considerably further in various training sessions and developed the Correctional Policy Inventory described in Chapter 5.

CHAPTER 5

1. Vincent O'Leary developed the ideas of correctional policies and developed several earlier forms of the questionnaire in a variety of training sessions. The author

helped to develop the final version of the policy questionnaire that was used in this research, conducted research on correctional management, and conducted the in-depth study of the Hilltop institution during a departmental training program conducted by O'Leary.

2. This is the same strategy used by James Q. Wilson for the differentiation of policy styles in *Varieties of Police Behavior* (Cambridge: MIT, 1968), pp. 4-9.

3. See the discussion on amplification of deviance in Leslie Wilkins, *Social Deviance* (Englewood Cliffs: Prentice-Hall, 1966), pp. 90-91.

4. Claire Selltiz et al., *Research Methods in Social Relations* (New York: Holt, Rinehart, and Winston, 1959), p. 366.

5. For example, classification and disciplinary decision behavior might be correlated with a policy profile in which a policy were deemed to exist (+) if the score were over the mean and deemed not to exist (−) if the score were under the mean. We might find that administrator X with policy profile (+ − + −) was likely to be conservative in his decisions while administrator Y with profile (− − − +) was usually liberal. This technique might be helpful in the analysis of why some parole board members favor incarceration *unless* there is a high chance of success on parole while other members favor release *unless* there is a high risk of violent behavior. The policy inventory, however, is aimed at the analysis of organizational variables rather than personal idiosyncracies, or at operating rather than case-by-case decisions.

6. I.e., the variety of prediction techniques used by the Gluecks, Burgess, and others all had rather similar results because raw data were poor. See Leslie Wilkins, *Evaluation of Penal Measures* (New York: Random House, 1969), pp. 63-73.

7. While this relationship has been well covered in the theoretical discussion Chapter 3, above, a more empirical explanation of the relationship between managerial and correctional behavior is necessary to validity of both the theory and the inventory. See Chapter 7.

8. I.e., Herbert Kelman, "Processes of Opinion Change," Public Opinion Quarterly, vol. 25, Spring, 1961, pp. 57-78. Jay Hall, Louis Tomain, and Martha Williams, "The Challenge of Correctional Change: The Interface of Conformity and Commitment," in Lawrence Hazelrigg, *Prison Within Society* (Garden City: Doubleday, 1969), pp. 308-328.

9. Louis Harris Associates, *Volunteers Look at Corrections* (survey for the Joint Commission on Correctional Manpower and Training, Washington, D.C.: Government Printing Office, 1968).

10. H.E.W., *Experiment in Culture Expansion* (Report of Proceedings of a conference called, "The Use of Products of a Social Problem in Coping with the Problem," at California Rehabilitation Center, Norco, California, July 10, 11, 12, 1963).

11. Selltiz, note 4, above, p. 161.

12. See ibid., pp. 181-182. However, as a training device, managers are asked to examine their individual profiles as a picture of their correctional stance, but they are warned that it is the principles that are important, and that the validity of the score as a picture of themselves is something that they should decide for themselves.

13. A concise discussion of advantages and disadvantages of different reliability measures is provided by Helen Walker and Joseph Lev, *Statistical Inference* (New York: Holt, Rinehart, and Winston, 1953), pp. 301-314.

14. For similar findings about conservative and liberal policy in relation to hierarchy and staff-line differences, see Elmer K. Nelson and Catherine Lovell, *Developing Correctional Administrators* (Final Research Report, Joint Commission on Correctional Manpower and Training, Washington, D.C.: Government Printing Office, November, 1969), pp. 77-80.

15. The value of participant feedback to the research component of the program is

an interesting corollary to the use of immediate feedback to participants about their training material. See Frank Heller, *Group Feed-Back Analysis* (Human Resources Centre, Tavistock Institute of Human Relations, 1969). The value to participants of either observational or data feedback during the training session is that it increases the impact of training information. They see where they stand personally in relation to concepts and managerial techniques presented. Researchers, it would seem, have the same need for immediate feedback. See generally, Argyris, note 1, above.

16. The results of which are reported in Chapter 8.

17. One particular goal of this survey was the selection of a demonstration institution, that appeared from the data to be an average case.

18. Data on this congruence and the specific actions required are reported in Chapter 7.

19. See Argyris, note 1, above, pp. 103-122.

20. Hilltop prison had recently been separated administratively from the maximum security unit. The Superintendent of Hilltop, who had previously been the Deputy Warden for Treatment and Training of both prisons, seemed eager to initiate programs that would identify the character of his institution. Many of his plans, which were initiated at the time of the formal separation, had been developing for several years.

21. Now that the research is completed, it would have been useful if inmates had also been asked how they act toward officials in certain situations.

22. The use of the Spearman-Brown formula in spite of the ordinal data is suggested in Charles R. Tittle and Richard J. Hill, "Attitude Measurement and Prediction of Behavior: An Evaluation of Conditions and Measurement Techniques," in Norman K. Denzin, *Sociological Methods* (Chicago: Aldine-Atherton, 1970), p. 163.

23. Much of the developmental activity that was conducted in the year after this research was completed is reported in David Duffee, *Using Correctional Officers in Planned Change* (Final Research Report, National Institute on Law Enforcement and Administration of Justice, grant no. NI 71-115-PG, September, 1972). A later use of the same material appears in David Duffee, Kevin Wright, and Thomas Maher, *Refunding Evaluation Report in Community Service Centers* (Harrisburg, Pennsylvania Governor's Justice Commission, January 2, 1975). The work on changing their variables is continuing in both the state system researched in the report as well as in the Pennsylvania Bureau of Correction Community Correctional Centers.

CHAPTER 6

1. Elmer K. Nelson and Catherine Lovell, *Developing Correctional Administrators* (Research Report of the Joint Commission on Correctional Manpower and Training, Washington, D.C., November, 1969), see discussion on p. 77 and the instrument on p. 128.

2. See Table 6.1 "Attitudes Toward Goals of Corrections: Now Emphasized and Should Be Emphasized in Administrators Own Organization," in ibid., p. 120.

3. There are sixteen Central Office managers in the interview data and seventeen in the questionnaire data because of the addition of the Parole Board Chairman in the latter.

4. David Duffee, *Final Report on Department Organization* (Department of Corrections, mimeograph, September 12, 1969), Section II, p. 24.

5. See the discussions concerning the functions of the executive according to Cressey, and Street, Vinter, and Perrow in Chapter 2.

6. Nelson and Lovell, note 1, above, p. 78.

7. An analysis of variance of officer scores demonstrated some differences in

officers' responses, but none that would appear in ordinal data. The shift on duty from 4 p.m. until midnight, when all the inmates were in the compound and most of the community volunteer groups were active, showed considerably *less* Reform-supportive behavior than the other two shifts. There were no significant differences during shifts on any of the other policies while the explanation for the lower Reform emphasis on the third shift is uncertain, it probably had a great deal to do with the shift captain, who used a considerably different "managerial style" than the other captains. On the concept of style and its measurement, see Chapter 7.

8. Duffee, note 4, above Section II, p. 14.

9. Ibid., Section III, p. 9.

10. Ibid., Section III, p. 10.

11. See Donald Cressey, "Contradictory Directives in Complex Organizations: The Case of the Prison," in Lawrence Hazelrigg, *Prison Within Society* (Garden City: Doubleday, 1969), pp. 477-496, and the discussion of Cressey's general analysis, Chapter 2.

12. Innovation is used here in Merton's sense of the man who uses "illegal" means to accomplish a legitimate end. Of course, the goal evidently pursued by officers is not of first importance in the eyes of administrators, but it may be in the larger social context.

13. The court consisted of the assistant superintendent, a counselor, a captain, and an officer. An effort was made to convene the court as soon as possible after the filing of a "conduct ticket." The reporting officer was *not* allowed at the hearing, a procedure that angered most guards. The adminstration explained that they did not want inmates intimidated by the presence of the officer as they attempted to give their version of the event. This kind of procedure as the statistical consequences reported above would seem to place Hilltop on the lenient end of the continuum of disciplinary practices reviewed by Glaser. See *Effectiveness of a Prison and Parole System* (Indianapolis: Bobbs Merrill, 1969), pp. 119-124.

14. See Keith Warner and Eugene Havens, "Goal Displacement and the Intangibility of Organizational Goals," Administrative Science Quarterly, vol. 12, no. 4, March, 1968, pp. 539-555.

15. It is a rather important point that officers who strongly hold the Reform values firmly believe that a rigid regime of change-by-compliance is exactly what inmates need. Because the officer is the agent holding the power in the compliance structure, Reform may also offer additional psychological benefits for some people. But it is questionable that the urge to wield power would be as strong if the faith in its beneficient effects was not present. While a strong resistance to change from a Reform behavior to something else may well be the loss of power such a change would appear to entail, stronger resistance seems to come from the fact that challenging Reform policy implies to Reform adherents a threat to dominant American ideals, as they see them.

16. According to Chris Argyris, this is a typical reaction in "fragmented or closed" organizational climates. See *Integrating the Individual and the Organization* (New York: Wiley, 1964), p. 313.

17. On the slowness of correctional systems to change see Elliot Studt, Sheldon Messinger, and Thomas Wilson, *C-Unit: The Search for Community in Prison* (New York, Russell Sage, 1968) and Harold Bradley, "Designing for Change: Problems of Planned Innovations in Corrections," Annals, vol. 381, January, 1969, p. 90.

18. An analysis of variance using the inmate scores rather than frequencies high-lighted *some* differences in perception of policy among inmate groups. None of these differences was so great, however, that chi-square would be sensitive to them. In other words, the great majority of inmates in all groups perceived Restraint as the most frequently supported policy, but when relative scores are considered, some groups

perceived Restraint as considerably more frequent and Rehabilitation and Reintegration as considerably less frequent than some other groups. Given the overall merits and detractions of the questionnaire on the inmate level, it seemed wise to be conservative and not go into these results, since the important point is difference of perceptions from one hierarchical level to another. The analysis of variance of the inmate scores can be adequately summarized thus: The inmates who were shortly to be released or who had recently entered were most likely to perceive Restraint very frequently while those inmates in the middle of a long period of incarceration were likely to perceive less Restraint and more Rehabilitation and Reintegration. The irony of these perceptions is that the inmates least in need of Reintegration are the ones most likely to notice it. The reason for this is not clear presently, but it probably has to do with the degree of risk an inmate is willing to take. Only long timers can afford to take the risk that open communication requires.

19. Gresham Sykes, *Society of Captives* (Princeton: Princeton University Press, 1971), pp. 58-62.

20. See ibid., pp. 33-37.

CHAPTER 7

1. For a detailed description of the modeling process, see Stafford Beer, *Decision and Control* (New York: Wiley, 1966), pp. 90-114; and for an analogous but more traditional explanation of the policy formulation-implementation-evaluation cycle, see Lemont J. Lyden, George A. Shipman, and Morton Kroll, *Policies, Decisions, and Organization* (New York: Appleton-Century-Crofts, 1969), pp. 1-4.

2. Gresham Sykes, *Society of Captives* (Princeton: Princeton University Press, 1971), pp. 34-58.

3. Ibid., pp. 56-58.

4. Ibid., see the warden's report on the purpose of the strict regime, pp. 36-37. A usually subterranean but important purpose of the plethora of prison rules is the exculpatory function they serve for the people in authority if something goes wrong. See Bensman and Gerver, "Crime and Punishment in a Factory: A Functional Analysis," in Rosenberg, Gerver, and Houton (eds.) *Mass Society in Crisis* (New York: Macmillan, 1964), pp. 141-152.

5. Ibid., p. 61.

6. On the importance of the changee's perception of the intention of the change program see Herbert Kelman, "Three Processes of Attitude Change," Journal of Conflict Resolution, vol. 2, 1958, pp. 51-60.

7. The question of organizational ineffectiveness has several facets: the goals that are to be implemented, and the way in which that is done. There are the information, the transmission of it, and the reception of it. They are not distinct parts, however, because information only is information as it is transmitted and received. See Jim L. Munro, "Towards a Theory of Criminal Justice Administration: A General Systems Perspective," Public Administration Review, no. 6, November/December, 1971, pp. 626-628.

8. W. W. Ronon, *Individual and Situational Variables Relating to Job Satisfaction,* Journal of Applied Psychology Monograph, vol. 54, no. 1, part 2 February, 1970; also Rensis Likert, *New Patterns of Management* (New York: McGraw-Hill, 1961), pp. 5-16.

9. F. E. Emery and E. L. Trist, "The Causal Texture of Organizational Environments," in F. E. Emery, *Systems Thinking* (Baltimore: Penguin, 1969), p. 254.

10. Douglas MacGregor, *The Human Side of Enterprise* (New York: McGraw-Hill, 1960), p. 6.

11. Ibid.

12. Likert, note 8, above.

13. Likert, *The Human Organization* (New York: McGraw-Hill, 1967).

14. Robert Blake and Jane Mouton, *The Managerial Grid* (Houston: Gulf, 1964).

15. Ibid., pp. 88-89.

16. Rensis Likert, note 8, above, p. 162.

17. Blake and Mouton, note 14, above, pp. 62-65.

18. Ibid., pp. 24-28, 69.

19. Ibid., p. 110.

20. Ibid., pp. 145-163.

21. Jay Hall, Jerry Harvey, and Martha Williams, *Styles of Management Inventory* (Austin: Teleometrics, 1964).

22. Elmer K. Nelson and Catherine Lovell, *Developing Correctional Administrators* (Research Report of the Joint Commission on Correctional Manpower and Training, Washington, D.C., November 1969), pp. 47-50.

23. Nelson and Lovell use Reintegration as it is described in the present study. Their source of the term and the trend are Daniel Glaser, "The Prospect for Corrections" (paper presented for the Arden House Conference on Manpower Needs in Corrections, mimeographed, 1964); and Clarence Schrag, "Contemporary Corrections: An Analytical Model" (paper prepared for the President's Commission on Law Enforcement and Administration of Justice, mimeographed, 1966).

24. The fit of 9/9 style and Reintegration remained an assumption on the part of Nelson and Lovell because they had no technique by which to measure policy and produce statistical correlations with the styles that they proceeded to measure. See ibid., pp. 77-97.

25. Ibid., pp. 33-36. The most significant relationship to the adult institution manager were internal relationships to peers, subordinates, superiors, and inmates. He placed much less significance on the outside world. This ranking of relationships is to be expected, but it does demonstrate lack of concern for control of environmental-organizational relations to which the manager is the key.

26. The managerial style data for the national sample are presented in Nelson and Lovell, note 22, above, pp. 47-50. No statistical comparisons are attempted because the raw scores for the national samples were unavailable. Nelson and Lovell report only the means on the 15-point scale. Ranking of the means seems sufficient to make the general point that the tendency toward 9/1 management at Hilltop is stronger than in other institutions. In order to get the officers' impressions of their managers qua manager, the *inventory* was also given to officers, and they were asked to rate their immediate supervisors. The officers did not seem to understand either the content or the format of this questionnaire, and it was dropped from the analysis. A less direct but supportive set of data concerning the subordinates' view of their superiors is available in the results of the "organizational profile questionnaire," reported in Chapter 8.

27. David Duffee, *Final Report on Department Organization* (Department of Correction, mimeograph, September 12, 1969), Section III, p. 10.

28. See Sykes, note 2, above, pp. 28, 55. For the general model of such bureaucratic deviance, see Robert Merton, *Social Theory And Social Structure* (Glencoe: Free Press, 1949), pp. 151-160.

29. Duffee, note 27, above, Section III, p. 15.

30. I.e., Warren Bennis, *Changing Organizations* (New York: McGraw-Hill, 1966), pp. 132-134. Daniel Katz and Robert Kahn, *The Social Psychology of Organization* (New York: Wiley, 1966), pp. 390-451, is an excellent review of a variety of change strategies in use and the degree to which they manipulate or fail to manipulate organizational rather than individual and small group variables.

31. Duffee, note 27, above, Section III, p. 15.

32. Street, Vinter, and Perrow found similar reactions in the two institutions that they classified as Obedience/Conformity. After their first wave of research took place, they conducted executive seminars in each institution. As a consequence of the seminar, changes were initiated in the Treatment institutions, but no changes took place in the Obedience/Conformity institutions. *Organizations for Treatment* (New York: Free Press, 1966), p. 266.

CHAPTER 8

1. Mayer Zald, "The Correctional Institution for Juvenile Offenders: An Analysis of Organizational 'Character'," in Lawrence Hazelrigg (ed.) *Prison Within Society* (Garden City: Doubleday, 1969), pp. 229-246.

2. David Street, Robert Vinter, and Charles Perrow, *Organization for Treatment* (New York: Free Press, 1966) see, for example, pp. 26-39.

3. Ibid., pp. 21-22.

4. See the discussion in Leslie Wilkins, *Evaluation of Penal Measures* (New York: Random House, 1969) pp. 25-26, on the resolution of the argument of "uniqueness" and measurement.

5. Rudolph Moos, "The Assessment of the Social Climates of Correctional Institutions," Journal of Research in Crime and Delinquency, vol. 5, no. 2, July, 1968, pp. 174-188.

6. Ibid., p. 175.

7. Ibid., p. 177.

8. Ibid., pp. 180-182.

9. Ibid., p. 186.

10. The Moos Scale became available when the School of Criminal Justice agreed to cooperate with the National Council on Crime and Delinquency concerning a national survey of social climates of institutions that N.C.C.D. was engaged in. In return for administering the Scale for N.C.C.D., the data were made available for use in this study. See Ernst Wenk and Thomas Halatyn, *Measuring the Social Climate of Correctional Institutions* (Davis, Calif.: National Council on Crime and Delinquency, 1973).

11. The substitutes for these inventories that were utilized at the other institutions will be described in the following sections.

12. The Continuum and the questionnaire are very similar to those developed by Rensis Likert, *The Human Organization* (New York: Wiley, 1967), pp. 197-211.

13. These three groups may be considered analogous to Likert's System III, II, and I management patterns, respectively, ibid., pp. 3-12.

14. For a general description of this process, see Leslie Wilkins, *Social Deviance* (New York: Prentice-Hall, 1966), pp. 88-95. Also see Amitai Etzioni, *Complex Organizations,* on the idea that where there is broad scope there is low pervasiveness. See discussion in Chapter 2.

CHAPTER 9

1. F. E. Emery and E. L. Trist, "The Causal Texture of Organizational Environments," in F. E. Emery, *Systems Thinking* (Baltimore: Penguin, 1969), pp. 241-257.

2. Raymond Studer, "The Dynamics of Behavior-Contingent Physical Systems," paper presented at the Portsmouth College of Technology Symposium on Design Methods (Portsmouth, England: December 4, 1967).

3. Generally regarded as the best volume on Blake's work is Northrup Frye, *Fearful Symmetry* (Boston: Beacon Press, 1962).

4. See Talcott Parsons, *The Social System* (New York: Free Press, 1964), pp. 516-517.

5. An interesting observation by an inmate about this fractional rather than synthetic approach to prison organization is Jackson's statement that counselors as well as officers function as guards. George Jackson, *Soledad Brother* (New York: Bantam, 1970), pp. 160-161.

6. The concept belongs to Chris Argyris, *Integrating the Individual and the Organization* (New York: Wiley, 1964), pp. 237 and 313-314.

7. On unionization analyzed in these terms, see Chris Argyris, *Personality and Organization* (New York: Harper and Row, 1957), pp. 103-107; and William F. Whyte, *Money and Motivation* (New York: Harper and Row, 1955), pp. 81-89, 130-133.

8. Perhaps the foremost document in this area is Richard McCleery, "Correctional Administration and Political Change," in Lawrence Hazelrigg (ed.) *Prison Within Society* (Garden City: Doubleday, 1969), pp. 113-149.

9. David Duffee, *Using Correctional Officers in Planned Change* (Washington, D.C.: National Technical Information Service, 1973), and "The Correctional Officer Subculture and Organizational Change" Journal of Research in Crime and Delinquency, vol. II, no. 2., July 1974, pp. 155-172.

BIBLIOGRAPHY

BOOKS

Angyal, A. *Foundation for a Science of Personality.* Cambridge: Harvard University Press, 1941.

Argyris, Chris. *Intervention Theory and Method.* Reading, Mass.: Addison-Wesley, 1970.

――― *Integrating the Individual and the Organization.* New York: Wiley, 1964.

――― *Personality and Organization.* New York: Harper and Row, 1957.

Beer, Stafford. *Decision and Control.* New York: Wiley, 1966.

――― *Management Science.* Garden City: Doubleday, 1968.

Bennis, Warren. *Changing Organizations.* New York: Wiley, 1967.

Bensman and Gerver. "Crime and Punishment in the Factory: A Functional Analysis," pp. 141-152 in Rosenberg, Gerver, and Houton (ed.) *Mass Society in Crisis.* New York: Macmillan, 1964.

Blake, Robert and Jane Mouton. *The Managerial Grid.* Houston: Gulf, 1964.

Blau, Peter. *Bureaucracy in Modern Society.* New York: Random House, 1956.

Buckley, Walter. *Sociology and Modern Systems Theory.* Englewood Cliffs: Prentice-Hall, 1967.

Clemmer, Donald. *The Prison Community.* New York: Holt, Rinehart and Winston, 1958.

Cloward, Richard. "Social Control in a Prison," pp. 20-48 in *Theoretical Studies in Social Organization of the Prison.* New York: Social Science Research Council, Pamphlet 15, 1960.

Cohen, Albert. "Multiple Factor Approaches," pp. 77-80 in Wolfgang, Savitz, and Johnston (eds.) *The Sociology of Crime and Delinquency.* New York: Wiley, 1962.

Cressey, Donald. "Achievement of an Unstated Organizational Goal," pp. 50-67 in Hazelrigg (ed.) *Prison Within Society.* Garden City: Doubleday, 1969.

――― "Limitations on Organization of Treatment in the Modern Prison," pp. 78-110 in *Theoretical Studies in Social Organization of the Prison.* New York: Social Science Research Council, Pamphlet 15, 1960.

Drucker, Peter. *The New Society.* New York: Harper and Row, 1962.

Emery, F. E. *Systems Thinking.* Baltimore: Penguin, 1969.

Emery, F. E. and E. L. Trist. "Socio-Technical Systems," pp. 281-296 in Emery (ed.) *Systems Thinking.* Baltimore: Penguin, 1969.

――― "The Causal Texture of Organizational Environments," pp. 241-257 in Emery (ed.) *Systems Thinking.* Baltimore: Penguin, 1969.

Etzioni, Amitai. *A Comparative Analysis of Complex Organizations.* New York: Free Press, 1961.

Fuller, Lon. *The Morality of Law.* New Haven: Yale University Press, 1964.

Gibb, Jack R. "Defensive Communication," pp. 191-198 in Leavitt and Pondy (eds.) *Readings in Managerial Psychology.* Chicago: University of Chicago Press, 1964.

Glueck, Sheldon and Eleanor Glueck. *Five Hundred Criminal Careers*. New York: Knopf, 1930.

Goffman, Erving. *Asylums*. Garden City: Doubleday, 1957.

Grusky, Oscar. "Role Conflict in Organizations: A Study of Prison Camp Officials," pp. 455-476 in Hazelrigg (ed.) *Prison Within Society*. Garden City: Doubleday, 1969.

Hall, Jay, Martha Williams, and Louis Tomaino. "The Challenge of Correctional Change: The Interface of Conformity and Commitment," pp. 308-328 in Hazelrigg (ed.) *Prison Within Society*. Garden City: Doubleday, 1969.

Irwin, John. *The Felon*. Englewood Cliffs: Prentice-Hall, 1970.

Katz, Daniel and Robert Kahn. *The Social Psychology of Organizations*. New York: Wiley, 1966.

Lewin, Kurt. *Field Theory in Social Sciences*. New York: Harper and Row, 1964.

Likert, Rensis. *The Human Organization, Its Management and Value*. New York: McGraw-Hill, 1967.

——— *New Patterns of Management*. New York: McGraw-Hill, 1961.

MacGregor, Douglas. *The Human Side of Enterprise*. New York: McGraw-Hill, 1960.

McCleery, Richard. "Correctional Administration and Political Change," pp. 113-139 in Hazelrigg (ed.) *Prison Within Society*. Garden City: Doubleday, 1969.

Mannheim, Herman and Leslie Wilkins. *Prediction Methods in Relation to Borstal Training*. London: H.M.S.O., 1955.

March, James and Herbert Simon. *Organizations*. New York: Wiley, 1958.

Merton, Robert. *Social Theory and Social Structure*. New York: Free Press, 1957.

Miller, S. M. and Frank Riesman. *Social Class and Social Policy*. New York: Basic Books, 1968.

Packer, Herbert. *The Limits of the Criminal Sanction*. Stanford: Stanford University Press.

Pearl, Arthur and Frank Riesman. *New Careers for the Poor*. New York: Free Press, 1965.

Selznick, Philip. *T. V.A. and the Grass Roots*. New York: Harper and Row, 1948.

Shipman, George A. "Role of the Administrator: Policy Making as Part of The Administering Process," pp. 121-134 in Lyden, Shipman, and Kroll (eds.) *Policies, Decisions, and Organization*. New York: Appleton-Century-Crofts, 1969.

Skolnick, Jerome. *Justice Without Trial*. New York: Wiley, 1967.

Street, David, Robert Vinter, and Charles Perrow. *Organization for Treatment*. New York: Free Press, 1966.

Studt, Elliot, Sheldon Messinger, and Thomas Wilson. *C-Unit: Search for Community in Prison*. New York: Russell Sage, 1968.

Sykes, Gresham. *Society of Captives*. Princeton: Princeton University Press, 1958.

Warner, Lloyd and J. O. Low. *The Social System of a Factory*. New Haven: Yale University Press, 1965.

Weber, George H. "Conflicts Between Professional and Non-professional Personnel in Institutional Delinquency Treatment," pp. 426-454 in Hazelrigg (ed.) *Prison Within Society*. Garden City: Doubleday, 1969.

Whyte, William F. *Money and Motivation*. New York: Harper and Row, 1955.

Wilkins, Leslie. *Evaluation of Penal Measures*. New York: Random House, 1969.

——— *Social Deviance*. Englewood Cliffs: Prentice-Hall, 1966.

Wilson, James Q. *Varieties of Police Behavior*. Cambridge: Harvard University Press, 1968.

Wolfgang, Marvin and Franco Ferracuti. *The Subculture of Violence*. London: Tavistock, 1967.

Zald, Mayer. "Power Balance and Staff Conflict in Correctional Institutions," pp. 397-425 in Hazelrigg, (ed.) *Prison Within Society*. Garden City: Doubleday, 1969.

——— "The Correctional Institution for Juvenile Offenders: An Analysis of Organizational 'Character'," pp. 229-246 in Hazelrigg (ed.) *Prison Within Society*. Garden City: Doubleday, 1969.

ARTICLES AND PERIODICALS

Adamek, Raymond and Edward Dager. "Social Structure, Identification, and Change in a Treatment Oriented Institution," American Sociological Review, vol. 33, no. 6, December, 1968. pp. 931-943.

Aiken, Michael and Jerald Huge. "Organizational Interdependence and Intra-Organizational Structure," American Sociological Review. vol. 33, no. 6, December, 1968. pp. 912-930.

Arnold, Thurmond. "Law Enforcement—An attempt at Social Dissection," 42 Yale Law Journal. I (1932).

Bradley, Harold B. "Designing for Change: Problems of Planned Innovation in Corrections," Annals, vol. 381, 1969. pp. 89-98.

——— "Community Based Treatment for Young Adult Offenders," Crime and Delinquency. vol. 15, no. 3, July 1969. pp. 359-370.

——— Glynn Smith, and William Salstrom. *Design for Change, A Program for Correctional Management*. Final Report, Model Treatment Program. Sacramento: Institute for the Study of Crime and Delinquency. July, 1968.

Braunstein, Daniel N. "Interpersonal Behavior in a Changing Organization," Journal of Applied Psychology. vol. 54, no. 2, 1970. pp. 184-191.

Cressey, Donald. "Contradictory Directives in Complex Organizations, the Case of The Prison," Administrative Science Quarterly. vol. 4, June 1959. pp. 1-19.

——— "Social Psychological Foundations for Using Criminals in the Rehabilitation of Criminals," Journal of Research in Crime and Delinquency. vol. 2, 1965. pp. 49-59.

——— "The Nature and Effectiveness of Correctional Techniques," Law and Contemporary Problems. vol. 23, Autumn, 1958. pp. 754-771.

——— "Contradictory Theories in Correctional Group Therapy Programs," Federal Probation, vol. 18, June, 1954, pp. 20-26.

Dession, George. "Psychiatry and the Conditioning of Criminal Justice," 47 Yale Law Journal, 319 (1933).

Fisher, Robert. "Total Institutional Commitment and Treatment Trends in English Corrections," Issues on Criminology. vol. 2, no. 1, Spring, 1966. pp. 61-78.

Galliher, John F. "Change in a Correctional Institution," Crime and Delinquency. vol. 18, no. 3, July, 1972. pp. 263-270.

Garabedian, Peter. "Social Roles and Process of Socialization in the Prison Community," Social Problems. vol. 11, Fall, 1963. pp. 139-152.

Grant, J. D. and Marguerite Q. Grant, "A Group Dynamics Approach to the Treatment of Non-Conformity in the Navy," Annals, vol. 322, March, 1959. pp. 126-155.

Griffiths, John, "Ideology in Criminal Process or a 'Third' Model of the Criminal Process," 79 Yale Law Journal 359 (1970).

——— "The Limits of Criminal Law Scholarship," 79 Yale Law Journal 1388 (1970).

Hagan, Charles and Charles Campbell. "Team Classification in Federal Institutions," Federal Probation. vol. 32. no. 1, 1968. pp. 30-35.

Heijder, Alfred. "The Function of Prison: A Study in Administrative Penology," International Journal of Offender Therapy. vol. 11, no. 2, 1967. pp. 56-63.

Kelman, Herbert. "Compliance, Identification, and Internalization: Three Processes of Attitude Change," Journal of Conflict Resolution. vol. 2, 1958. pp. 51-60.

——— "Processes of Opinion Change," Public Opinion Quarterly. vol. 25, Spring, 1961. pp. 57-78.

King, Roy and Norma Raynes. "An Operational Measure of Inmate Management in Residential Institutions," Social Science and Medicine. vol. 2, 1968. pp. 41-53.

Mathiesen, Thomas. "A Functional Equivalent to Inmate Cohesion," Human Organization. vol. 27, no. 2, 1968. pp. 117-124.

Messinger, Sheldon L. "Issues in the Study of the Social System of Prison Inmates," Issues in Criminology. vol. 4, no. 2, Fall, 1969. pp. 133-144.

Moos, Rudolph. "The Assessment of the Social Climates of Correctional Institutions," Journal of Research in Crime and Delinquency. vol. 5, no. 2, July 1968. pp. 174-188.

Morrison, June. "The Inmate Volunteer: A Study of Paradoxical Assumptions," Journal of Research in Crime and Delinquency. vol. 4, no. 2, July, 1967. pp. 263-268.

Nasati, Michael, D. Dezzani, and Mimi Silbert. "Atascadero: Ramifications of a Maximum Security Treatment Institution," Issues in Criminology. vol. 2, no. 1, Spring, 1966. pp. 29-46.

Packer, Herbert. "Two Models of the Criminal Process," 113 University of Pennsylvania Law Review 1 (1964).

Perrow, Charles. "The Analysis of Goals in Complex Organizationa," American Sociological Review. vol. 26, no. 6, 1961. pp. 854-866.

Reich, Miriam. "Therapeutic Implications of the Indeterminate Sentence," Issues in Criminology. vol. 2, no. 2, Spring, 1966. pp. 7-28.

Scheurell, Robert P. "Valuation and Decision Making in Correctional Social Work," Issues in Criminology. vol. 4, no. 2, Fall, 1969. pp. 101-108.

Schick, Allen. "From Analysis to Evaluation," Annals. vol. 394, March, 1971. pp. 57-71.

Schmideberg, Melitta. "Re-Evaluating the Concepts of 'Rehabilitation' and 'Punishment'," International Journal of Offender Therapy. vol. 12, no. 1, 1968. pp. 25-28.

Scrag, Clarence. "Leadership Among Prison Inmates," American Sociological Review. vol. 19, Fall, 1954. pp. 37-42.

Selznick, Phillip. "Foundations of the Theory of Organization," American Sociological Review. vol. 13, 1948. pp. 25-35.

Slesinger, Jonathan and Ernest Harburg. "Organizational Change and Executive Behavior," Human Organization. vol. 27, no. 2, Summer, 1968. pp. 95-109.

Street, David. "The Inmate Group in Custodial and Treatment Settings," American Sociological Review. vol. 30, 1965. pp. 40-55.

Terryberry, Shirley. "The Evolution of Organizational Environments," Administrative Science Quarterly. vol. 12, no. 4, March, 1968. pp. 590-613.

Wallace, Robert. "Ecological Implications of a Custody Institution," Issues in Criminology. vol. 2, no. 1, Spring, 1966. pp. 47-60.

Warner, W. Keith and A. Eugene Havens. "Goal Displacement and the Intangibility of Organizational Goals," Administrative Science Quarterly. vol. 12, no. 4, March, 1968. pp. 539-555.

Wheeler, Stanton. "Socialization in Correctional Communities," American Sociological Review. vol. 26, October, 1961. pp. 697-712.

Wilson, Thomas. "Patterns of Management and Adaptation to Organizational Goals: A Study of Prison Inmates," American Sociological Review. vol. 74, no. 2, September, 1968. pp. 146-157.

Wolf, Martin G. "Need Gratification Theory: A Theoretical Reformulation of Job Satisfaction/Dissatisfaction and Job Motivation," Journal of Applied Psychology. vol. 54, no. 1, 1970. pp. 87-94.

Zald, Mayer. "Comparative Analysis and Measurement of Organizational Goals: the Case of Correctional Institutions for Delinquents," Sociological Quarterly. vol. 4, no. 3, Summer 1963. pp. 206-230.

MONOGRAPHS, REPORTS, AND MISCELLANEOUS

Duffee, David. *Using Correctional Officers in Planned Change.* Final Report L.E.A.A. grant NI 71-115-PG (Washington, D.C.: National Technical Information Service, 1973).
— — — *Final Report on Department Organization.* (Department of Correction, mimeo., September, 1969): The identification of this report by state would violate conditions of anonymity under which this present research was conducted.
Gottfredson, Don. *Measuring Attitudes Toward Juvenile Detention.* (New York: National Council on Crime and Delinquency, 1968).
Governor's Special Committee on Criminal Offenders. *Preliminary Report.* (New York: State of New York, June, 1968).
Hall, Jay, Jerry Harvey, and Martha Williams. *The Styles of Management Inventory.* (Austin: Teleometrics, 1964).
Heller, Frank A. *Group Feed-Back Analysis,* (London: Tavistock Institute of Human Relations, 1969).
Nelson, Elmer K. and Catherine H. Lovell. *Developing Correctional Administrators.* Research Report of the Joint Commission on Correctional Manpower and Training (Washington, D.C., 1969).
President's Commission of Law Enforcement and the Administration of Justice. *Challenge of Crime in a Free Society.* (Washington, D.C.: G.P.O., 1967).
— — — *Task Force Report: Corrections.* (Washington, D.C.: G.P.O., 1967).
Ronan, W. W., *Individual and Situational Variables Relating to Job Satisfaction, Journal of Applied Psychology Monograph.* vol. 54, no. 1, part 2, February, 1970.
U.S. Department of Health, Education, and Welfare. *Experiment in Culture Expansion.* Report of proceedings of a conference called "The Use of Products of a Social Problem in Coping with the Problem," held at California Rehabilitation Center, Norco, California, July 10, 11, and 12, 1963.

INDEX